A REALISTIC PHILOSOPHY
OF RELIGION

A Realistic Philosophy of Religion

By

A. CAMPBELL GARNETT

Associate Professor of Philosophy
University of Wisconsin

19 42

WILLETT, CLARK & COMPANY

CHICAGO   NEW YORK

Dedicated in parental affection and hope to

FRANCIS CAMPBELL GARNETT

Royal Canadian Air Force

Reported " missing " on active service

March 10, 1942

16650

Preface

RELIGION is a fact of individual and social life. The philosophy of religion is an attempt to understand it. Understanding must begin with analysis, which distinguishes the various features that make up the fact and observes how they are related to form its strucure. But every fact is related to other facts, and the understanding of these further relations constitutes the interpretation of the fact. So the understanding of religion must involve analysis and interpretation.

The first part of this book is devoted almost exclusively to analysis. It endeavors to discover the distinctive features and essential structure of religion as a living personal and social phenomenon. The second and third parts are concerned with questions of interpretation. This falls into two parts because religion is practice as well as theory, and the practice of religion is at least as important as the theory. In practice religion seeks to be good. So the question here is first, what goodness is, and second, what constitutes good religious practice, both in relation to society in general and in the operation of a religious organization. In theory religion seeks to be true. So the question here is that of the validity of the ideas that enter into the structure of religion. In this section, chiefly for reasons of space, we have confined our attention to the ideas of God and immortality. In the epilogue one further religious idea is examined — the Christian concept of faith.

The primary purpose of this book is to present an original analysis and interpretation of religion which, as to both theory and practice, the author believes to be particularly pertinent to the distressing problems of our day. From the analysis of religious experience there issues the finding that what men have called God is a factor within themselves that they naturally distinguish from the familiar self of private desire. It is that within each of us that demands of us that we concern ourselves with the good of others besides ourselves. The history of religion is the story of man's effort to understand and adjust himself to this element of the divine within him. Traditionally he has believed that the divine within comes from a divine being without, and religious communities have divided over their interpretation of that divinity. But it is the thesis of our interpretation of religious practice that, providing we rightly understand the nature of the divine within, as a will to universal good, we can and should co-operate as a religious community without insisting on further agreement in matters of religious theory. Here is the basis for a universal religion, maintaining the essence of Christianity, united in the faith and practice of human brotherhood, finding the basis of that faith and practice in a verified knowledge of the divine nature, and agreeing to differ on its further interpretation.

Yet these further questions are not unimportant. They are relevant to human hopes and affect the power of human faith. So in the third section of the book we attempt an interpretation of religious theory. And here we find in the moral nature of man empirical evidence that the human spirit is organic to a larger spiritual reality much as the human body is organic to a larger physical reality. In this organismic philosophy we find a conception of God and a hope for human destiny that are adequate to religious needs and aspirations and free from the fears, constraints and false hopes whereby religious beliefs have too often depressed, enslaved and deceived the human race.

In the presentation of this thesis alternative views have been duly considered and thus care has been taken to develop the discussion in a form suitable for use as a college textbook for courses in the philosophy of religion. It is hoped that many teachers may regard its central thesis as sufficiently important to select it for intensive study, gathering around it other reading material such as that suggested in the bibliography. Others may set it, or some part of it, for supplementary reading and discussion. The greater part of the book is non-technical and will be found to be easy reading for any educated person. Chapters 8 to 10 are necessarily philosophical and require more careful study. So, too, may parts of chapters 1 and 5. But no part of the book should be beyond the capacity of the average college student, even without previous training in philosophy.

The title of the book indicates its philosophical standpoint, temper and tone. It is realistic in its theory of knowledge and of values, in its acceptance of the reality of the physical world, and in its concepts of God and human mental life. In these respects it is in accord with the metaphysical argument presented by the author in *Reality and Value*. It is also realistic in its frank facing of the darker facts of life, of the problem of physical evil, of the sense of sin, and of the uglier features of religion. But its realism is not pessimism and does not end in skepticism. It finds instead, in known reality, the ground for a lively faith in God and man. This viewpoint was foreshadowed and outlined by the author in an article in the *Hibbert Journal* for October 1939 on "The Natural Form of Religious Experience." The book is, in large part, based on lectures given in a course on the philosophy of religion at the University of Wisconsin during the past five years. Parts of chapter 6 have been published in an article, "Liberalism as a Theory of Human Nature," which appeared in the *Journal of Social Philosophy and Jurisprudence,* January 1942.

A. CAMPBELL GARNETT

The University of Wisconsin
Madison, Wisconsin

Contents

PREFACE   vii

INTRODUCTION

I. METHODS AND VIEWS   1

PART I

ANALYSIS

II. THE BIRTH OF RELIGION IN THE INDIVIDUAL   35
III. THE BIRTH OF RELIGION IN THE RACE   60
IV. TYPICAL BELIEFS AND PROBLEMS   90

PART II

INTERPRETATION OF PRACTICE

V. THE ESSENTIAL IDEAL   123
VI. THE GREAT SOCIETY   151
VII. THE RELIGIOUS COMMUNITY   178

PART III

INTERPRETATION OF THEORY

VIII. THE NATURE OF MAN   209
IX. THE NATURE OF GOD   244
X. THE NATURE OF GOD (continued)   269

EPILOGUE

XI. THE CHRISTIAN FAITH — 301

    BIBLIOGRAPHY — 323

    INDEX — 327

INTRODUCTION

Methods and Views

THE TASK AND METHOD OF PHILOSOPHY

IN THE twentieth century the tide of philosophical thought has turned from speculation to criticism. It is customary to distinguish two types of philosophical question, synoptic and critical. The former is the attempt to take the conclusions of all the special sciences and weave them together into a consistent synoptic view of the world as a whole. Because there are gaps in our knowledge unfilled by the special sciences the task is essentially speculative. But science is constantly closing these gaps, and new sciences are constantly springing up to explore, by their own special methods, fields over which speculative philosophy formerly ranged with little restriction from organized knowledge of facts.

Thus the mansion of synoptic philosophy has been left impoverished. It is like a fine old house, once the center of a great estate, when the family has had to dispose of one part of the land after another to younger sons and enterprising strangers, until there is too little left to maintain the traditional scale of activities. When that happens the only hope of the family is to turn its resources and energy to some new enterprise. Fortunately, the members of the philosophical family have been able to do this. Among the resources of their tradition they have found and refurbished the old instruments of critical analysis; and amid the confused abundance of our modern intellectual production they have found a useful and interesting sphere of activity. At first this new trend in philosophy looked like complete abandonment of the old synoptic program; and there were many who were quite willing to make the sacrifice. But as the work of critical analysis goes on, working down to deeper levels and on to wider issues, the possibility and the need of a synoptic view seem to return in another way and with a better prospect of success.

The program of critical philosophy calls for a critical examination of the fundamental assumptions of every science and of the concepts it uses to describe the phases of experience with which it deals. The assumptions call for clarification and frank recognition. The concepts call for analysis to bring out all the variations of their meaning. And the experience they are used to describe also calls for analysis in order to insure, on the one hand, that our concepts make a distinction in thought wherever there is a difference in experience and, on the other hand, that they do not make a distinction where there is no difference. This has to be done for the sensory-motor experience whereby we acquire our knowledge of the physical world, for the intellectual experience of our logical thinking, and for all those elusive ranges of feeling that affect our social, moral, aesthetic and religious life. Then, as a further problem, the results of critical analysis call for definition, definition calls for comparison, and comparison for a fitting together of the resultant concepts into the kind of whole that most naturally or reasonably describes the experience from which they are derived. Thus synoptic philosophy begins to emerge again, not as the major task of philosophy, but as the outgrowth and final discipline of the whole endeavor. It is more restrained; but its foundations are better laid, by reason of the more thorough spadework of critical analysis. Something of the old spacious dignity and exhilaration has thus returned to the mansions of philosophy, but without the flamboyance and pretentiousness of former days. As this discussion proceeds we shall see this tendency work itself out in the critical analysis of religious concepts and the experience from which they are derived.[1]

Before we actually begin our study of religion, however, perhaps an illustration from another field may help to make this matter of method clearer. In the Platonic dialogue called the *Meno* Socrates, having shown Meno that he does not know what virtue is, and having admitted that he himself does not know either, proposes that they start an inquiry upon the subject. To this Meno objects that, if they do not know what virtue is, they cannot know what they are inquiring about and will not recognize it if they find it. Socrates replies by stating the conviction that the human mind has resources of knowledge of which it is not clearly conscious, and that these can be brought to light in the course of reflection if only we can ask ourselves the right questions.[2] In proof of this he takes an ignorant Greek slave and, by judicious questioning, leads him to the discovery that the square on the diagonal of a given square is twice the area of the given square. All that was necessary was to take familiar examples of the concepts derived from ordinary experience of space, such as squares and lines, relate them together in various ways, and by careful observation discover that they had properties and relations not previously recognized. Socrates was mistaken in thinking that some mystical explanation of the phenomenon is necessary. The concepts used were obtained by an

[1] This method, which combines the logical analysis of concepts with the phenomenological analysis of experience, seems to me to be the distinctive and proper method of philosophical investigation. It is, in a strictly proper sense, both empirical and scientific, yet distinguishes the philosophical sciences by their method and task from the empirical sciences in the narrower sense. Broadly speaking, in " science " the problem is generalization and the method inductive; in " philosophy " the problem is definition and the method analytic.

[2] Socrates' own explanation of this phenomenon is that the soul must have learned these things in a previous existence and recollects them in the course of the inquiry. This is an excellent example of the way synoptic philosophy often closes inquiry by overhastily jumping to some far-reaching conclusion.

elementary analysis of the spatial character of experience. The further information was obtained by an analysis of the logical implications of these concepts. It is in this way that all our mathematical knowledge has been developed; and in the course of it the definitions, even of the original concepts, have been greatly refined and made more adequate to the description of the relevant types of experience.

But if Socrates was wrong in his explanation of the reason why analysis is able to discover new knowledge, he was certainly right in his contention that it is a genuine method of discovery. There are innumerable relations and properties involved in our common experience of space and number that we ordinarily fail to notice; and these, when noticed, constitute structures involving further relations and properties that may or may not be noticed. The same is true, as Socrates contended, in the realm of our moral experience. But here the experience itself is vaguer than that of space and number, and the common concepts with which we attempt to describe it are much less adequate. As Socrates tirelessly insisted, when the man in the street (not to mention the philosopher) talks about virtue he contradicts himself so frequently that he demonstrates that he has no adequate conception of what it is. Yet Socrates was right in insisting that, by persistent questioning of himself in the light of all his relevant experience, he can clarify those concepts. He can show that they stand for something intelligible to himself and his fellows as descriptive of certain common features of human experience, and that he can define those concepts with sufficient clarity to draw from them deductions and interpretations of great significance for life.

PROBLEMS OF METHOD IN THE PHILOSOPHY OF RELIGION

The question of method in the philosophy of religion is very similar to that in ethics. Indeed, as we shall see, the two studies are closely interrelated. Ethics may, for the most part, be conveniently separated from religion, but it is disastrous to try to separate religion from ethics. And just as, in ethics, a little inquiry raises the question whether anyone really knows what virtue is, so too one soon finds a similar or worse confusion as to the nature of religion. Professor Leuba, writing in 1912, listed forty-eight definitions of religion,[3] and scholars have been so busy with the subject since then that they must have added at least as many more. The contradictions and conflicts that people find when they begin to discuss religion are notorious.

From all this one may well conclude that we do not know what religion is. But one would be wrong to argue, with Meno, that therefore it is fruitless to inquire about it. The numerous conflicting definitions offered, even in the last quarter of a century, have added much to our knowledge and greatly clarified our thinking. By their very differences they have brought to light neglected features, and by their critical analyses they have gone far to distinguish the essential from the unessential. Research in the philosophy of religion is simply the task of carrying this process further and doing it more and more thoroughly and systematically. In this way we grow to understand more exactly and more fully what it is to be religious, and what this capacity or feature of human nature implies for the rest of human nature. We may come to see, too, that this feature of human nature has implications that affect our view of the rest of nature, of which human nature is a part. Finally, the deeper insight thus gained into human nature and the rest of nature may reflectively illuminate religion.

In this investigation we have to begin with the rough-and-ready concept of religion that we have picked up from our

[3] J. H. Leuba: *A Psychological Study of Religion* (New York: The Macmillan Co., 1912) , Appendix.

social environment and filled with meaning from our own experience. We soon discover that we all have different concepts and differences of experience. But if my concept and experience were entirely different from the reader's, then what is here written would be entirely unintelligible to him. So if we can understand each other at all when we talk about religion we have *some* experience of it in common. But when we speak thus of " religious experience " we do not mean by it anything highly unusual or esoteric. It is simply a term to describe the kind of experience people have when they engage in religious activity, including the thinking about religious matters. That, of course, varies from time to time and from person to person. But we shall be looking for the most common and distinctive and significant elements in it. We shall try to define them and work out their implications. Everyone who is willing to give careful and critical attention to religious ideas and practices can thus join in such an inquiry and make his contribution out of his own experience. People who do this will understand each other just in so far as they have a common, or similar, experience and succeed in elucidating and communicating it. Each, by his own and other people's efforts at elucidation and communication, will add content, definiteness and significance to his concept of religion. He adds to his knowledge of religion. He learns from others; but he does so only in so far as they enable him to find something comparable to their experience in himself. In the last resort, phenomenological analysis is analysis of one's own experience; and it is communicable only because each person's own experience of facts and values is an experience of the facts and values of a common world.

But though our whole understanding of such concepts as religion and morality has, in the last resort, to be wrought out of our own experience, it would remain very poor without the illumination we receive from others. It is necessary to bring to bear upon our own experience, therefore, a description of a great variety of the experiences of others, and to seek to enter into sympathetic understanding of them. We need to inquire, not merely how others have felt about certain facts and ideas, but why they have felt that way about them, and why we, perhaps, feel differently. The materials for analysis, therefore, need to be gathered from history and from a wide range of religious experience and activity different from our own. We must not confine ourselves to our own religious tradition, even though that tradition probably does contain everything necessary for a complete understanding of religion. The trouble is that we are sure to fail to see the significance of much of it, and to overemphasize the significance of other features, unless we compare it with other religious traditions. In particular, much can be learned from a study of the religion of primitive peoples. This is not because religion is there seen in its simplest and most essential form, for that, as we shall see, is not the case. Primitive religion is so thickly overlaid with adventitious accretions, and so confused with nonreligious features and motives, that the genuine core of religion in it is difficult to detect. Its distorted emphases carry us far astray if we take them for the most essential features. But the very poverty of primitive religion, when we have cleared away the rubbish, helps us to evaluate the essentials. And the extremes of religion, such as that of the primitive and that typical of the modern scholar, and those of the saint, the prophet and the neurotic, constitute test cases for every theory of religion. They are variants from the common type that the theory of the type must explain. Each of them, when properly understood, casts a flood of light upon obscure phases of the common and undistinguished type of religious experience that most of us share. Thus history, anthropology, psychology and theology all combine to bring grist to the mill of the student who would undertake a philosophical analysis and interpretation of the concept of religion.

RATIONALISM AND SYNOPTIC PHILOSOPHY

This empirical and critical approach to the philosophy of religion leads to a very different conception of religion itself from that assumed when the synoptic task of philosophy is undertaken without first finding a basis for it through thoroughgoing critical analysis. The critical approach issues in an empirical theory of the basis of religion. It leads to an emphasis upon will and the sense of values as constituents of religion at least as important as the intellectual. The synoptic approach inevitably emphasizes the intellectual content and even suggests that religion is primarily and basically a system of thought — a theology. This theory of religion is commonly known as rationalism.[4] It means that man first comes to *believe* something about the existence of gods, spirits or other higher powers, and then, on the basis of this belief, concludes that it is right or prudent to worship and obey them. Everything is thus made to depend upon the truth of these beliefs. And the beliefs have to be supported by reasoned argument from the facts of nature and history, i.e., upon a synoptic philosophy or an alleged revelation attested to by historical and supposedly reliable witnesses.

This is probably the commonest theory of religion and is maintained by dogmatists the world over. Since religious beliefs are so various and conflicting, these dogmatists usually maintain either that all religions are false or that all are false except their own. Further, this rationalistic theory of religion means that the motive of religion is ultimately and essentially that of self-preservation.[5] Man is depicted as cul-

[4] For a critique of rationalism, cf. John Baillie: *The Interpretation of Religion* (New York: Charles Scribner's Sons, 1928) , especially Part II, chap. 2.

[5] This conclusion is explicitly and logically drawn from the rationalistic premises by George Foot Moore in *The Birth and Growth of Religion* (New York: Charles Scribner's Sons, 1923) .

tivating religious beliefs and practices as a way of meeting practical problems of life that are beyond his natural means of control. Of course, it is true that this is often *one* motive of religious activity. But for rationalism it is the fundamental motive; others are merely adventitious. This reverses the conclusion that, as we shall see, develops from an empirical and analytical inquiry, for this seems to show that religious practices (including thinking and believing) are performed for the sake of the values immediately found in them, and that other motives enter in only as the development of belief lays a basis for them. Thus for rationalism religion is first a belief and secondarily a pursuit of values; for empiricism it is first a pursuit of values and secondarily a system of beliefs.

Only a thoroughgoing analysis of the concept of religion and of the experience on which it rests can disprove the rationalistic theory. But three preliminary considerations may be cited as suggesting its falsity. First, the fact that religion itself has survived such tremendous changes of belief. If the whole superstructure rested upon a basis of belief, one would expect that destruction of the beliefs would cause the whole structure to collapse. But it does not. When people find even their most fundamental religious beliefs proved false they more often retain as much of their religious activity as they can, modifying the total structure as seems necessary and finding new beliefs to fit in the places of the old. A person may be very deeply distressed at losing his religious beliefs, but he often develops just as fine and satisfying a religion with a mere fraction of his original and traditional system, or with none of it. Indeed, many who have gone through that experience claim — as do, for example, the liberal Protestants and humanists — that they have found the way to a finer religious life than before. At the same time it must be admitted that some sort of belief forms an integral part of every person's religion. Many fail utterly to reconstitute their religious life after the shattering of their beliefs, yet these often look back on their former religion with a sense of loss and need. It is a very superficial kind of religion that can be lost with the loss of belief and never missed, and it is only the bad types of religious belief that can be lost with a sense of relief and gain. Thus the familiar phenomenon of continuity of religion in spite of forced abandonment of religious beliefs, strongly indicates that belief is *not* the most fundamental element in religion.

The second and third considerations may be dealt with together. Religion shows its independence of any specific belief in the fact of the enormous variety of beliefs that may be incorporated in a religion, and in the fact that the practical manifestations characteristic of religion may be present even where all the generally recognized characteristic beliefs are absent. There may be one God or many gods, or no gods but only a vague multitude of spirits. Even the belief in spirits does not seem to be essential to religion, for the religious ceremonies of the Australian aboriginals, though they believe in the existence of spirits, are in no sense a worship or even a cajoling of them. Further, in the teaching of Buddha and Mahavira [6] we have religious systems which were very vital to their founders and their immediate followers. Yet in these systems religious activity is entirely dissociated from the gods and spirits in which, on naturalistic and traditional grounds, they believed. Again, in the thought of Spinoza, Auguste Comte and the modern humanists we have religion dissociated from all its characteristic forms of belief except the ethical. Yet in these leaders of ancient and modern life and thought there is a rich and strong spiritual life; and it finds sustenance in its own distinctive vision and practice to a degree matched only by the best in more traditional religions. Religion is made to be something very poor indeed

6 The founder of Jainism.

if the essence of it is not recognized to be present in these cases. And if it is, then we must also recognize that the essence of religion is not to be found in any of its characteristic forms of thought. Religion, of course, always *involves* some thought, some belief. But it is religion that produces the characteristic forms of thought, not the characteristic forms of thought that produce all the rest of the religion. These other features of religion, of course, are experience and action. Religious thought interprets and directs them. At the level at which they are religious they are not devoid of thought; but it is they, and not the varying thoughts that interpret them, that are fundamental.

THE RESULTS OF RATIONALISM

If the rationalistic theory of religion is adopted then the characteristic forms of religious thought have to be treated as the only genuine forms. Others are irreligious or only pseudoreligious. It becomes a problem to explain how the fruits of a religious life can be brought forth from such non-religious soil. Further, in defense of religion it becomes necessary to prove the truth of its characteristic forms of thought. These are so various that a certain omnipresent core has to be extracted as the essential minimum. This, it is generally agreed among rationalists, is the belief in a spiritual power or powers, higher than man and able to affect his welfare. If the religion is to be ethical it must be added that this power (or powers) is concerned with man's moral behavior. Everything then appears to rest upon the question whether these basic beliefs are true. The evidence for this must, for the most part, be drawn from outside the religious life itself. For the religious life, if it rests upon belief, can do little to prove the truth of the beliefs upon which it rests. The mystical experiences to which it can point are too easily explained away as psychological results of the antecedent beliefs. At best it can show the practical value of those beliefs and so justify the will to believe. But the will to believe requires that other considerations shall at least have established an open possibility of the belief's being true. And the will to believe must be very strong if it is not to demand probabilities to support it in addition to mere possibilities open to it. So these, too, have to be sought in nonreligious considerations.

This makes religion dependent upon synoptic philosophy. Religion is represented as depending on the truth of certain metaphysical propositions, and, notoriously, no propositions are more difficult to prove. The fact that they are also just as difficult to disprove does not help unless the will to believe is strongly present. But people who pride themselves on being tough-minded scorn to be influenced by the will to believe. Many others, who are not tough-minded, are emotionally influenced by the spirit of the age, which likes to be thought tough-minded; so they too scorn the will to believe. Thus all metaphysical propositions are rejected as offering no basis for action and no justification of belief. Religion is left to those who are " tender-minded " and influenced by the will to believe. In reality, of course, tough-mindedness is simply a tendency to do one's thinking without paying much attention to the values involved in the situation, and tender-mindedness is a tendency to pay considerable attention to values. One type tends to make the mistake of ignoring the relevance of values, and the other of allowing its thinking to be unduly influenced by them. But an age that is proud of its tough-mindedness is unconscious of its blindness. The metaphysic that pays little attention to values seems to it the more reasonable. That which gives primacy to values seems like an expression merely of the will to believe. And since religion, on the common rationalistic interpretation of it, seems to be based upon such a metaphysic, it is treated with a lofty skepticism.

Yet another reason why rationalism leads to skepticism is found in the history of religion. Most religious beliefs are obviously false. So if belief is the foundation of religion its foundations are mostly false. Even if the so-called " essential " belief in a higher spiritual power should be true, it is certain that most of the reasons upon which it has been based in the past are bad reasons, now shown to be false. People have based their belief in gods upon all sorts of stories of revelations and manifestations and upon theories of how the world was made — stories and theories which will not bear investigation. These the rationalistic supporter of religion now rejects and in their place puts more modern metaphysical arguments, some very ingenious, learned, profound and obscure. But these arguments, even if sound, are not the ones on which religious beliefs originally rested. The original arguments were bad. But by fortunate accident, the rationalist has to maintain, they led to some sound conclusions. Thus, if belief is the basis of religion, and the original beliefs were based on errors, religion was originally based on error. Yet it flourished and grew. So, if this be the case, the skeptic may be pardoned for doubting that the new underpinning, supplied by the rationalist to support the tottering structure, is any sounder than the old.

But the situation is very different if religion is based on experience. Religious thought or belief is then an interpretation of that experience, and religious activity a response to it. The response may be more or less appropriate; the interpretation may be more or less correct. Both are questions for careful investigation. The fact that many interpretations are certainly wrong and many responses inappropriate does not eliminate the need of finding the right ones. It means that the task has difficulties, but not that it is impossible. If there are " characteristic " interpretations and responses, then these, in their essential features, have a certain probability in their favor if they do not conflict with other evidence. They, of course, need careful and constant re-examination. But the fact of error in the past, though it indicates the need for caution and the folly of dogmatism, does not of itself cast doubt upon the interpretations of the present. On the contrary, the predominant interpretations of the past, since they (on this theory) grow out of experience, constitute important material to guide our search for the correct interpretation. So, with this in mind, we may take a preliminary glance at some of the empirical interpretations of religion.

ROMANTIC EMPIRICISM: SCHLEIERMACHER

The father of modern religious empiricism is Friedrich Schleiermacher. His revolt against rationalism is an important part of the romantic movement which succeeded the Age of Reason. In harmony with the spirit of the times it expressed the conviction that the roots of religion are to be found neither in reason nor in morality but in feeling. Religion, he pointed out, is not a matter of knowledge but of piety. "True religion," he asserts in the second of his famous *Speeches on Religion,* " is a sense and taste for the infinite." [7] In his major work, *The Christian Faith,* he maintains that "the essence of piety is a feeling of absolute dependence or, which is to say the same thing, a consciousness of our relation with God." [8] This is said to be the highest grade of feeling, but it is indescribable. It is an " intuition," an " immediate self-consciousness " which one may contemplate but cannot express. It is something psychologically more fundamental than ideas. Ideas and words are inadequate to describe it. Ideas, therefore, are not necessary to religion — not even the idea of God. " Christian doctrines are expressions of the Christian religious emotions set forth

[7] *Schleiermachers sämtliche Werke* (Berlin: Reimer Verlag) , I, 188.
[8] *Ibid.,* III, 14.

in speech." [9] Such accounts are necessary though always inadequate. "The manner in which the Deity is present to man in feeling is decisive of the worth of his religion, not the manner, always inadequate, in which it is copied in idea." [10]

Schleiermacher, in revolt against both Scholasticism and Calvinism, had gone for his inspiration to Plato and Spinoza. The practical piety of common men had shown him that a living religion is independent of theological knowledge. Plato and Spinoza had convinced him that the divine immanence is more important than the divine transcendence. The skepticism in which the Age of Reason ended impelled him to look deeper for the roots of religion. His psychology suggested just three possible alternatives in the tripartite division of mental life into perception, feeling and activity. The first, he said, issues in science, the third in morality, the second in religion. Thus religion seemed to be saved from the attacks of science. It had a world of its own to cultivate. It had an acquaintance with the divine as immediate as that of the senses with their world. In that acquaintance it had the basis for tentative affirmations about the spiritual world (the world discovered in the inner self, but not confined to it) which science could not gainsay.

Schleiermacher's revolt started a vital new movement in religious thinking. But it was only a beginning. He had pointed to the fact that religion does not begin or end with dogmas, whatever part they play in between. He had asserted the need of a clear analysis of the inner religious life if the true nature of religion is to be understood. But that problem of analysis has proved very elusive, and Schleiermacher's was only a first attempt upon it. To criticize, refine and correct his work has been the task of his successors. His

9 *Ibid.*, p. 94.

10 Schleiermacher: *Speeches on Religion to Its Cultured Despisers,* translated by John Oman (London: Kegan, Paul, Trench, Truebner & Co., 1893), p. 97.

notion of "feeling," "intuition" or "immediate self-consciousness" has proved too vague. Feeling, in the strict sense, as James Ward has pointed out,[11] involves a subject that feels and an object upon which the activity of that subject is directed; i.e., I always feel *somehow* about *something*. And that something is always some *particular* object. We do not directly *feel* the Infinite. Only after we have thought about it do we have any feelings *about* it. Schleiermacher in his earlier writings used the term "intuition" as synonymous with feeling, but later dropped it in order to get rid entirely of the notion that religion must have an intellectual basis. But to fall back on feeling as the explanation does not suffice. It cannot account for the fact that religion is always vitally concerned with objective conditions and registers the conviction that its object, which it calls "God," is objective. If feeling alone were primarily concerned then religion should be merely a problem of inner personal adjustment. Yet it is never merely that. Schleiermacher's theory tends to degenerate into a vague pantheism in which the vital distinctions of good and evil, truth and falsehood, are lost. But with such interpretations of itself religion never can be content. So an empirical theory of religion, if it is to make the vitality of religion intelligible, must return to its problem of analysis to seek the root of religion in something more definite and less subjective than a vacuous feeling of dependence.

MYSTICAL EMPIRICISM: WILLIAM JAMES

Schleiermacher, by reason of his references to intuition and the vagueness of his concept of a feeling of the divine, is often called a mystic. A more distinctively mystical turn is, however, given to empirical religious thought by William James. He finds that, amid all the variations of creed and practice,

11 In *Psychological Principles* (London: Cambridge University Press, 1920), chap. 2, § 3.

the religious consciousness universally bears witness to a certain common nucleus of testimony. First, there is a vague uneasiness, a sense that there is something wrong about us as we actually are; and second, the solution of this uneasiness lies in " a sense that we are saved from this wrongness by making proper connection with the higher powers." [12] But this sense of a contact with higher powers is merely mystical, ineffable and transient. It cannot be subjected to close analytic and scientific inquiry. However, James has a hypothesis that fits this mystical experience into place among a mass of known and ordered psychological facts, and at the same time suggests that the religious conviction concerning contact with higher powers may be true.

This hypothesis is based on two sets of psychological facts. First, there is the commonly experienced division within the self, wherein a person feels that his neglected and unfulfilled ideals are really a part of his " better self," so that the division can be overcome by wholeheartedly identifying himself with that better part. Second, there are the facts of the marginal consciousness and the subconscious mental process. These reveal a great reservoir of feeling and meaning from which influences flow into the attentive consciousness in ways not explicable in terms of the consciously present sense experience, logical thought and associative connections. In the solution of that inner conflict, says James, whereby the individual identifies himself with his higher self,

he becomes conscious that this higher part is coterminous and continuous with a *More* of the same quality which is operative in the universe outside of him, and which he can keep in working touch with, and in a fashion get on board of and save himself when all his lower being has gone to pieces in the wreck.[13]

[12] William James: *Varieties of Religious Experience* (New York: Longmans, Gréen & Co., 1902) , p. 508.
[13] *Ibid.*

When we ask what is this " more," and whether it is really external to the individual, James replies: ". . . whatever it may be on its *farther* side, the ' more ' with which in religious experience we feel ourselves connected is on its *hither* side the subconscious continuation of our conscious life." [14]

But the subconscious was, in James's day, beyond the pale of scientific research, for Freud had not yet given to the world the key to its investigation. So, for James, empirical inquiry ended there. However, beyond the reach of science he ventured an " overbelief " that the wider self of the subconscious is, on its *farther* side, continuous with a wider spiritual reality, the unconscious being that part of the human mind susceptible to influences from that transcendental region. This hypothesis he found to be suggested by the empirical fact of the continuity of the narrow and egoistic part of the self with " a wider self through which saving experiences come," [15] for why, otherwise, should these finer influences well up from these subliminal regions of the mind? Beyond this, James found pragmatic support for his overbelief in its psychological value, it being beyond the range of scientific facts to prove or disprove and thus a proper place for exercise of the will to believe.[16]

There has been no greater master of psychological analysis than William James, and his description of the facts here is beyond cavil. However, much work has been done, especially upon subconscious phenomena, since James wrote, and we now know that, in so far as the *intellectual content* of the unconscious includes a " more " that is " of the same quality " with the " higher part " of the self, it is a deposit of previous activity of the conscious self. Thus it is not in this region that

[14] *Ibid.*, p. 512.
[15] *Ibid.*, p. 515.
[16] For a very valuable discussion of James's conception of the will to believe see R. B. Perry: *In the Spirit of William James* (New Haven, Conn.: Yale University Press, 1938) , chap. 5.

we should look for the roots of the better self. There certainly is a tendency of the self to reach out after values that are not merely egoistic, and this tendency does come into conflict with other, more prominent tendencies. This conflict, as we shall see, comes close to the heart of religious experience. But more light on the whole process from normal religious experience, of both civilized man and the primitive, is needed, and a better understanding of the unconscious is required. It is not satisfactory to pass the whole problem over to an inscrutable " unconscious " region of mind and leave religion floundering in the ineffabilities of mysticism. James, following up with keen analysis the vaguer beginnings of Schleiermacher, has ably pioneered. But further empirical inquiry is needed.

Following in the trail that James blazed, a great many investigators have become convinced that the roots of religion are to be found in a more or less mystical experience that may be isolated by psychological analysis. Notable among these are Ernst Troeltsch and Rudolph Otto. Space forbids that we should investigate them all, though concerning Otto's theory we shall have more to say later. This general trend, however, is to be noted among those who, more recently, have attempted these analyses. There is a growing tendency to give more and more definite shape to religious experience as essentially a type of value experience, though opinions differ as to how far it is purely subjective and how far its objective features are spiritual in nature. This tendency to recognize the object of religious experience as an object of value is, at the same time, a tendency away from mysticism toward concreteness of the religious object.

SYMBOLISTIC EMPIRICISM: AMES AND WIEMAN

Those empiricists who have been influenced strongly by the instrumentalist philosophy of Professor John Dewey and, more recently, by its less profound but more precise Anglo-

German counterpart, logical positivism, have, quite naturally, seen in religious symbolism a key to the value and power of religious experience. In Dewey's philosophy, mind is a system of meanings, and meaning is an organic process functioning symbolically. Further, the growth of meaning is practically equivalent to the increase of value.[17] Thus symbols are not only real, but are objects of supreme importance. With this philosophy as a mental background Dean Edward Scribner Ames [18] turned to a psychological inquiry into the roots of religion and found its origin in primitive ceremonial, but emphasized that that which gives a religious character to a ceremony is not the mere fact that it is symbolic but its relevance to the values of the group life. Belief in spirits is not the root of religion, but spirits find their place in religion as symbols of the vital interests of the group. The same is true of totem and myth and sacrifice. The religious consciousness, Ames claims, is not essentially distinguishable from the social consciousness, the practices and beliefs characteristic of religion being due to its tendency to pursue social aims through the influence of symbols. The idea of God is a socially developed symbol into which a group of people have projected their highest interests and ideals. At its best it signifies the totality of human values, and its power over the human mind is the power of the meaning society has poured into it.

This same point of view, in essentials, has been developed, corrected and deepened by Professor H. N. Wieman in a series of brilliant and stimulating books culminating in his contribution to a co-operative volume with Professor W. M.

[17] " Good consists in the meaning that is experienced to belong to an activity when conflict and entanglement of various incompatible impulses and habits terminate in a unified orderly release in action." — John Dewey: *Human Nature and Conduct* (New York: Henry Holt & Co., 1932) , p. 210.

[18] Cf. his *The Psychology of Religious Experience* (New York: Houghton Mifflin Co., 1910) and *Religion* (New York: Henry Holt & Co., 1929) .

Horton.[19] His instrumentalist theory of knowledge and posi-
tivistic presuppositions, of course, make it impossible for him
to arrive at a belief in a personal God,[20] but the penetration
and breadth of understanding of his analysis of the religious
life are all the more striking for being free from any such influence upon his thinking. The term " God," he contends, is
correctly used for whatever rightfully commands the supreme
devotion of man, whether personal or supernatural or not.
This, he finds, points beyond the range of immediate experience, of the world as known, to a system of real processes of
the natural world pregnant with a meaning and value yet unrealized but in course of realization. " God (or the work of
God) is unlimited growth of meaning and value," [21] a creative
synthesis that is superhuman and suprapersonal, though, so
far as we know, unconscious.[22] The lack of consciousness
Wieman refuses to regard as a serious deficiency, while the
nonpersonal nature of God, he claims, removes from our conception of the divine nature certain limitations that are alleged to go with the notion of personality.

These negative elements in Wieman's conception of God
are due chiefly to the limitations of his starting point in philosophy.[23] The positive elements are due to his profound
analysis of religious experience. " There is," he says, " a pe-

[19] Wieman and Horton: *The Growth of Religion* (Chicago: Willett, Clark
& Co., 1928) .

[20] Instrumentalist philosophy seeks to interpret the difference between the
mental and nonmental as a mere difference of function developed by organisms
in the course of evolution. For a discussion of this question see chap. 8 of this
book.

[21] Wieman and Horton, *op. cit.*, p. 323.

[22] *Ibid.*, p. 365.

[23] In an article, " God is More than We Can Think " (*Christendom*, I,
433) , Wieman says: " The empirical method requires, as I understand it,
that every belief be formed and tested by sensory observation, experimental behavior and rational inference." Here, like so many other empiricists, he fails
to give due weight to the fact that mental acts and values are also data of
observation, though not sensory.

culiar quality of living, incommensurate with anything else, which religion alone can give." It is " to live only ' for the will of God,' " and the will of God is " the creative synthesis of each unique situation." It is marked by a life-transforming decision to pursue a good that transcends the established order of specific human desire. " It is a self-commitment to the service and enjoyment of something that is better, greater, richer than any definite thing or objective which can be brought fully within our understanding." It brings " a sense of alienation between the order of life's abundance and the established order of human existence," a recognition that specific human desires are maladjusted to the total goodness of God, a " sense of sin " which is simply the obverse side of the recognition that the continuous remaking of personality is always capable of further heights and riches. Finally, it involves a " world-transforming interest," a " radical instrumentalism " that seeks " to make all things means to an end that cannot as yet assume definite form in our experience because we have not attained it." It is a propulsive movement of life that finds release and specific direction only through crisis and decision and requires for its cultivation the communion of a group of kindred spirits.[24] This, of course, is presented as an analysis of religious living at its purest and best, but, for that very reason, as involving what is most *essential* to and characteristic of religion. It is a self-surrender and devotion in which

one gives up specific self-direction as at present established and commits himself to the direction of the best that is unpredictably brought forth in the ceaseless innovations and creative syntheses of actual living. . . . In religious phraseology, this means to be seeking always God's will and not one's own.[25]

What, then, is the nature of that to which the truly religious person is thus devoted and which he calls " the will of

[24] Wieman, in Wieman and Horton, *op. cit.*, chap. 10 *passim.*
[25] *Ibid.*, p. 304.

God "? Wieman rightly insists that it is not merely an "ideal" in the ordinary sense of some specific goal framed by the imagination. It is both too fluctuating and too close to us for that. Yet it is more than merely the progressively unfolding values of the real world. It is these and the continuous promise of something more beyond. Perhaps we might interpret Wieman's meaning by saying that it is a feature of reality that always points beyond itself to a vague and *fluid ideal* that calls us to reach actively beyond the present and actual to something of supreme worth not yet realized but realizable.

Three features, he declares, must be possessed by anything that can be regarded as worthy of that supreme devotion of man which alone is religious in quality: It must be superhuman, having a power for good greater than the intelligently directed efforts of men. It must be the best reality in existence, supremely worthful, the sovereign good. It must be that which exercises the greatest power for good and must be limited to that which does good. Is there any such reality? Certainly the universe as a whole is not such. But it is to be found, says Wieman, *within* the universe. It is the process of "unlimited connective growth," connective growth being distinguished from competitive growth by its harmony with, and support of, all further connective growth. Competitive growth is the root of evil. Connective growth is purely good. "God is the *growth of connections between* activities which are appreciable," which for us is equivalent to the "growth of value and meaning in the world." [26] In Wieman's instrumentalist philosophy this growth of value and meaning is growth of symbolic behavior (including language), for it is symbolic behavior that is creative of mind, personality, society and all their values.[27]

[26] *Ibid.*, pp. 350 ff.

[27] In a privately circulated paper from which he permits me to quote, Wieman says: "Symbolic behavior is the outgrowth of sublinguistic developments which reach very far down into the total process of existence. The

Of God thus conceived Wieman speaks with a personal pronoun, for He is declared to be suprapersonal, and the impersonal " it " implies something infrapersonal. But this usage, and a certain rhetorical freedom, make it possible to present this unconscious, nonpersonal system of social, biological and physical tendencies to connective growth, which he calls God, as something much more satisfying to the religious consciousness than it really is. God, Wieman says, responds to the intimate needs and attitudes of each individual personality.[28] He is a source of human personality and fellowship, giving to personalities all their enrichment and fullest flowering. He catches up the intimate and secret outreaching of the human heart. " We know the mighty gentleness, we know the tender care which characterize his being." [29]

Now if we agree — as I think we may and as our own analysis will proceed to show — that religious living involves all that Wieman says of it, then we must also agree that it demands for its object of devotion a being with at least all the positive characters that he has ascribed to God, including these last named. A God that could not be believed to be all this would scarcely call forth, or be worthy of, the kind of devotion Wieman has described as religious. But one may question whether a God that is nonpersonal and unconscious could really fulfill these demands of the religious consciousness if the personal pronoun and the rhetoric did not cover up its deficiencies. Can the religious person be satisfied with the " response " of a blind and unfeeling cosmic activity, or with the " fellowship " of an unconscious process? Take away the personalization involved in the use of such terms as " will," " tender care " and " gentleness," and that which is

---

reality of God is this sublinguistic process which sustains and promotes the growth of symbolic behavior, plus the growth itself, and all the infinite possibilities of enrichment to which it points and leads."

[28] *The Growth of Religion*, p. 361.

[29] *Ibid.*, p. 365.

left is something too poor to call forth the devotional feeling earlier described.

The cultivation of the religious life, as Wieman well recognizes, requires the fellowship of kindred spirits to sustain us in the crises and draw the best out of us. But the severest test of the religious life comes when the good that a man would do is not appreciated and the kindred spirits who should stand by him fail to understand. It is then that the religious person needs to find strength in the conviction that the good he does is shared by One at least who does appreciate, and whose approval outweighs all the rest. Without that conviction few if any of us can scale the heights of human devotion and stand alone. Without it most of the prophets would have failed to face the hostile multitudes. And such is the shyness of human beings about their deeper aspirations, and such the obtuseness of those who should understand and appreciate, that the need is commoner than might at first be thought. It is the need of a God with whom the individual may feel a sense of communion. But there can be no real communion with an unconscious process. There can be no sympathetic understanding, approval and appreciation from that which neither feels nor knows. It fails to give support to the religious life just where that support is most needed. If this be truth then religion would certainly seem to be the poorer for it.

But there is another consideration that is even more important. Personality is the highest thing we know. It is the vehicle in which all values are realized; and the " good," as we shall see, defines itself for us most clearly and concretely as personal development. What gives its unique value to personality is the fact of consciousness. Values no being is conscious of are as worthless as jewels lost in the depths of the ocean. No amount of rhetoric, therefore, can give to an unconscious entity a higher value than attaches to a conscious being. A deity that is unconscious is therefore infrapersonal in value, however suprapersonal it, or " he," may be in other respects. The creature that is *conscious* of value is the creature that *has* value in the only sense that is of ultimate importance. And if man is the creature most fully conscious of value then it is he who, in the last analysis, is the creature that *has* the greatest value. Either God must be a conscious being or he cannot be the object of supreme devotion. We only fool ourselves with rhetoric when we try to pay devotion to something allegedly superhuman that, being unconscious, is in reality infrahuman in value.

Unless, therefore, a deeper analysis still can reveal a basis for some form of belief more adequate to the requirements of a high devotion, then devotion on that level is likely to fade out of human society. But perhaps we may take further courage from the fact that most of Professor Wieman's negative pronouncements concerning God are based on a theory of mind and knowledge which is far from commanding universal assent even among naturalistic philosophers. And, in any case, we must be grateful to him for a profoundly sympathetic and penetrating analysis of religious experience, which is all the more convincing for its obvious freedom from any bias due to prior convictions of the personality of the divine being. At the same time, one may question whether such insight would be possible for a mind that had never, at any time, experienced the influence of such convictions.

MORALISTIC EMPIRICISM: JOHN BAILLIE

The tendency to find the roots of religion in our sense of values is by no means confined to those who view those values as attached merely to nonpersonal processes and symbols. Much the more common tendency is to regard the values with which religion is concerned as rooted far more deeply in the nature of things, conditioned by a spiritual reality that transcends human society. When values are given this objective foundation in the world order, then their claim upon us as presenting moral obligations forces itself to the front. Those thinkers who have regarded the whole pursuit of social values as religious, without distinguishing carefully between the religious, the irreligious and the merely secular pursuit of such values, have paid attention almost entirely to the distinction of good and evil within the religious consciousness. This is the point of view of Dean Ames and, though somewhat less decisively, of Professor Wieman.

But the thinkers who now come under discussion find the fact of greatest significance for the religious consciousness, not merely in the distinction of good and evil, but in that between right and wrong. It is in the moral consciousness, above all, that they find the roots of religion. This insight we owe, in the first place, to Immanuel Kant. But Kant was still under the influence of the Age of Reason and tried to make the passage from morality to religion by the rationalistic approach. It took the form of his moral argument for the existence of God. Since Schleiermacher and James first pioneered the empirical approach, however, there has been a growing body of investigators who have expressed the conviction that religion grows out of morality, and that in the very nature of the moral-religious consciousness of man there is direct evidence of the existence of a superhuman spiritual reality.[30]

Probably the most thorough and illuminating analysis arriving at this conclusion is that of Professor John Baillie.[31] In the course of a brilliant discussion of rationalism, romanticism, and the empiricisms which we have classified as mystical and symbolistic, he traces the essential core of the religious consciousness to our consciousness of value. By bringing out

[30] Among the leaders in expression of this view may be mentioned A. S. Pringle-Pattison, W. R. Sorley, A. E. Taylor, D. C. Macintosh, A. N. Whitehead, F. R. Tennant, John Oman, and John Baillie.

[31] *The Interpretation of Religion,* especially Part II, chaps. 5–8.

the distinction between the religious attitude and the non-religious, from certain of the Greek Sophists to Huxley's Romanes Lecture [32] and Lord Bertrand Russell's *A Free Man's Worship,* he shows that the line of cleavage is defined by the question of the objectivity of values. Have the higher human values any support and sanction in the nature of things beyond the conventions and conditions of the social order? Where the conviction is emphasized that there is something beyond ourselves, something in the nature of independent reality, that puts us under *obligation* to be true to the highest values we know, there religion flourishes and tends to develop a belief in a moral and personal God. Where values are believed to have no deeper ground than human decisions, conventions and occasional preferences, there irreligion flourishes, or religion pales into humanism.

This means that the religious consciousness is grounded in the moral consciousness. The further question is as to the nature of the transition from the one to the other. Here, Baillie's exposition seems to me to be less convincing. He points out that human beings are very deeply convinced of the truth of at least the broad outlines of their system of moral values. He argues (and most people will agree with him) that if we could be as certain of our principal religious beliefs as we are that it is right to help our fellow traveler out of the ditch, we might well be content. But Baillie further contends that any belief in the objectivity of our values implies that " the ultimate reality must . . . be One Who loves the Good." And this is grounded in the assertion that " if reality demands these things of me, then reality must be interested in moral value; . . . it must be on the side of the good and against the unworthy and the evil. But that is to say that it is a moral Being itself." [33]

[32] On *Evolution and Ethics,* delivered in 1893.
[33] *Op. cit.,* p. 352.

Now it must be admitted that most thinkers, on both sides, have been inclined to agree with Baillie here. It is for this very reason that opponents of theism have usually sought the ground of moral obligation in individual necessity or in the requirements of the social order. Any admission of a deeper ground of the moral order in nature itself was felt to imply that the natural order is somehow spiritual or divine. But this implication is by no means necessary. It has, for example, recently been boldly challenged by Professor Nicolai Hartmann in what is certainly one of the most significant works on ethics for several decades.[34] Values, and the distinctions of higher and lower within the scale of values, Hartmann treats as part of the order of nature; and the sense of obligation he regards as part of the response of personality to this natural order of values. Thus there is teleology and interest manifested in the course of human behavior but, he contends, no evidence of teleology on the cosmic scale. It must be admitted that Hartmann's hypothesis undermines the cogency of Baillie's argument that " if reality demands these things of me then reality must be interested in moral value."

However, though his final proof of theism is thus met with an alternative hypothesis, another part of Baillie's thesis may still remain sound. This is his suggestion that man *arrives* at the belief in a higher spiritual reality by implicitly supposing that that which makes moral demands of him must itself be a moral being, so that, if the moral demands come from beyond himself and beyond human society, there must be a moral being beyond himself and human society. This, as we have seen, is a perfectly natural, though not a necessary, inference. Baillie regards it as the source of the belief in God. He recognizes that it is not " a conscious piece of deductive reasoning," but rather holds that " under the long tuition

[34] Nicolai Hartmann: *Ethics,* translated by Stanton Coit (3 vols.; London: George Allen & Unwin, 1932) .

of moral experience, the consciousness of the moral claim comes, by an almost imperceptible transition of thought, to be interpreted as an awareness of a Divine Reality." [35] Baillie is content to rest the matter there, for to him this transition of thought, when made clearly explicit, seems a perfectly sound inference. To one who feels that the major premise of this inference does not exhaust the possibilities, this will not seem so satisfactory an explanation of the origin of religious belief. In any case the transition of thought involved is left extremely obscure. Further analysis seems to be called for if any greater light on the problem is to be obtained.

CONCLUSION: THE FURTHER TASK

In the remaining chapters of this book an effort will be made to carry that analysis further. And this will mean that we shall have to begin it all over again. The new feature that this further analysis, if sound, discloses is the fundamental part played in the religious life by the experience of the altruistic will (in the sense of a will to secure the good of others) in its conflict with egoistic tendencies and in its integration in harmony with the self as a whole. If this analysis is sound it means that the moralistic empiricists, such as Baillie, have stated correctly the most essential point, for this conflict and this integration are the most vital features of the moral life and are undoubtedly felt as involving a personal relation to an objective moral order. At the same time a full measure of justice may be done to those features of the religious experience emphasized by the other empirical points of view. With Schleiermacher we may recognize the part played by feeling, and the particular significance of the sense of dependence on something of infinite worth beyond ourselves. With Ames and Wieman we must recognize the tremendous importance of religious symbolism, and the social

---

[35] *Op. cit.,* p. 348.

nature of the values with which religion is primarily concerned. We can also account for the element of mysticism emphasized by James and others, for religious experience, as we shall see, involves a sense of contact of the ego with a will that seems to be more than merely its own.

Our method in this undertaking will be, in Part I, to analyze phase after phase of religious experience, gradually making its essential characteristics more and more clear, and then, in Parts II and III, to consider the significance of the understanding of religion at which we have arrived. This will be done first for practical conduct and, second, for questions of belief. In the epilogue we shall examine the essential significance of the Christian faith in the light of the foregoing analysis and interpretation. This analysis and interpretation will summarize the grounds for belief in God as a superhuman spiritual reality so far as such grounds are to be found in the philosophical examination of religion itself.

PART I

ANALYSIS

The Birth of Religion in the Individual

THE INITIAL PHASES OF RELIGIOUS LIFE

BIRTH is not the beginning of life. It is simply the occasion when we come forth into the light of day. Similarly, by the birth of religion in the individual mind we do not mean the beginning of the religious life, but simply the occasion of its coming forth into the full light of consciousness. The absolute beginnings of religion are too obscure to be described and too early to be remembered. Their nature can only be guessed at from what we know of religion when it begins to assume definite shape and consciously to affect the course of thought and motivation. But this coming of religion into full consciousness is an event sufficiently definite, in the mental life of great numbers of people, to permit of fairly clear characterization, and it usually occurs late enough in the life of the young person to be fairly well remembered. It is therefore a phase of religion, and of the mental life generally, clearly open to scientific study both by external observation of others and by reflective analysis of one's own immediate experience and memory.

Its importance for our study is not that religion is any stronger or better in its beginnings than in its mature development. It even has the disadvantage of emphasizing tendencies to certain weaknesses and confusions due to lack of maturity. But it is usually a fairly vivid stage of religious development; and it has the great advantage, for us, of standing in close contemporary contrast with the antecedent stage when religious factors were little evident and little influential.

Here, therefore, we should be able to see what is essential to the nature of the religious life, its true meaning as distinguished from the life in which religion is undeveloped. From these essentials we can go on to follow its growth and achieve an understanding of its fuller possibilities.

The metaphor of " birth," however, contains certain dangers of misinterpretation. Physical birth is a comparatively sudden and complete change of status. The psychological birth of religion is, normally, not sudden. In his physical birth the individual is passive. In his religious " new birth " he is active; he is " born again " by his own labors. This labor may involve some travail of soul, or it may not. The metaphor is picturesque and suggestive but, like most metaphors, apt to be misleading if pressed too far. The one excuse for it is the fact that the religious life does and, if it is to develop normally, must, come forth into clear and definite consciousness. The individual actively undergoes certain inner mental adjustments. There is a change and enrichment of his system of values. Life acquires fuller meaning. All these influences affect, more or less completely, his system of beliefs and his habits of action.

The fact that this change may take place suddenly, and may be accompanied by abnormal psychological phenomena such as spiritual anguish and ecstasy and even by visions and voices and strange physical impulses, has been given a great deal too much attention. This mistake has been committed both by religious people who are concerned with the practical religious results and accompanying beliefs, and by students concerned with the interpretation of religious phenomena. On the other hand, the fact that many people grow to spiritual maturity without passing through any marked period of storm and stress, responding very easily and naturally to appropriate new spiritual stimuli from the environment, has led some religious educators to believe that under proper processes of

" conditioning " moral and religious development may take place without effort from within, being purely a matter of passive responses to stimuli from without. A fair consideration of the whole range of evidence, however, strongly suggests that both extreme views are wrong. Spiritual anguish and ecstasy are abnormal and unnecessary. They are either pathological or due to the stress of unusual moral trials. Yet full religious and moral development is a prize that can no more be won without effort, struggle and occasional failure than can excellence in any other form of human achievement.

THE TYPICAL CONVERSION CRISIS: SOME HISTORICAL EXAMPLES

The literature of this subject is very full and has been so frequently reviewed, with the same general conclusions, that we need not do more than briefly recount some typical examples and some statements of those who have made a special study of it. The cases of conversion accompanied by exceptional psychological experiences, whether gradual or sudden, do not usually belong to the earliest phases of religious development. There are several minor Protestant sects and religious movements that make a special cult of the " second blessing," obtained by prolonged prayer and other forms of religious activity. Similar to these are cases where the most significant feature is a new doctrinal conviction or religious insight. The apostle Paul had been for a number of years a zealous Pharisee, and because of his religious zeal was persecuting the new sect of Christians, when his remarkable conversion occurred.[1] Al-Ghazali, the great Moslem theologian who revivified Islam in the eleventh century, was a theological professor at the height of his career when he entered upon his years of spiritual crisis. Oppressed by philosophic doubts he suffered a breakdown of health and resigned his position.

[1] Acts 9:1–22; 22:1–22; cf. also 6:9–15; 7:55–8; 4.

Later he was brought back to faith in Allah and his Prophet by mystical experiences which, he says, were beyond description, but which were obtained through exercises involving the mastering of desire, the combating of passion, the purifying of the soul and the perfecting of the character.[2] Ramakrishna, one of the most important Indian religious leaders of the nineteenth century, was twenty years of age when, a very proud Brahmin but with a deep religious interest, he began his worship at a shrine of Kali founded by a Sudra (low caste) woman. After three years of storm and stress and unsatisfied longing for the divine, mingled with occasional visions, and after much earnest thought and genuine moral self-culture, this led him to a triumph over human pride and worldliness and lust. The love of what he called " the little self " was overcome, and he came to a realization " that God is walking in every human form and manifesting Himself alike through the saint and the sinner, the virtuous and the vicious." [3]

These cases parallel, in their general outlines, those of St. Augustine, Tolstoi, Bunyan, Gautama Buddha and others of lesser fame, but equal intrinsic interest attaches to such experiences as William James has recorded in *Varieties of Religious Experience* or such as are found in books like Harold Begbie's *Twice-Born Men*. In order to have one example before us in a little more detail we may take the personal account of his conversion given by the Hindu Christian, the Sadhu Sundar Singh:

When I was out in any town I got people to throw stones at Christian preachers. I would tear up the Bible and other Christian books and put kerosene oil on them and burn them. I thought this was a false religion and tried all I could to destroy it.

[2] G. F. Moore: *History of Religions* (2 vols.; New York: Charles Scribner's Sons, 1913–19) , II, 456–66.

[3] J. B. Pratt: *The Religious Consciousness* (New York: The Macmillan Co., 1920) , pp. 129 ff.

I was faithful to my own religion, but I could not get any satisfaction or peace, though I performed all the ceremonies and rites of that religion. So I thought of leaving it all and committing suicide. Three days after I had burnt the Bible, I woke up about three o'clock in the morning, had my usual bath, and prayed, " O God, if there is a God, wilt thou show me the right way or I will kill myself." My intention was that, if I got no satisfaction, I would place my head upon the railway line when the five o'clock train passed by and kill myself. If I got no satisfaction in this life I thought I would get it in the next. I was praying and praying, but got no answer; and I prayed for half an hour longer hoping to get peace. At 4:30 A.M. I saw something of which I had no idea at all previously. In the room where I was praying I saw a great light. I thought the place was on fire. I looked round, but could find nothing. Then the thought came to me, " Jesus Christ is not dead but living and it must be He Himself." So I fell at His feet and got this wonderful Peace which I could not get anywhere else. This is the joy I was wishing to get. This was Heaven itself. When I got up the vision had all disappeared; but although the vision disappeared the Peace and Joy have remained with me ever since. I went off and told my father that I had become a Christian.[4]

MENTAL CONFLICT AND THE CONVERSION CRISIS

Modern abnormal psychology enables us to understand these extraordinary experiences. In every case there is mental conflict; and mental conflict, when prolonged and severe, generates repressions. Mental conflict is conflict of interests; and in the cases that lead to conversion there is always involved some conflict with moral interests. Saul of Tarsus, for example, had been fighting a growing conviction that the Christians were right. His persecution of them had been a case of persisting in a painful duty and nursing a bitterness that were contrary to the strong human elements of his nature.

[4] B. H. Streeter and A. J. Appasamy: *The Sadhu* (London: The Macmillan Co., 1921) , pp. 5–7.

This is expressed by the voice in the scene on the Damascus road: " It is hard for thee to kick against the pricks." He had heard the preaching of the martyr Stephen and had held the coats of those who stoned him, without himself participating in the deed — a picture of hesitation. As a Jew of Tarsus he was probably a member of the synagogue of Cilicia with which Stephen had held discussions. He had rejected the doctrine of the Christians because he saw that it meant the end of Jewish exclusiveness and of the high hopes of Jewish messianism, as well as for its intrinsic improbability. It was because he saw, perhaps more clearly than most of the Christians, that it meant the end of Judaism, the equality of the Gentiles before the one true God, that he felt so strongly that the sect must be crushed. And probably, as C. G. Jung suggests,[5] it was because he felt himself half convinced by the testimony of the Christians and strongly attracted by the Christian ideal that he was so zealous in their suppression. There was a conflict in his soul between the pride of the Hebrew in being the chosen people of God and the Christian ideal that opened the love and forgiveness of God equally to all. He hated the growing Christianity in his own mind, and he fought it by fighting the Christians. But on the Damascus road he had several days of enforced inactivity in which to think, and when he came in sight of the walls of Damascus, where the hateful business of persecution was to begin again, a revulsion of feeling set in. The repressed Christian ideal of a universal religion that made all men alike before God took possession of his mind, and with it came a conviction of the truth of the martyr's witness to the doctrine of the risen Christ. There flashed upon his mind a vision of the heavenly triumph of the teacher whose followers he was persecuting, and there rang in his ears a call to become an apostle of the new truth to the

[5] " The Psychological Foundations of Belief in Spirits," *Proceedings of the Society for Psychical Research,* May 1920.

Gentiles whom he had been seeking to shut out of the King-dom of God.

A very similar conflict, resulting in a similar stage of bit-terness toward the new religion and a similar symbolic seeing of the light in the vision, is to be observed in the case of the sadhu. Each of the other cases reveals its own distinctive kind of conflict. With al-Ghazali it was between doubts that the scientific and philosophic reason had raised and a faith that rested on a moral foundation; and the conflict was not solved until reason found a new foundation in a new sort of experi-ence that led to convictions in harmony with those that the moral life seemed to him to require. With Ramakrishna it was chiefly the pride of the Brahmin as opposed to a generous recognition of the spiritual equality of others, suggested by the fact that a Sudra, and a woman, had erected the shrine at which he was worshiping. St. Augustine's conflict was chiefly with sensuality, a difficulty that remained after intellectual doubts had been satisfactorily resolved. In the case of Tol-stoi the trouble was that he had lost all religious belief and given himself over to enjoy the superficial and artificial life of the idle aristocracy. But these things after a time failed to satisfy. His deeper moral nature demanded that life should have a meaning, and his thought and mode of life had made it meaningless. He tells, in *My Confession,* how the problem was solved with a growth of insight into the values of simple things and of the life of common helpfulness toward one's fel-low men. And with this insight there came back to him the belief in God and immortality. Bunyan was afflicted by a sense of sin which was typically psychopathic — vague, gen-eralized and acute. Of the inner conflict and dissatisfaction that underlay the religious experience of Gautama we know little save that it was sufficient to move him to renounce his position as a petty rajah and take up the life of an ascetic in search of peace of soul.

This examination of cases of conversion and exceptional religious experience, among persons of importance in history and literature, leads thus to the same conclusions as Professor Starbuck arrived at from his study of numerous cases, chiefly in American evangelical circles, by the method of the questionnaire.[6] The more pronounced types of religious experience arise out of conflict; they are preceded by a period of " storm and stress "; and the conflict is essentially a moral one. Conversion, Starbuck found, is principally a phenomenon of adolescence. Its periods of greatest frequency coincide with the three periods [7] within adolescence when the most serious problems of personal adjustment arise, though adolescence as a whole is a period of rapid adjustment and thus always more or less of conflict. It is the time of the awakening of the sexual life. But, much more important, it is the period of the chief development of the moral understanding, requiring constant adjustment to new moral insights and the constant solution of new moral problems. In his examination of the motives for what his subjects called their " conversion," Starbuck found considerable percentages attributed to fear of hell, social pressure and other nonmoral motives, due to the type of evangelism prevailing in America in the latter half of the nineteenth century, when his subjects had the experiences they recorded for him. But even so, in the majority of the cases the principal motive was moral, and the moral motive tended to acquire greater predominance as the age of conversion advanced. In their comments on their experience it is the moral motive and the moral conflict that his correspondents stressed. Starbuck sums up the importance of conduct as an organizing center for religious belief in the following statement:

[6] E. D. Starbuck: *The Psychology of Religion* (London: Charles Scribner's Sons, 1900).

[7] These occur at the ages of 12, 15½, and 18 or 19, and are characterized by a quickening of emotional, physical, and intellectual development, respectively. Cf. Starbuck, *op. cit.*, chap. 16.

The ethical instinct, the effort to do right, is far the most constant and persistent of all the forces that are active in the child life. In adolescence, when the new life bursts forth, its most important content was ethical. During storm and stress and doubt that which remained firmest when life was least organised was this same instinct. And now we find, in describing their fundamental attitudes toward life, that the respondents already in the late teens and twenties mention conduct almost as frequently as at any later time in life.[8]

NORMAL CONVERSION AND MORAL AWAKENING

But over against these more striking cases and the emphasis on conflict arising from them, there must be placed a great multitude of cases of religious development apparently devoid of crisis. William James, with his usual felicity of phrase, termed these the " healthy-minded " type to distinguish them from the " sick souls " and the " twice-born." In these cases the close interrelation of the religious and the moral development is the fact of major importance, though there are some cases where there is nothing that the subject will recognize as religious at all. Where there is a religious consciousness, it is the smoothness of its relation to the moral consciousness that seems to explain the absence of the experience of conflict. As an outstanding example of this type James (and many others after him) quotes the reply of Dr. E. E. Hale, an eminent Unitarian minister, to one of Starbuck's circulars:

I observe, with profound regret, the religious struggles which come into many biographies, as if almost essential to the formation of the hero. I ought to speak of these, to say that any man has an advantage, not to be estimated, who is born, as I was, into a family where the religion is simple and rational; who is trained in the theory of such a religion, so that he never knows, for an hour, what these religious or irreligious struggles are. I always knew that God loved me, and I was always grateful to him for

[8] *Ibid.*, p. 321.

the world he placed me in. I always liked to tell him so, and was always glad to receive his suggestions to me. . . . To live with all my might seemed to me easy; to learn where there was so much to learn seemed pleasant and almost of course; to lend a hand, if one had a chance, natural; and if one did this, why, he enjoyed life because he could not help it. . . . A child who is early taught that he is God's child, that he may live and move and have his being in God, and that he has, therefore, infinite strength at hand for the conquering of any difficulty, will take life more easily, and probably will make more of it, than one who is told that he is born the child of wrath and wholly incapable of good.[9]

This statement, however, must be taken as asserting a *relative* absence of conflict compared to the experiences common in the conversion crises of the time. No person could achieve moral perfection without experiencing even a single temptation, and it must not be supposed that the Rev. Dr. Hale was making any such claim. Furthermore, it is obviously the statement of a person for whom the path of life had been set in pleasant places. It would not be so easy to be " always grateful " to God for the world he has placed one in if one had to endure economic want, pain, disease, loss of loved ones and frustrated ambitions; and to " lend a hand " would not always seem so " natural " if one could do it only at the cost of bitter personal sacrifice. Nevertheless, Dr. Hale's experience is much nearer to that of the average religious person than is a Bunyan's or a Tolstoi's.

Starbuck's investigations alone are sufficient to show that in normal circumstances, among young people who are not subjected to theological teaching seeking to provoke a crisis, the religious awakening is gradual. It is connected with the progressive development of moral ideals and the practical adjustment of conduct to the expanding moral vision. From 273 personal accounts of their religious development by peo-

---

[9] William James: *Varieties of Religious Experience,* pp. 82–83.

ple who had no " conversion crisis," he gathered the following general conclusions:

(a)   That before the age of ten or eleven " religion is
distinctively external . . . rather than something which possesses inner significance." [10]   This means that religion consists in beliefs accepted on authority, and in the performance
of rites without an inner sense of their significance and value.
God is an external being who, like Santa Claus, brings good
gifts and watches to see whether we are good, and to whom
petitions may be sent up a chimney called " prayer."   Much
of what is thus called religion has, for the child, no basis in
the spontaneity of his own moral interests.   The genuine religious awakening has not yet taken place.   Morality itself is
largely a matter of conformity to rules under social pressure.
It lacks insight into values and responsive appreciation of
them.   But belief in supernatural beings like Santa Claus,
fairies, miracle-working saints and creator-gods does not constitute religion.   It is on a level with belief in the virtues of
a horseshoe or a rabbit's foot, or in the universal beneficence
of Dr. Quack's Cure-all and the rigid laws of political econ-
omy.   Beliefs, whether in the supernatural or in natural elements, and the practices that go with them, become religious
only by virtue of their connection with a deeper and more inward experience.   Children under ten are not always devoid
of this experience, though in most of them it is not sufficiently
clear and vigorous to make vital connection with religious
belief and practice.   Where this connection is not made
(either because of intellectual objections to the beliefs or
because of continued indecisiveness of the inner experience) ,
the beliefs tend to fade in adult life, and the practices tend
to be dropped as meaningless.   It is important, therefore, to
grasp the nature of the kind of experience that makes religion
real and vital.   This usually comes into prominence between

[10] *Op. cit.,* p. 194.

the ages of ten and twenty-five, though it may manifest itself earlier or be delayed until later.

(b)   A second conclusion drawn by Starbuck points to the nature of this inner experience, which usually manifests itself first during adolescence.   He calls it a " spontaneous awakening " whereby the ideas of God, duty and religious observance, which have hitherto been external, take root in the inner life and assume a vital significance.   In so far as the subjects were able to point to any special incidents in this connection they tend to emphasize one or more of three elements: fresh intellectual insight, first-hand perception of right and wrong, and emotional responses.   But it is the moral development that is central.   Starbuck sums up his study of these phenomena by saying: ". . . *back of the whole adolescent development, and central in it, is the birth of a new and larger spiritual consciousness.*" [11]   It is " the birth of a larger self."   And the birth is an active process, usually difficult at some points, though not necessarily critical.   In some individuals, such as Dr. Hale, the advance of the moral consciousness and the growth of habits are so skillfully directed and so little strained by adverse circumstances that there are no marked stages, no obvious patches of light and shade.   But always there are some " difficulties " of a moral nature and a need " to live with all one's might," even though, as in the doctor's case, a confidence in the availability of infinite resources of divine strength to overcome them may make the task seem always " easy."

One feature of the conversion process as described by Starbuck and James seems to have received a false emphasis by these writers, due to the fact that their materials were so largely drawn from people influenced by the Protestant evangelical tradition.   This is the interpretation of the element of " self-surrender " in the final stage of conversion, and the descrip-

[11] *Ibid.*, p. 252.

tion of the whole process as one of " struggling away from sin
rather than of striving toward righteousness." [12]   Professor
Pratt [13] has done good service in pointing out that this is
true of only a limited number of cases, and is due to theological emphasis on the necessity of " conviction of sin " in order
to the attainment of salvation.   He rightly points out that
in those remarkable cases of conversion by the Salvation Army
in London which are reported by Harold Begbie,[14] though
the subjects were shockingly bad sinners, they were not so
much oppressed by a sense of sin as animated by a positive
moral ideal.   They were seeking righteousness and its fruits
rather than a divine remission of the sins of the past.   The
" surrender " they made was not, as Puritan theology used to
teach, a cessation of all effort in a complete reliance on the
saving grace of God, but a surrender of the old passions and
desires to the new moral aspirations, a surrender of the lower
self to the higher.   This sort of positive effort and moral idealism is the *sine qua non* of all religious development.

RELIGION AS AN OUTGROWTH OF MORALITY

From all this evidence one fact stands out clearly — that the
roots of religion are in the moral life.   If man had no moral
consciousness he might have superstitions and he might even
have science and a philosophy, but he would have no religion.
Yet morality and religion are not just the same thing.   Religious activity manifests a persistent tendency to a speculative
reaching out of thought to solve the mystery of life.   It tends
to postulate the existence of intangible personal agencies beyond the realm of natural human beings.   It issues in efforts
to achieve harmony with a power outside the self, on which
the self feels itself in some way to depend.   It emotionalizes

---

[12] Starbuck, *ibid.*, p. 64; James, *op. cit.*, p. 209.

[13] Pratt: *The Religious Consciousness*, chap. 8.

[14] In *Twice-Born Men* (New York: Fleming H. Revell Co., 1909) .

and emphasizes the moral life. It finds something in its experience that arouses awe and reverence. It attributes to what it recognizes as the moral law the authority of a superhuman will. These tendencies are not typically a part of the moral consciousness, as they are of the religious. Many people live good moral lives without any special experiences, activities or beliefs of this sort, and say they have no religion. If we assert, as we must, that religion is rooted in morality, we are yet forced to admit that not all moral experience is religious in quality or tends to involve or depend upon religious beliefs. Is there then something *added* to the experience of the moral consciousness that transforms mere morality, or morality *simpliciter*, into religion? Or is there some special phase of the moral experience that contains elements which tend to lead to the development of the distinctively religious features, making religion something more than morality, something arising out of it though not essential to it?

It has been usual to adopt the former of these alternatives. The traditional religions have taught that this additional element is belief in the supernatural, founded either on reason or on revelation, or on both. Sometimes they have added that religious experience depends also on a special divine activity in the human soul. Philosophers, psychologists and anthropologists have, for the most part, agreed that some kind of belief in higher powers is necessary to religion. Most have regarded these beliefs as derived, more or less reasonably, from reflection on problems external to religious experience itself; others have thought that they arise from reflection on a distinctive (but nonmoral) element in experience, which is thus the peculiar root of religion.[15] The humanists, on the other hand, have insisted that belief in superhuman powers is quite

---

[15] In this category come Schleiermacher, with his emphasis on " the sense of dependence "; Rudolph Otto, with the theory of the " numinous "; and Ernst Troeltsch, with the doctrine of " the religious *a priori*."

unnecessary to religion, that moral experience alone is enough. Their difficulty, however, has been to defend themselves against the charge of obliterating the distinction between morality and religion, for it scarcely seems sufficient to regard religion, as did Matthew Arnold, as " morality touched by emotion."

Humanism, with its insistence that moral experience (of our relation to our fellows and of the social values involved in that relationship) is sufficient basis for the religious life, might find an answer to its problem in the second alternative view. But this second view does not necessarily lead to humanism. It asserts (a) that religious belief, feeling and activity arise in response to certain distinctive phases or features of moral experience; (b) that these beliefs, feelings and activities then tend to develop their own distinctive life in relation to other features of experience, and in such a way that there is often considerable independence and lack of correlation between morality and religion; but (c) that these intellectual, aesthetic and practical phases of religion, when strongly developed, tend to gather the whole of the moral life into their embrace.

If this interpretation of the roots of religious belief is correct the question still remains which, if any, of those beliefs are correct. It may still be the case that humanism is right in its rejection of all belief in anything higher than man. Or it may be that the moral argument for the existence of God achieves a new cogency from the recognition that moral experience is the *actual* as well as a *logical* basis for religious faith.[16]

The questions mainly at issue between the humanists and the theists will not concern us until we reach chapters 8 to 10 of this book. The problem with which we shall be chiefly occupied until then is the question, What is the *actual* basis

[16] This position is ably defended by John Baillie: *The Interpretation of Religion*.

of the distinctively religious activities and beliefs? Is it reason, or revelation, or a feeling of dependence? Is it an experience of the numinous, or a religious *a priori,* or some phase of our moral experience? We shall devote little space to a dialectical discussion of the alternatives, but shall try to find the answer by continuing our analysis of the various individual and historical phases of the development of religion, and by applying the thesis to which our analysis directs us in the interpretation of those developments. That thesis is a form of the second of those referred to; i.e., that religion arises from certain distinctive features of our moral experience. It affirms that religion is rooted in the experience of moral conflict.

Now in cases where the birth of the religious consciousness is delayed until later adolescence and adult life, and in cases of later religious crisis, such as those of St. Paul and of the " second blessing " cultivated by the Holiness movement, the moral issue most prominent in consciousness may concern specific sins or ideals, or it may rest on a vague state of moral dissatisfaction without any definite content. But in the normal, youthful development of religion the moral issues involved tend to be the general, and yet quite definite, problems of human relationships. The first moral problems of which we are aware are not those of sex or doubt or pride, but those of justice and kindness. The moral ideals that first inspire us are not those of chastity or humility but those of service to the common good. The moral heroes of youth are those who show courage, resource, energy and self-sacrifice in loyal support of the common cause or devotion to some ideal of altruistic service. Where such ideals, rather than repentance and submission, are exalted in connection with religious belief, there is a natural and ready response on the part of young people at an early age, and religion develops naturally — not without effort, but happily and without undue distress. It is marked by emotional peaks of social and missionary enthusiasm rather than by valleys of despair.

Because of this essentially social nature of our early and fundamental morality (and of the healthy-minded type of religion that arises from it) , and because of the predominantly social nature of primitive religion, Professor E. S. Ames goes so far as to say, not merely that " the origin of religion . . . is to be sought in the origin of the social consciousness," but also that " the religious consciousness is identified with the consciousness of the greatest values of life " and that religion may be viewed as " participation in the ideal values of the social consciousness." [17]   But if this is an adequate account of the matter, then the tendency of religious thought and activity to reach beyond humanity to find the divine must be due to extraneous influences and cannot be regarded as an essential feature of religion; and if that is the case then its persistence in the history of religion calls for much explanation.   When people find that their gods are false they usually do not give up all gods; they reshape their conceptions of them or search for new ones.   The persistence of the god idea, through all its changes in history, indicates that there is something in human experience that seems very strongly (even if wrongly) to demand it.   So if the origin of religion is in the social consciousness, the consciousness of the greatest values of life, or, as I would prefer to put it, in our consciousness of our moral relationship to our fellow men, then there must be something in that consciousness that strongly suggests a relationship of man to the suprahuman.

MORAL CONFLICT AND THE DIVIDED SELF

This brings us to the main thesis of this book: *that man's consciousness of God rests upon the element of conflict that exists within the moral life, a conflict that is first felt as be-*

[17] Ames: *The Psychology of Religious Experience*, pp. 168, 356.

tween the egoistic and the altruistic tendencies of our nature.

In the past those writers, such as James and Starbuck, who have drawn attention to the element of mental conflict in the birth of the religious consciousness, have been too much influenced by those features of the conflict in the majority of the cases studied which were due to the special influence of evangelical theology and to pathological repressions. These suggested that the struggle was away from sin rather than toward righteousness, and that it ended in surrender rather than in victory. In wholesome reaction against this placing of the highest value on features of the conflict which manifest themselves only when its nature is warped by mental disorder or harsh theology, those writers who have treated the religious awakening as essentially a moral phenomenon have pointed to the religion of the healthy-minded as indicating that conflict is unnecessary. But this too is an exaggeration. Conflict is *undesirable,* but it is necessary, for the simple reason that there are opposing psychological factors that have to be overcome if there is to be any growth of the moral personality. If we could grow into full perfection of character without effort on our own part we would be either automatons or divinities. And in neither case would we be likely to discover that there is anything in the universe higher than ourselves. But it is because we recognize ourselves as imperfect and strive to do and be something better that the conviction tends to grow that something higher than ourselves there really must be. To discover how this comes about and why it takes the form it does, we must examine the conflict more closely.

Now it is important to recognize that ethical principles cannot be stated simply as an issue between altruism and egoism. There are altruistic actions that are wrong and egoistic actions that are right. Nevertheless, it is this issue that constitutes the moral conflict as it first emerges in the consciousness of the individual; and it remains the fundamental moral problem throughout life. By an altruistic action I mean one aiming at an objective result selected because seen chiefly as a good-for-some-other-person, while an egoistic action is one where the objective is selected because seen chiefly as good-for-me. Personal satisfaction, of course, will be found in successfully attaining both results; but in the former case one has the satisfaction because one sees (or believes) that a good has been obtained by some other person; in the latter case one has satisfaction in achieving what seems to be a good for oneself. In brief, the altruistic motive rejoices in seeing others prosper, the egoistic in attaining one's own prosperity. The fact that there is rejoicing in the attaining of both goals does not alter the nature of the distinction. Altruistic and egoistic motives are not always in conflict; and egoistic motives are not always regarded as wrong, even where there is conflict. It is where one's own good is sought at the cost of a definitely greater good of others that the moral conscience begins to condemn; and it is where the individual pursues the greater good of others at the cost of his own that the moral conscience begins to commend.

Thus the altruistic will commends itself to the moral consciousness, upon mature reflection, when it takes the form of a disinterested will to the good, a will that is no respecter of persons but seeks equally the good of all. But this balance and universalism of the moral consciousness is achieved only after much reflection. It is also a matter of moral judgment rather than religious experience. What gives its religious character to moral experience is simply the striking contrast and conflict between the will to seek one's own good and the will to the good of others. As matter of fact, the will to the good of others rarely has the strength to create a conflict except where the good of others concerned is much the greater. Thus, in practice, the conflict between altruism and egoism, as it emerges within the consciousness of youth, is a conflict between the will to seek one's own good and the will to seek the *greater* good of others.

This conflict presents itself as between a lower self and a higher, between an old self and a new. This phraseology is more than mere metaphor, for though, in a strict sense, each individual is only one self, one personality, yet the self or personality is not a simple, indivisible, substantial soul. It is a composite psychological structure, having its unity in its habits and capacity for attention and in the systematic interrelation of its purposive life. It is a composite form of will that grows and changes, and the various elements in its structure are never in perfect harmony. When conflicts of will occur within it they destroy the unity and order of its functioning. They tear it apart and may even create that peculiar phenomenon known as an alternating personality. The completely integrated self is an ideal. The " divided self " is a matter of degree, the pathological condition that goes by that name being simply an exaggeration of a common defect that has reached a point of breakdown in some respects.

The conflict between egoism and altruism is always with us, but it needs must pass through a more or less acute stage, beginning usually in later childhood. The earliest formed self is a system of tendencies to respond to physiological drives and immediate experiences of pleasure and pain, satisfaction and dissatisfaction. The idea of the self grows slowly, and only *pari passu* with it grows the idea of other selves. The child's own satisfactions and dissatisfactions are prominent in his consciousness, and (in so far as he distinguishes self and notself) he responds to them as his own. He thus forms a strong body of purely egoistic habits, a tightly knit egoistic self, before he develops sufficient imagination to think of the satisfactions and dissatisfactions of other people and look at matters from their point of view. This natural, childish system of egoistic habits, which I shall call the original ego, is the " old Adam " that the altruistic desires have to contend with when they arise.   It is well fixed and does not readily give way. Generous impulses arise spontaneously when the young person thinks of the needs of others; and gradually a system of habits, both of thinking of the good of others and of responding to the thought, develops.

This new system of purposive tendencies is a new part of the self; and in so far as it is not integrated with the original ego it is apt to come into conflict with it.   There are conflict of will, emotional conflict, and a vaguely felt need of integration, creating inner dissatisfaction.   Somehow the newer elements of the self, the altruistic, are felt as higher, as having a certain authority above that of the other desires, as pointing to obligations.[18]   But these altruistic or social interests, when followed out, bring their own rewards.   There is joy and satisfaction in them.   Even when they have called for sacrifice and there has been hesitation, even when it has required a fight to overcome the original ego, it is usually felt as worth while, in later reflection, to have been true to the higher self. Gradually new ideals of unselfish devotion to causes of social value thus take firm hold.   These broader ideals may at last become the dominant element in the personality and the original ego may sink into a place of proper subordination.   But even then the higher self retains its power only by eternal vigilance.

THE ALTRUISTIC WILL AND THE IDEA OF GOD

Now all our studies of the birth of religion in the individual show that it tends to occur during this period of the awakening moral life, when the conflict between the altruistic will and the original ego is at its height.   Our study of the special religious experiences in adult life of outstanding personali-

[18] The reasons for this, and its significance, are discussed in chap. 8.

ties in history and literature, also showed that the new religious convictions that they obtained were wrought within them through a period of deep moral conflict — and almost all morality is ultimately concerned with the welfare of our fellow men. Thus those beliefs and activities wherein religion tends to transcend morality always seem to rise in the experience of moral conflict, a conflict which is originally and ultimately between the will to the good of the private self and the will to the greater good of others. It means that man, in this moral conflict, tends to feel that the will to the good of others, when it conflicts with the original ego, is not his own. He identifies himself with the original ego. The will to the greater good of others, usually relatively weak in itself, appears as something he should be able easily to subordinate. But it will not be subordinated. It asserts its authority. It hangs over him as an obligation. If he rejects it, it accuses him. If his ego at last surrenders to it, if he makes it his own and follows it out, it fills him with an unexpected joy, a deep sense of satisfaction and a rare feeling of power.

Is it any wonder that when earnest and thoughtful minds have reflected on this experience they have concluded that the agency which makes these demands upon the ego is more than human, that it is indeed some higher power that constrains us to devote ourselves to the common good? And when, in deeper reflection, the moral demand has been seen to be no respecter of persons, and it has been felt that obedience to it is in itself a great good, that higher power has been defined as one that seeks in and through each of us the good of all. It is this interpretation of religious experience, worked out by the religious geniuses of the race, that has, with relatively unimportant variations and exceptions, become the common Christian tradition. And it is fairly closely paralleled by all the great ethical religions. When it is taught to children, and when in the unfolding of their moral experience they find its suggestions very fully realized, then the childish beliefs merely externally held attain new meaning and acquire internal conviction. Only if elements that ring false to their experience have been incorporated into the traditional beliefs taught to them, or if there is a clash between the religious interpretation and beliefs that seem to be based on a scientific foundation, or if their moral experience for some reason does not conform to the normal pattern, do doubts tend to arise. But even those doubts may often be set aside if the later development of their moral experience reawakens the appeal of the ideal, or if in some other way the upward moral striving is renewed.

If this analysis is sound then the immediate datum of religious experience, whence the belief in a superhuman moral agency arises, is the altruistic will itself, with its claim to present an obligation and its power to suffuse life with new interest and deeper satisfaction. This means that what men immediately feel as the divine agency, as God within them, is this element of their own personality, the altruistic will. To this extent at least God is real and personal. He is that within us which goes beyond the seeking of our own good to seek the good of others. The divine is immanent within us. The question whether it is also transcendent can be answered only after a much wider study of its operation and of the world within which we find it.

If we ask whence comes this element in themselves which men have distinguished as divine, one answer is that it may be a natural product of a continuous course of evolution, entirely reducible to laws operative at the lower levels. Another answer is that it may be an emergent property of life, new to the world in man, but something more than a continued operation of the forces that produced his animal nature and intelligence. Or it may be that it belongs to the eternal structure of the universe, and is the creative power that has

made man what he is and works still within him to make him
something better. Or it may be that some more traditional
type of theism holds the truth; for this interpretation of religious experience is not necessarily inconsistent with·a religion
which teaches that " it is God that worketh in you both to will
and to do of his good pleasure," and that " in him was life and
the life was the light of men . . . which lighteth every man
coming into the world." [19]

Few theists will object to the view that the moral will in
man is God within us; but many are likely to object that the
altruistic will is not always moral, i.e., not always right. Its
intentions are good, but it may sometimes lead us to undue
sacrifice of ourselves, sometimes to a falsity to higher values
or to socially important principles in order to please some
narrow or unworthy group or individual, sometimes to mistakes as to what is the true good of those whose good we seek.

But this objection misses the point. If this altruistic element of our personality which we have called divine is, indeed, the immanence of a transcendent deity within us, then
it only means, so far, that he is immanent as *will*. It remains
another question whether he is also immanent as *knowledge*.
The theist usually recognizes that there are features of human
will that have developed independently of, and even contrary
to, the will of God. The view here presented would mean,
for theism, that that element of human will which seeks the
good of other personalities than our own is not one of these
independent developments, but is derived unchanged from
the creative source. But the fact that it makes mistakes and,
while always pursuing good, sometimes destroys a greater
good, would simply indicate that in this derivation it did not
bring with it a divine omniscience. In that case it must be
understood to pursue the greatest good of all as seen from the
fallible human viewpoint and so, sometimes, to make mis-

[19] Phil. 2:13; John 1:4, 9.

takes in that pursuit. The fact that the altruistic will cannot be identified with the moral will is therefore no objection, even from the theistic standpoint, to its being viewed as the divine element in human personality and the primary and immediate datum whence we attain to a knowledge of God.

But it must be emphasized that our analysis thus far has found no arguments to advance in favor of a belief in the divine transcendence, and has not sought to find them. We have been concerned to discover the distinctive element in religious experience, the actual empirical datum, that gives rise to this belief. From our analysis of the genesis of the belief in the individual we have been led to conclude that that datum is the altruistic will. This conclusion would also imply that it is this will that, in the course of the moral conflict due to it, transforms the external (nonmoral and really nonreligious) beliefs of childhood into the internal and genuinely religious and moral faith of youth; and, further, that it is this same type of experience that results in those restorations of faith, convictions of new religious truth, recoveries of reality in the religious life, and deepenings of religious experience that mark the religious crises of adult life. It explains why the sick soul has a more vivid and convincing religious experience than other people, and how a full religious development is yet possible without such crises. In general it fits the facts of the birth and growth of religion in the individual so far as we have yet studied them.

Our next task is to test this theory of the roots of religion by seeing how it fits a wider range of religious experience. We must inquire how it can account for the earliest forms of religious belief known to man, and how far it can illuminate the typical beliefs and problems disclosed in the history of religion.

The Birth of Religion in the Race

THE ORIGIN OF RELIGION: DIFFICULTIES OF THE PROBLEM

CAREFUL STUDY of the documents of the great ethical religions shows that their development can, without exception, be traced back to polytheisms and tribal worship closely akin to those of existing primitive peoples. A comparative study of all religions shows so many parallel features of belief and custom, and so much survival of early forms in the later, that it becomes clear that in its fundamentals religion is essentially one in spite of its multifarious forms. Consequently students of the subject feel entirely justified in going to primitive peoples of the present day for information concerning the earliest forms of religious belief and practice. But even so the question of origins is not simple. The practices of the most primitive peoples represent a long era of evolution before they attained their present form. And there is no people that has a pure religion. Waves of cultural influence have spread in all directions over the earth, and the peoples now most isolated and primitive have gone to their present homes from regions far away,[1] absorbing traces of religious belief and practice and disseminating their own as they passed.

Thus the problem of discovering the earliest forms of religious belief is by no means simple. We cannot take the religion of the most primitive people as necessarily constituting

[1] For example, the scattered groups of Negritos are found as far apart as central and south Africa, the Andaman Islands (Bay of Bengal) and the Philippine Islands; and small groups or traces of Australoids still exist in India, Ceylon, the Malay Peninsula and the Celebes Islands.

the most primitive form of religion.   It may contain much that is borrowed and may in some respects even be decadent. Every practice and belief requires interpretation, and it is by no means easy to enter into a sympathetic understanding of people so far removed from ourselves.   Also, the understanding of other peoples' religious experience requires that one have a religious experience of one's own and understand that experience.   Professor Malinowski has recently pointed out that both the fundamentalist and the atheist are at a special disadvantage here, the former because his own intensity and dogmatism make it difficult for him to appreciate the genuineness of a religious experience the conditions of which differ so much from his own, the latter because much of the ordinary religious man's experience is unintelligible to him.[2]   Another recent writer points out another difficulty in the fact that, even to two people of the same primitive tribe, as to two people of a modern city, the same religious beliefs and practices may mean something very different.[3]   One person has not as much religious interest and sensitivity as another.   Thus generalization is rendered all the more difficult.

It is for this reason that we began our study with an examination of the birth of religion in the individual rather than with its origin in the race.   Only when we understand what are the most essential features of the religious experience, and have analyzed it critically and thoroughly where we know it best, are we in a position to interpret the religion of those farthest removed from ourselves.   There is no surer way to arrive at the wrong conclusions than to begin with a description of primitive religions (which are the most difficult to understand because so far removed from us) , formulate theories of the nature of religion based on these descriptions, and then

[2] B. Malinowski: *Foundations of Faith and Morals* (New York: Oxford University Press, 1936) , p. 1.

[3] P. Radin: *Primitive Religion* (New York: Viking Press, 1937) .

try to reduce all religion to this theoretical formula. Yet that has, undoubtedly, been the method adopted by many investigators who have approached the problem primarily from the standpoint of anthropology. It is no wonder that many of these have seen in religious belief nothing but a tissue of hoary superstitions and survivals of primitive magic which civilized man should long ago have outgrown. Among theories of this kind we may refer briefly to those of Tylor, Durkheim, and Westermarck.

E. B. TYLOR: THE ANIMISTIC THEORY

The first of the modern anthropological interpretations of religion was that of E. B. Tylor, published in 1871.[4] He regarded the belief in spiritual beings as lying at the basis of all religion, and so felt that the fundamental problem was to explain the origin of that belief. This he attributed to two factors, the first being primitive man's observation of the difference between the living body and a corpse, leading to the conclusion that there must be something present in the former and not in the latter. Now the primitive conception of a spirit is that of a filmy, unsubstantial replica of the body which is capable of a separate existence and is the possessor of the consciousness and will of the person. Tylor recognized that the sheer invention of such a hypothetical entity to explain the difference between the dead and the living would involve a tremendous leap of the imagination. Therefore he looked for a second factor to bridge this gap, and he thought that this could be found in the experience of dreams. He discovered that primitives commonly believe that in a dream the soul leaves the body and actually goes through the experiences envisioned. Thus, since dreams had suggested to the savage that some conscious replica of himself could leave his body and wander abroad while he slept, this concept could explain the

---

[4] E. B. Tylor: *Primitive Culture* (7th ed.; New York: Brentano's, 1924).

difference between the living and the dead. From man this concept of a spirit was easily spread to animals and to such inanimate objects as impressed the primitive as having any unusual power. Thus the world became peopled for him by spirit agencies of all sorts in nature, and by the spirits of the innumerable dead, including his own ancestors, chieftains and enemies. Some of these were obviously injurious and others might be beneficial. Thus religion, Tylor believed, arose as an effort to propitiate these spirits by offerings and to win their favor by prayers.

It may well be doubted whether Tylor's ingenious explanation of the origin of belief in spirits is the true one, for it is surely a very far-fetched theory to explain so simple a matter as dreams, the true explanation of which is constantly present to the experience of every savage and every child. Tylor, like most people who engage in much abstract thinking, probably had little capacity for visual imagery in daydreams. But primitives, like children and the majority of practical people, do have that capacity. And the difference, for a vivid visualizer, between a half-awake daydream and an ordinary dream is not very great. So the savage had no real need to invent the remarkable theory of a soul to explain the fact that he had mistaken imagery for reality in his sleep. After the belief in a soul had been developed it could easily, of course, be applied to those dreams to which it was appropriate. And Durkheim has shown that it is not applied to all dreams.[5] A more plausible explanation of the belief in spirits is that it arose as a hypostatization and personalization of the notion of *mana;* but we shall refer to that later.

Whatever the explanation of the origin of the belief in spirits, however, it is now very widely agreed among students of the subject that this belief is not the earliest form of re-

[5] E. Durkheim: *Elementary Forms of the Religious Life,* translated by Joseph Ward Swain (New York: The Macmillan Co., 1915), pp. 59–60.

ligion. There are other forms of religion that seem to be more primitive. The elaborate religious ceremonies of the Australians, for example, though these people believe in the existence of spirits, have nothing to do with this belief. The same may be said of the daily ritual of the Todas of India, reported by W. H. R. Rivers.[6] The fetish of the African is sometimes occupied by a spirit, but at other times only possessed of an impersonal supernatural power. Again, as R. R. Marett has clearly shown,[7] many objects of worship, especially nature deities, are not regarded as having spirits but simply as being alive and possessing remarkable powers. Thus it is evident from the earliest vedic poems that the sun and other nature deities were not spirits but simply living beings of great majesty and power, "magnified nonnatural men," in the picturesque phrase of Matthew Arnold and Andrew Lang. Later they are addressed as having spirits, and later still as anthropomorphic high gods to whom the natural object originally worshiped is merely a home.[8] But in all these cases the object worshiped is believed to be imbued with a peculiar, sacred and supernatural power, the mana to which we have already referred.

Thus Tylor's theory that animistic belief is the root of religion does not square with the facts concerning the most rudimentary types of religion now known. It is also, as Durkheim again points out,[9] unsatisfactory in that so persistent and deep-rooted a social phenomenon as religion can scarcely be believed to rest upon a mere intellectual error. Indeed, its intellectual forms are so varied, and it is so capable of surviving the overthrow of one intellectual formulation after another, that it is not reasonable to think that its thought content, the element of belief, is really the foundation of the

[6] In *The Todas* (New York: The Macmillan Co., 1906).
[7] In *The Threshold of Religion* (1st ed.; London: Methuen & Co., 1914).
[8] E. W. Hopkins: *The Religions of India* (Boston: Ginn & Co., 1895).
[9] *Op. cit.*

structure. It expresses itself in thought, and when one intellectual formulation proves unsatisfactory it seeks another; but its roots would seem to lie deeper in experience than any intellectual interpretation of events.

E. DURKHEIM: THE COLLECTIVIST THEORY

From these disadvantages Durkheim's sociological theory of religion is free. It explains away religious belief as entirely illusory, but since it does not rest religion upon belief it does not make religion itself illusory. It claims rather to purify religion by freeing it from mere superstition. It finds the roots of religion in man's sense of his relation to his fellows, and therefore is much better able to do justice to the essentially moral nature of most religious practice and to salvage its values from the wreck of its intellectual content. To modern humanists, Durkheim's theory has proved very attractive and, indeed, it has close historical connections with the forerunner of the humanist movement, Auguste Comte. Durkheim's definition of religion emphasizes two things: a felt distinction between the sacred and the secular, and the moral union of individuals in a religious society. " A religion is a unified system of beliefs and practices relative to sacred things, i.e., things set apart and forbidden — beliefs and practices which unite into one single moral community called a Church all those who adhere to them." [10]   Beliefs and practices therefore may change. But religion remains so long as other beliefs and practices can be found to perform this important ethical and social function.

Because of their isolation and the simplicity of their material culture, Durkheim assumes the Australian aboriginals to be representative of religion in its most primitive form. They believe in spirits and have traditions concerning certain beings who came from the sky, taught them their culture,

[10] *Ibid.,* p. 47.

and returned thither. But there is neither worship nor prayer offered to the spirits or other divine beings. The aboriginal religious consciousness is absorbed in a mere totemic ritual, each clan or social group having its own totemic symbol. The use of these symbols Durkheim believes to be a necessity for social cohesion, for the concept of the clan is too complex to be completely grasped without it. The religious feeling attached to the symbol, he claims, is derived from the actual feeling toward the clan itself. The social group in which the individual lives and moves and has his being bears, in actual fact, he argues, the relationship toward the individual which religion attributes to God. It dominates him by its superior authority. On the other hand, when he feels himself in harmony with it, it is a source of strength and courage. It calls forth his highest devotion, and in its fellowship he finds his deepest satisfaction.

These feelings aroused by the social group become attached, says Durkheim, to the totemic symbol. To it is attributed the mystical force that arouses them, the moral authority and power that really belong to the group itself. It becomes an object of devotion, inspiring awe and reverence. Its peculiar mystical power is generalized in the concept of mana and attached to everything connected with the cult and to other objects similarly inspiring awe. Gradually it is personalized, becoming first an animal deity and later an anthropomorphic god who appears in the animal form of what was once the totem — a course of development plainly recorded in Egyptian religion. Thus religious belief in the supernatural is presented as developing out of a tendency, commonly manifested in religion, to take the symbol for the reality, thus imbuing it with an unreal, mystical power and authority, personalizing and exalting it. But the reality of religion is man's relation to his fellow men, the real power and moral authority of the group, and all the values that accrue from sharing in a common life and devotion to the common good.

Criticism of Durkheim's theory by both theists and naturalists centers round the explanation of the notion of the sacred, as distinct from the secular, and that of the mystical power commonly called mana. These are attributed by Durkheim directly to the felt influence of the group. The mana of the totem is the mana of the group; its authority is that of the clan; the sacred is neither more nor less than the social. Professor Goldenweiser points out [11] that there are many social ceremonies of primitive people which are distinctly not sacred, so that the sense of the sacred certainly involves something more than a mere feeling inspired by the presence of the group; it must at least be some distinctive kind of group relationship that is sacred. Further, it is by no means the case that, as Durkheim assumes, all peoples are, or have been, totemic. Even some of the most primitive food-gatherers, such as the Andaman Islanders, the Congo pygmies and the South African Bushmen, are not totemic,[12] yet they have a religion, they distinguish between the sacred and the secular, and they possess the concept of mana. Totemism would seem to be a matter of social organization, incorporated into the religious practices of a people, rather than the most primitive expression of religious feeling. There is much evidence that the culture of the Australian aboriginals has been greatly influenced by diffusion of magical practices and social forms from outside the country.[13] The sky-beings to whom they attribute so much of their culture were probably real

[11] A. A. Goldenweiser: *Early Civilization* (New York: Alfred A. Knopf, 1922).

[12] R. H. Lowie: *Primitive Religion* (New York: Boni & Liveright, 1924).

[13] This is emphatically the opinion of Professor A. P. Elkin, of the University of Sydney, who probably knows the aborigines better than any other living authority. See his *The Australian Aborigines: How to Understand Them* (Sydney, Australia: Angus & Robertson, 1938), pp. 159, 198, 200 ff.

people of a higher culture, who believed that their own spirits came from the sky and returned thither, and who sometime in the dim past were in sufficiently close contact with the Australians to impress some of their practices upon them.

Thus the anthropological evidence upon which Durkheim's theory is based breaks down. Nor is it adequate as a theory of the nature and origin of religion. Religion is so much a matter of individual spiritual culture that Professor Whitehead described it as " what we do with our solitariness." [14] This is to go to the other extreme, but it points to a feature of religion to which the sociological theory cannot do justice. When religious feeling is cultivated intensely apart from all relation to society it becomes distorted; but it may still be very intense, and this would not be possible if its real root were simply in the social relationship. Further, the tendency in religion to reach out beyond man to find a relationship with something deeper in the universe, cannot be adequately explained as due simply to a tendency to treat symbols as reality. Long after thought has abandoned those symbols which merely represent the social group, man, instead of reverting to society itself for his religious sustenance, seeks some deeper root than the social for his moral and religious satisfaction. This must be due to something in religious experience itself, for it is too persistent to be merely a social habit created by false ideas long abandoned. Indeed, if we refer again to the birth of religion in the individual as we know it today, we see how inadequate the collectivist theory is to explain it. This process is certainly rooted in moral experience, but certainly not merely in a feeling derived from the influence of society. Finally, the whole tendency of religion and morality to reject the verdicts of society as not ultimately authoritative in their sphere shows how inadequate it is to attempt to trace religious

[14] A. N. Whitehead: *Religion in the Making* (New York: The Macmillan Co., 1926) .

feeling to nothing deeper than the impression made on the individual by the group.[15]

E. WESTERMARCK: THE NATURALISTIC THEORY

We may take Westermarck as exemplifying what is commonly called the " naturalistic " [16] theory of religion — that it is primarily natural objects that stir primitive man to superstitious awe, reverence and worship, so that religious belief and practice are to be regarded as the outcome of a very natural but mistaken interpretation of nature.   Religion is defined as " a belief in and a regardful attitude towards a supernatural being on whom man feels himself dependent and to whose will he makes an appeal in his worship." [17]   Thus religion is interpreted as resting on belief in the supernatural, and the primary problem is to explain the origin of this belief.   The distinction between natural and supernatural phenomena, Westermarck says, is quite clearly made by primitive people. Familiar phenomena are taken for granted and ascribed to " natural causes," but the unfamiliar and mysterious arouses fear and the whole attitude toward it is different.   Further, the primitive distinguishes between mechanical causation and volitional activity.   Even among supernatural phenomena he makes this distinction, those mechanically caused being treated as magical but not made objects of worship.   It is only those supernatural phenomena that impress him as being voluntary that the savage treats with religious respect and makes his objects of worship.   And in order that this should

---

[15] For a very thorough critique of the theories of Durkheim and his school in this connection see C. C. J. Webb: *Group Theories of Religion* (New York: The Macmillan Co., 1916) .

[16] A less ambiguous term would be " naturistic," for in the ordinary philosophical sense such theories as those of Tylor and Durkheim are also " naturalistic."

[17] E. Westermarck: *Origin and Development of the Moral Ideas* (2 vols.; New York: The Macmillan Co., 1906–8) , II, 584.

happen these distinctions need not be conceptualized in abstract terms. The emotional response of man to the unfamiliar is even compared to the shying of a horse; and it is pointed out that even a child responds differently to the animate and to the inanimate.

In proof of his contention that mystery is the essential characteristic of supernatural beings Westermarck presents an imposing array of facts. He gathers evidence from primitive language to show that everywhere the word for the divine tends also to mean the mysterious and wonderful. Thus the *manitou* of the American Indians is " a spiritual and mysterious power thought to reside in some material form "; the Fijian *kalou* means a god and may also be applied to anything marvelous. Since Westermarck wrote, this phenomenon has come to be recognized as the most universal feature of primitive religion. It is the belief in mana. " Mana " is a Polynesian word, though found also in Melanesia and Indonesia. It is translated by such terms as power, might, influence, authority, prestige and glory. It signifies an efficacy going beyond that encountered in everyday life.[18] Mana sometimes appears to be impersonal, sometimes personal, and it resides not only in gods, spirits, priests and magical and religious ceremonies but also in chiefs and even in ordinary persons, animals and things so far as they seem to possess a power beyond that ordinarily intelligible. It is the explanation of all that is mysterious and wonderful. There can be little doubt that the concept of mana represents the most primitive, as well as the most universal, belief that is of definitely religious origin.

For further evidence that the belief in the supernatural arises from the sense of mystery and awe Westermarck points to the type of object that is commonly deified. Here the evidence is overwhelming. Men do not make gods of ordinary

[18] For an illuminating account of the usage of the word see H. I. Hogbin: " The Word ' Mana ': A Linguistic Study," *Oceania*, Sept. 1938.

things until they have found something remarkable about them. But, especially among the more primitive peoples, everything that is strikingly unusual, even a twisted stick or a peculiarly shaped rock, is apt to be regarded as possessing supernatural attributes and may be deified. Gods are made of anything that is awe-inspiring, mysterious or dangerous. The snake, alcoholic liquors, great waterfalls, mountains, thunder, storms, great heroes and rulers, the seasons, objects of remarkable utility such as the cow, objects used in magical ceremonies such as the totem, the groves and caves and other places where such ceremonies are held, strange diseases, persons afflicted with mental disorder — in short, everything strange and wonderful is apt to be regarded as either itself divine, possessed of a spirit, or at least the seat of mana.

With Westermarck's contention that everything mysterious tends to be thought of as supernatural we may, then, agree. But, as he himself points out, merely to be supernatural is not necessarily to be a religious object. Magic is distinguishable from religion. Religion involves worship, devotion and a moral attitude, while magic is simply an effort to use supernatural forces to attain human ends. Westermarck explains this by saying that it is those supernatural objects that are personalized, regarded as voluntary agents, that are made objects of the religious approach. Religious activity is an appeal to the will of a supernatural being. But if this were so then there could be no religion (there could be only magic) where the ceremonial is not directed toward a being conceived as personal, i.e., capable of a voluntary response. This would make the Australian aboriginals actually devoid of religion, for, though they believe in the existence of spirits and other supernatural personal beings, they offer to them no prayers or sacrifices; yet they carry out their totemic ceremonies and initiations with a truly religious fervor and find a genuine spiritual encouragement and moral strength in them. Again,

Westermarck's theory would deny the name of religion to the thought and devotion of Spinoza and Gautama, for the object of their devotion was conceived as impersonal. It would deny the name of religion also to the modern humanist movement.

But the first half of Westermarck's argument is in itself really fatal to his position, for it points out that, to the primitive, the divine and the mysterious and wonderful mean the same thing. Mana is not to be distinguished from the sacred and divine. Yet it is in itself impersonal and is often attached to impersonal objects. The divine is therefore something mysterious and wonderful in the universe, but not necessarily personal. Yet, even when not personal, it is something to be treated with reverence, something sacred, something it would be sin to ignore or treat lightly, something that may be very precious. It is something not clearly conceived but intensely felt. Above all it is felt in the ceremonies themselves, and because it is felt there these are to be performed with intensive attention and zealous care. Thus the ceremonies, as in Australia, can be developed into an elaborate system long before the imagination has personalized objects of nature and thought of appealing to these imaginary powers for support in the battle of life. The notion of mana then stands out as the most elementary of all religious concepts, and religion is seen to have its basis in something immediately felt, not in a mere illusory personalization of the mysterious and wonderful.

A still more fundamental deficiency in Westermarck's theory is its failure to do justice to the moral element in religion. He regards religion as simply an effort of the superstitious person to utilize supernatural forces to secure his ends or to prevent them from injuring him, an effort differing from magic only in that it is directed toward supernatural agencies believed to possess feeling and will. It thus takes the forms of prayer, sacrifice and other types of personal appeal instead of the impersonal methods of magic. On this view man, in religion, is merely concerned with getting what he wants. The moral element is secondary.

Now it must be frankly recognized that much of the so-called religious activity of people, both in civilized communities and among savages, is of just this character. But, though it observes religious forms, is it really religion? In all the great ethical religions such mere pursuit of the loaves and fishes is repudiated as a simulation and prostitution of religion. It contains no real devotion, no worship from the heart, no moral earnestness; and these things are the essence of religion. The "true believer," who possesses them, may ask material favors of his God, but he feels a duty that does not derive from his mere need of these favors. This deeper and distinctively moral element in the relation of the worshiper to the object of his worship is not superficially obvious in the religious practice of primitive peoples, but it is certainly there. Their ceremonials are not merely means to securing material ends and social and military prizes, but duties to be performed. The Australian aboriginal insists that his ceremonies "make everybody better." Those who know them well assert that the ceremonials are performed with great reverence as well as zeal, and that they are regarded as a moral obligation as well as acts of prudence to insure the life and safety of the tribe.

To neglect them is a specific disloyalty to the welfare of the tribe, and leaves a feeling of vague uneasiness, of loss of contact with the great heroes and the source of life; moreover, disloyalty to the tradition and rules means unworthiness, with the result that the old men will not hand on esoteric knowledge to such unworthy young folk.[19]

[19] Quoted from private correspondence of Professor A. P. Elkin, anthropologist at the University of Sydney and editor of *Oceania*. See also his *The Australian Aborigines: How to Understand Them*, especially chaps. 7, 8.

In his evaluation of religion as essentially moral in character by reason of its fundamentally social nature, Durkheim is much nearer the truth than either Tylor or Westermarck. This fact has recently been strongly emphasized by another great anthropologist. He speaks of " the ethical element intrinsically inherent in all religious activities," and continues:

They always require efforts, discipline, and submission on the part of the individual for the good of the community. Taboos, vigils, religious exercises are essentially moral, not merely because they express submission of man to spiritual powers, but also because they are a sacrifice of man's personal comfort for the common weal. But there is another aspect which, as we shall see, makes all religions moral in their very essence. Every cult is associated with a definite congregation: ancestor worship is primarily based on the family; at times even on a wider group, the clan; at times it becomes tribal when the ancestor spirit is that of a chief. The members of such a group of worshippers have natural duties towards each other. The sense of common responsibility, of reciprocal charity and good will, flows from the same fundamental idea and sentiment which moves clansmen, brothers or tribesmen to common worship.[20]

Thus, even in the most primitive forms of religion we must recognize a moral element, which Westermarck's explanation of its origin would make secondary and unessential. In the developed religious consciousness of civilized man, however, it is primary and fundamental. Religion is the *service* of the divine, not its utilization for our human purposes. So much is this the case that we say a man makes a god of money or position if he acts as if those things were worth being made the supreme ends of his life. It is a secondary matter, though a natural and important corollary, that that which is so worthy of our service is able to serve us and may be appealed to for that purpose. People who are not deeply sensitive to

[20] Malinowski: *Foundations of Faith and Morals*, p. 7.

religious values, and sufficiently reflective, are apt to put this secondary matter first; and we must not think harshly of the primitive if, in the difficulty and uncertainty of his life, he does so most of the time. But even he perceives the other side and feels his religion as primarily a duty, though a duty from which he expects to reap benefits.

RUDOLPH OTTO: THE THEORY OF THE NUMINOUS

In Professor Rudolph Otto's well known book, *Das Heilige*,[21] an attempt is made to do justice to both the mystical and the moral elements in primitive religion, while still regarding the mystical element as primary. This work is also important for the influence it has had in the rejection of the notion that religion rests primarily upon an intellectual content of belief, and in directing the search for its basis in something immediately felt. The idea of the holy, as found in the developed religious consciousness, contains, Otto says, two elements: a rational element, the idea of the good; and an irrational element, the sense of the sacred, a dim awareness of an aspect of reality which is mysterious, terrible, fascinating. This is the distinctive and original element of the religious consciousness. To it he gives the name of the "numinous." In the course of its development religion becomes more and more rational and moral and this mystical element sinks into the background; but if it is lost altogether our experience ceases to be religious.

Now there is much of importance in this emphasis on the mystical element in religion. It is probably true that religion can never dispense with mysticism altogether. But it does not follow that that which is intuitively grasped in the mystical element of religious experience is nonmoral. In primitive religion as we know it today the element of fear, awe and

[21] Translated by John W. Harvey under the title, *The Idea of the Holy* (New York: Oxford University Press, 1925).

fascination is undoubtedly predominant. But primitive religion as we know it today is not the beginning, but the end, of a long process of evolution. It is religion stalemated, religion at a dead end, religion in which the vital element that would make it dynamic, changing, progressive, has been overlaid by elements that render it static, adapted to its environment, but no longer adaptable, no longer a power to change the environment itself and the vehicle of its own expression. Religious evolution, like other forms of evolution, runs into a cul-de-sac along many of its lines of differentiation. In only a few directions, and perhaps ultimately only in one, is continuous progress possible. That is the lesson of evolutionary history in animate nature and human civilization. We must not expect, therefore, that the most prominent element in primitive religion can reveal the essential genius of all religion.

The vital element in religion is the moral element. The dead hand everywhere upon it, but heaviest upon primitive religion, is magic. The features of the numinous to which Otto points as the original and distinctive features of the sacred and holy are those derived from the magical element in religion — the *mysterium tremendum et fascinans*. From this, he rightly points out, there is no *logical* transition to the ethical.

How should it be logically inferred from the still " crude," half-demonic character of a moon-god or a sun-god or a numen attached to some locality, that he is a guardian and guarantor of the oath and of honorable dealing, of hospitality, of the sanctity of marriage, and of duties to tribe and clan? [22]

Yet Otto recognizes that it is always felt as axiomatic that the divine should be regarded as to some extent concerned with the moral. Here, he admits, is a problem; and his solution

[22] *Ibid.*, p. 140.

is a lame one: " we are forced to assume an obscure *a priori* knowledge of the necessity of this synthesis, combining rational and non-rational." [23] Surely, before we leave the matter there we should try every alternative hypothesis.

R. R. MARETT: THE CONCEPT OF MANA

It becomes obvious from these studies that any satisfactory theory of the origin of religion must be able to account, not only for the prominence of magic and mysticism in religion, but also for the connection of these, from the beginning, with a vital moral element. The attempt to explain how the moral could have grown out of, or become tacked on to, the magical and mystical has signally failed. The suggestion therefore arises that we might succeed better by approaching the problem from the other side. It may be the case that the moral element is really primary and the magical and mystical a natural outgrowth from it; and perhaps some element of the mystical is also a necessary and permanent feature of all religion. An interpretation of this kind may, I think, be developed through an examination of the contribution to our knowledge of the subject made by Professor R. R. Marett. Marett finds in the notion of mana not only a preanimistic stage of religion but also a stage more primitive than that of the mystical reverence for natural objects emphasized by Westermarck.[24]

If we adopt Westermarck's approach then we must believe that it was the mysterious and wonderful phenomena of external nature that first led man to formulate the hypothesis of a strange and marvelous energy resident in many things, whereby they were able to exercise an influence or power beyond anything ordinarily intelligible. We must believe that,

[23] *Ibid.* The rational is, for Otto, the moral, and the nonrational is the nonmoral; both are elements in the holy.
[24] Marett: *The Threshold of Religion,* chaps. 1, 4.

having formulated this hypothesis, he persuaded himself that, by various extraordinary dramatic and symbolical actions, he could somehow control this force and turn it to his benefit — and, as we have learned from the Australian aborigines, that he could do this without any thought of help from superhuman personalities or spirits. And we must conclude that the mana he attributed to the ceremonies and religious objects themselves was a second thought, due to their association with mysterious objects of nature and the mysterious power he had persuaded himself that they would exercise.

Now Marett's theory reverses this. Religion, he points out, has abundantly proved its survival value for the primitive. But its value is due, not to the soundness of its intellectual element, which is mostly absurd, but to its wholesome effect upon his *feelings*.

After all, to feel like winning in the battle of life is always more than half-way to a victory which, in the biological sense, can never be complete. . . . Neither to know nor to do, but to feel that he can do is the deepest aspiration of the savage. He seeks from cult neither truth nor works so much as a sense of power. . . . Though a withdrawal from real life *in esse,* religion retains the sense of being real life *in posse* — real life mastered in advance. . . . Herein, then, lies the truth of religious symbolism — not in what it says, for it speaks darkly, but in what it makes a man feel, namely, that his heart is strong.[25]

The most primitive religious exercise is a response to feeling, not to thought, and it takes the form of dance and dramatization rather than prayer and sacrifice. It works wonders — real wonders — upon the state of mind of those who participate in it. And because of this they tend to believe that it works wonders in an objective fashion too. The subtle

[25] Marett: *Faith, Hope and Charity in Primitive Religion* (1932) , pp. 12–15 *passim.* By permission of The Clarendon Press, Oxford.

influence that has made the tribesman confident of success is credited with a more direct part in the success that follows. Mana is a name for the power that uplifts his heart in the tribal dance. And when he comes home flushed with victory he believes that the same power strengthened his arm in the battle or the hunt for which the dance prepared.

On this interpretation the notion of mana arises in reflection upon the emotional experience of the primitive group ceremony and is first attached to the ceremonies themselves. From this beginning the subsequent development may be readily inferred. The vaguely conceived mysterious power felt in the ceremony must be given a locus, and it tends most naturally to be localized in the ceremony itself and, as these become regularized in practice, in the properties used in the ceremony. The churinga stones, the clan symbol or totem, the symbolic garb worn by the participants, the bull-roarer and all other instruments come to be regarded as imbued with mana. The ceremonies are held in places that have a suitable atmosphere — in groves or caves, on mountaintops, in the shadow of great trees and quaint and impressive rock formations — and those places become full of mana. Eventually everything that arouses feelings at all similar to those of the ceremony — feelings of awe and mystery — and anything that seems to possess an extraordinary power are regarded as having mana. Living in a world believed full of this mysterious power, the primitive looks expectantly to the mana of his ceremonies to prevail over the mana of other things, to ward off dangers and contribute to his food supply. He develops ceremonies which, by their symbolic meaning and dramatization, persuade him of their efficacy in these ways. All of these are magical, relying for their objective efficiency on their mana. Some of them, performed solely for their supposed objective effect, lose that effect upon the *feeling* of the performer which was the source of the belief in mana, and magical practice is developed more or less in divorce from religion.

This means that the magico-religious ceremonies of the primitive are not originally founded on any kind of belief, but magical and religious beliefs are outgrowths from the ceremonies and, in particular, from the feelings underlying the ceremonies, expressed in them and stimulated by them. The ceremonies themselves must have been gradual growths beginning in spontaneous expressions of feeling. These spontaneous feelings, whatever they were, must be regarded as the ultimate source and permanent foundation of primitive religion. The feelings were, and are, probably very complex, since they issue in both magic and religion. But whatever they are, the secret of primitive religion is to be found in them. And if religion is a unified growth from the primitive to its highest modern forms then its most essential feeling elements must be the same throughout. We have seen in our previous chapter that, at the higher levels, religion is rooted in feelings concerned with the moral life. The question therefore formulates itself as the problem as to where the moral element enters into religion. Is it an integral part of the feeling-states out of which the earliest ceremonies arose? Or are they, in their origin, nonmoral, the ethical element becoming incorporated into them in the course of their development?

Marett hesitates between these alternatives, but inclines toward the latter — " that the excitement generated by cult is almost unmoral in its initial phase." It generates a passion which can transform a cold ethical code into a hunger and thirst after righteousness, but which may also prove itself dangerous and devilish. " *Mana* is, as Freud would say, ambivalent. Possessed by it a man is moved to let himself go whether for better or for worse. . . . It looks, then, as if religion apart from morality was neither good nor bad, but just a neutral force." [26]

This may, and must, all be granted — if one agrees that religious beliefs and practices apart from morality are still really religion. But it may be the case that the feeling in which these beliefs and practices arise is essentially a feeling for moral values, so that religion is fundamentally rooted in morality. If this is the case, as I will try to show, it could not be expected to involve, as a consequence, that religious beliefs and practices could never become separated by primitive people from their moral roots. This happens all too often, among civilized people, with beliefs and practices which we know have a moral origin. The elaboration of belief and ceremonial proceeds under impulsion of a great variety of motives — and this elaboration has slowly proceeded among primitive peoples for thousands of years. The sheer intensity of feeling-states cultivated in ritual and dance has been enjoyed for its own sake and directed toward all sorts of nonmoral and immoral ends. But if we look for those feelings which were most fundamental and for those in which the ceremonies must have spontaneously originated, we shall find, I think, that their central constituents must be recognized as feelings for moral values.

THE BEGINNINGS OF RELIGION

We may sum up the evidence from anthropology as culminating in the view that the most primitive religious idea is that of mana, that this arises in the actual ceremonial performances of the primitive groups, and that subsequently, as Marett says, "Gods start, in fact, as no more than portions of the ritual apparatus." [27] What then is the nature of the ceremonial performed before there had developed even so

---

26 *Ibid.,* pp. 18–19.
27 *Ibid.,* p. 11.

primitive a religious notion as mana — the ceremonial out of which that notion arose? It must have been a type of performance that originated in spontaneous expressions of feeling. But what expressions of feeling could have been so taken up by the group as to result in the development of group ceremonial to express them? Obviously, they must have been feelings concerned with the common welfare of the group. So we reach the conclusion that religion was a moral exercise in its first beginnings. It arose out of the expression of feeling for the common welfare.

A little further reflection will show how deep in the moral life these feelings must have gone. It must have been the strongest feelings and the strongest expressions that came to be cultivated and formalized in ceremonial. But strong expressions of feeling are called forth only in times that are more or less critical — for example, when the food supply is endangered or when dangers have to be faced from fierce neighbors, animal or human. Furthermore, expressions of feeling for the common welfare and of intention to play one's part in contributing to it, if made under circumstances that cost nothing, are merely trite or idle boasting; they arouse no appreciative response. It is when the fears and difficulties are so great that individuals hesitate to do their part, when each has reason to doubt the adequate courage and co-operation of his partner and neighbor, when circumstances are so hard and dangerous that each man doubts even himself — it is then that men take courage from each other's expressions of boldness; it is then that they welcome their comrades' assurance of devotion to the common cause. His language being undeveloped and inadequate, primeval man could not have been very eloquent. He must have expressed himself as much in gesture as in words, especially when his feelings were strongly aroused. So these early expressions of courage and devotion to the common cause, of faith and hope against a dark future, of moral indignation and vengeance against the enemy, must have taken the form of symbolic gesture and dramatized action rather than words. It was from such simple but vital and human things that the ceremonies of religion grew.

Here at last we can see the connection between the birth of religion in the individual and its birth in the race. We have seen that the religious life of the individual begins as he becomes conscious of the duality within himself — of the will to secure the good of other persons distinguishing itself from the will to secure his own good, of the resultant inner conflict and the sense of obligation. It is essentially the same experience that would underlie those primitive, dramatic expressions of feeling with which tribal ceremonies began. Before man acquired the intelligence to distinguish between his own private good and the good of others, the cohesion of the group was secured by instinctive, animal, gregarious tendencies. Each individual responded, like an animal or an infant, to the immediacy of his own feelings; but nature had so organized those feelings that the group held together with mutual aid. Intelligence first made selfishness possible. The cunning of homo sapiens made it possible to break the instinctive bonds of common action, to pursue private self-interest. It brought moral conflict into being. When primeval man met this conflict in his soul with a gesture of courage and a symbolic declaration of adhesion to the common cause, religion was born. Religion was necessary to save the race from destruction by an egoistic individualism created by its very intelligence.

A little sober imagination and knowledge of primitive peoples enables us to reconstruct the rest of the story. There were dramatic expressions of courage in the face of danger; and these developed into the ceremonies whereby the primitive works up his enthusiasm and beats down his fears before the battle or the hunt of dangerous animals. In the face of despair wrought by dwindling food supplies and long delayed rain there were symbolic expressions of hope; and these developed into the ceremonies whereby the primitive buoys up his spirits and persuades himself that he is helping forward the forces of nature in their benevolent tasks. There were vivid warnings and preachments from the grown men to the fast maturing youths, and responsive demonstrations of zeal and endurance from the young; and these developed into the initiation rites whereby the savage warriors ceremonially and psychologically " make a man " out of a boy. From our standpoint there seems to be much in these ceremonies that is vicious and cruel, as well as much that is superstitious and shortsighted. But to the understanding of the primitive these things are appropriate and good in both intention and effect. They have grown with little design, but upon them he has lavished his best thought and artistic skill. He enters into them with zeal, feels their meaning rather than thinks it, and finds that the effect upon him is good.

That effect is powerful; yet it is no ordinary power such as he feels in his arm and sees at work in animals and things around him. In the rites he finds a peculiar and extraordinary power. That he calls mana. Before the rite perhaps he is dubious, fearful, inclined to shirk. But in the midst of the wild dance or solemn ceremony something grips him, uplifts him, draws him out of himself, fills him with zeal and courage, thrills him with the sense of kinship with his people. It is not a mere abstraction but a concrete power that he feels. It goes with him into the battle, gives him strength and skill, and brings him home victorious. It is a *thing* — vague but real, mysterious but powerful, overpowering and terrible but helpful and needed. He does not personalize it, but naturally he localizes it. It is in the ceremonies, in the symbolic objects used in them, in the places where they are held. Finally, it is in all objects that impress him as possessing a nature or power that is not of the ordinary kind. It becomes a convenient concept that explains the happening of all that has no other explanation. Then it becomes something that it is necessary to control, something that may perhaps be used to good effect. Naturally it is objects that have mana that must be used to control the mana of other things. So he takes something that has acquired mana from its use in the ceremonies — a feather, a bone, a shell, a tuft of hair — and uses it as a charm. Thus magic grows, both within the religious ceremony and the ideas associated with it, and outside of religion, more or less detached from it.

Once mana is localized, the objects thus dignified, singled out for special attention and credited with peculiar power, would often easily lend themselves to imaginative animation and personalization. Thus the totem, the grove, the waterfall, the mountain, the intoxicating drink, the mysterious snake and the fierce bull become quasi-personal seats of mana. The stage of animatism [28] has been reached. But since mana explains all mysteries it explains those of life and death. It is the mana of something that generates the child in the womb. And when a man dies his mana goes from him. Mana is always an intangible power, and it is this intangible power that has left the body. In its disembodied state the mana of the person is greater than ever, for it is more mysterious. With these beginnings of animism mana is no longer so definitely localized. There are intangible powers of a personal, or at least animate, nature; and mana everywhere tends to be interpreted in animistic form. From animism and animatism the more imaginative peoples passed readily enough to polytheism. The Egyptians gradually personalized and spiritual-

---

[28] This is the stage where natural objects are worshiped as living personal beings rather than as the seat of spirits separable from their physical existence. Belief in spirits is " animism."

ized the semitotemic animal symbols of each nome, or district, until they became high gods who appeared and were worshiped in an animal form.   The Syrians turned the vaguely conceived and multitudinous fertility spirits into definitely characterized deities — the *ba'alim* became Ba'al or Bel.   The Hindus transformed the early animatistic vedic nature deities of sun, sky, etc., into personal, spiritual beings who made these places their home.   A few departed heroes, such as Krishna, were raised to the rank of high gods.   Tribal deities were developed out of the animatistic gods of the locality inhabited by the tribe.   So, in one way and another, according to circumstances and the imaginative capacity of the people, the pantheons of polytheism have grown.

But while magic and superstition, crude guesses at the mysteries of nature, poetic fancy and the scheming of priests have influenced the development of religious ideas, the moral element has never been entirely absent.   It is because of its real moral value that religion survived despite the load of magic and trickery that was thrust upon it.   It is the cement that has bound human society together, buttressed its mores, curbed the worst extremes of its tyrants though often a tool in their hands, inspired its reformers, and generally prevented the cunning and selfish from completely disintegrating the social whole.   If testimony is needed on this point we might bring together the verdicts of two great British anthropologists, neither of whom can be accused of having any theological ax to grind: " The comparative study of civilisation teaches that the core of all sound communal life has always been a strong, living faith." [29]   " But to shed religion has surely never helped a people to prosper." [30]

[29] Malinowski: *Foundations of Faith and Morals,* p. viii.
[30] Marett: *Faith, Hope and Charity in Primitive Religion,* p. 4.

RELIGION AND ETHICS

Our analysis has done more than merely reaffirm the social value of religion and solve the interesting intellectual problem of its origin. It has shown us why religion is of social value; and it has clearly distinguished, within religion as ordinarily conceived, that which is essential and valuable from that which is adventitious and evil. The important thing is that it is the adventitious element — magic — that is evil, and the essential element — the moral — that is valuable. And again it is important to recognize that the magical element can be sloughed off from religion without leaving us with nothing but an ethic. For the moral element in religion is not an ethic. It is not a body of moral teaching. It is rather a mode of response to natural and inevitable feelings for social values. It is that mode of response which gives acknowledgment and expression to the ideal; and indeed, communal or group expression. It recognizes and inwardly meditates upon the objective character of the ideal. It seeks to achieve the integration and reintegration of personality by sharing a common spiritual experience with the group.

Our study of the birth of religion in the individual revealed it as a process of inner personal integration achieved largely through private meditation; our study of its origin and development in the race reveals it as a process whereby that integration is maintained by cultivating a spiritual integration with the religious society. And the whole process of inner personal integration is revealed as having its social value in that it involves the integration of the whole personality under control of a single master motive — the disinterested will to the good of others.

This last feature is, of course, not clearly visible in the religion of the primitive. There we have a conflict between the ego and the will to the common good of a small group, or the particular good of a friend.   But it is the same essential conflict of egoism and altruism however small the group, and even though the means of achieving its good is robbing or destroying some neighboring group.   Sensitivity to the larger good of the larger group, like sensitivity to the higher values possible for the small group itself, is a plant of slow growth.   It is with these developments that the great religious innovators are chiefly concerned.   Religious progress is only in smaller part a progress in scientific and metaphysical understanding achieved by philosophers.   It is, for the greater part, a progress in the widening horizon of values, to which the disinterested will aspires; and this is the work of the prophets.   It is also, to no inconsiderable extent, a matter of improvement in the modes of worship, of spiritual expression, whereby the vision of wider and higher values is propagated and maintained; and this is the work, chiefly, of poet, artist and priest.

Thus religion gathers into itself the thought and knowledge of the times, their modes of social organization, their artistic and poetic expression, and, at its best, devotes them to the external integration of society and the internal integration of the individual.   And, as with progressive insights it discovers the true goal of its own essential motive, this integration becomes more and more determined by the disinterested will to the good of all — that other and higher will that the religious man finds within himself and which, long before he has understood completely its nature and its end, he has come to call the will of God.

But finally we must recognize that, having done full justice to the paramountcy of the practical moral element in religion, we cannot neglect its conceptual interpretation.   It is not enough to see clearly the goal toward which religion moves.   Rational man will ask the reason for the goal.   We have seen that it is intelligence that opens the way for the conflict to develop within man's soul, that makes him a creature capable of *moral* evil and thus of a *moral* good. We have seen that religious activity buttresses and supports the altruistic elements in personality. We have seen man's incipient egoistic individualism checked by these influences.

But is the check permanent? We see today an intelligent egoistic individualism triumphing in a widespread neglect of the traditional means of spiritual culture, a neglect fostered also by a perception of the moral deficiencies, perversions and intellectual errors in traditional religion. The name of God no longer arouses the awe that once it did. Among millions the symbols of narrow racial and class cults arouse more enthusiasm and reverence. Religion, if it is to perform its social function, must be able to give a reason why men *ought* to devote themselves to that ideal of universal good that is the flower of its finest development. It becomes of vital importance that we should be able to clarify the nature of that ideal, to see precisely what it means in its practical application, and to see how deep it is rooted in the structure of reality.

This is the historic quest of religion for righteousness and truth. In pursuing it ourselves we shall next briefly review the way in which religion has, in the past, faced some of the chief problems involved. It is a quest that has been pursued with as much vigor in the Orient as in the Occident, but for reasons of space we shall confine ourselves chiefly to our own tradition, growing out of Egypt, Palestine and Greece into the Christian forms with which we are today familiar. At the same time this review of some of the historic answers man has given to the problems raised by his religious experience will help to confirm the accuracy of the analysis we have made of the essential nature of that experience.

Typical Beliefs and Problems

THE IDEA OF REVELATION

WE HAVE SEEN how natural, and almost universal, was the development of the belief in anthropomorphic deities. Equally natural and widespread was the expectation that such deities would occasionally communicate with human beings. This is such a reasonable assumption that atheists have often urged the absence of any universal and absolutely certain revelation as a reason for not believing in God. On the other hand, supporters of the traditional belief in revelation used the argument against the deists of the eighteenth century, who proclaimed a belief in God on rational grounds but rejected the dogmas of " revealed religion." It is not therefore surprising that from prehistoric times man has looked for communications from his deities and has lent a ready ear to anyone who could plausibly support a claim to have received them. In these circumstances, too, it is natural that many people should have come forward with such claims. The wish is father to the thought, and a lively expectation, amidst intense emotional excitement such as religious exercises often induce, is a fertile source of self-deception. In addition, the prestige and power and even economic advantage obtained by those able to convince their fellows that they possess such revelations, become a further inducement both to self-deception and to deliberate fraud. Divine revelations have been sought and seen in every unusual phenomenon of nature, in the effect of drugs, in psychological abnormalities, in incidents and experiences of religious ceremonial, in solemn vigil and quiet meditation. Priests, soothsayers and prophets have acquired reputations for a capacity to receive and interpret these communications. And records of special revelations in varied forms have been preserved and elaborated in oral tradition and sacred scriptures.

The record of what men have believed to be revelations from God is a strange mixture of sordid deception, fantastic nonsense, tragic error, well intentioned fraud, pleasant illusion, wholesome legend, enslaving tradition, stimulating faith, lofty idealism and penetrating moral insight. Among the human intermediaries of these alleged revelations, however, it is important to distinguish two types: First, the priests, who carry on a tradition, teaching an accepted form of revelation or practicing a traditional method of receiving and interpreting divine communications. They perform their functions *voluntarily* and are intermediaries by profession, often inheriting their traditional office and usually being specially inducted into it by their predecessors. Second, the prophets, who receive their alleged revelations *involuntarily* and frequently introduce innovations upon the tradition. One and the same person may sometimes perform both functions, but the prophet is usually outside the ranks of the professional intermediaries and, for this reason and because of his innovations, often finds himself in conflict with the established priesthood. The motives and the emotional grounds of belief in the two classes are often mixed, including fear, wishful thinking and moral conviction. But this distinction of motives is important, especially in the case of the prophets. Progress in religion is made through the work of the prophet who is moved by moral conviction. We need not make any assumptions regarding the source of his revelations to recognize in him the *genuine* prophet, compared to whom the other is a mere pseudo prophet or soothsayer. The genuine prophet has a message that is new to him and his hearers, a message that impresses him with its distinctive moral importance; and he labors under the conviction that it is given to him of God to preach it.

The moral genuineness of the great prophets is beyond question. Mohammed preached with high courage against the idolatry and low moral standards of his pagan compatriots, working under a conviction of his mission that had come upon him after many years of " seeking " in which scraps of Christian and Jewish teaching had convinced him of the inferiority of the paganism of the Arab tribes. For long he feared that he and all his people must be consigned to hell by the one true God for their sins and idolatry. The hardness and bitterness of traditional racial and religious lines long inhibited any other solution, for it was very little indeed that Mohammed knew of the higher religions. It was a revolutionary thought, and a genuine moral insight, that came to him in his vigil, with a vision of the angel bidding him to recite:

> Thy Lord is most gracious,
> Who taught by means of the pen,
> Taught man what he knew not.[1]

To the earnest but ignorant caravan leader it was a wonderful illumination — that the great God of the sacred writings would be gracious even to the sinful pagan.

To Gautama, the founder of Buddhism, the problem of salvation presented itself in a different light. The doctrine of transmigration, with its endless chain of lives in each of which the individual atoned by his suffering for the sins of the previous existence, presented itself to the Indian mind, then as now, as a threat rather than a hope. It was something

[1] Koran, Sura 96, 3–5. According to tradition this was the first revelation Mohammed received. His call to preach came later. The Lord " who taught by means of the pen " was, of course, the God who revealed the Hebrew and Christian scriptures, for this, to the illiterate Mohammed, was a very impressive fact.

from which one must try to escape. The Brahmanism of
the day sought this release in mystic contemplation, the cultivation of trance states and the practice of severe asceticism.
Gautama tried these without success, subjecting himself to
terrible privations, before there came to him the enlightenment that revealed a better way. The great need, as the Upanishads [2] taught, was to overcome the desires that maintained
the chain of being. But the true way to do this, Gautama
now became convinced, was by the life of simple faith, purity,
righteousness and kindliness, comprised in what he defined
as the " eightfold path." It was this insight into a better way
that gave to him his sense of a prophetic destiny. It obtained
for him, among his followers, the title of " the Enlightened
One " and eventual deification. The " path " is not beyond
criticism from the standpoint of the developed social consciousness of the twentieth century, but it was a wonderful
advance on the traditions of the day, and Gautama's faithful
teaching and practice of it have earned for him a place among
the very greatest of the moral and religious leaders of mankind.

These and many other figures from non-Christian religious
literature can be set beside the great prophetic figures of the
Hebrew-Christian tradition. Even from as early as 3500 B.C.,
in ancient Egypt, we have records preserved of prophetic ut-
terances earnestly expounding ethical teaching in the name
of religion.[3] In Pythagoras and others, including Socrates
with his *daemon,* Greece had prophets as well as philosophers. That these great prophetic leaders are genuine, in the
sense that they earnestly believed in their own prophetic mission and made important contributions to the moral and religious life and thought of their times, there can be no doubt.

[2] The philosophic writings of religious teachers of the time.
[3] J. H. Breasted: *The Dawn of Conscience* (New York: Charles Scribner's
Sons, 1933).

Whether their spiritual insight was in any sense a revelation to them from some form of spiritual reality independent of their own and other human minds, is quite another question. They certainly were often mistaken as to the *kind* of spiritual being from whom they believed their revelations to come. The conflicting views they express indicate that the so-called process of revelation, though it has led the way in the unfolding of higher and higher ideals, is far from being a source of pure and absolute truth. The orthodox theologies have usually struggled to explain away the contradictions within their own tradition, and have maintained that the revelations of their own prophets are true and that the others are not genuine revelations at all. But the ethical teaching of East and West, of Greek, Hebrew, Indian and Chinese sages, rises at its best to a height so nearly the same that such insular arrogance is precluded. If the ethico-religious development of any one people has been achieved by the human mind, unaided by any superhuman power, then the same must be true of all. And if any superhuman power has been at work, aiding in this moral and religious development of mankind, then it certainly succeeds in no more than instilling a very gradual enlightenment amid much illusion and error.

Yet the claim of the genuine prophet that his teaching is not merely his own, but is given him by a Source beyond himself, is too persistent to be dismissed without explanation. However, in our recognition of the division within the self that lies at the root of religious experience, and of the effect of the persistent presence of the altruistic will, we have at hand an adequate explanation of the prophetic phenomenon. The genuine prophet works under the compelling influence of a *moral* conviction. And it arises not merely from the social tradition around him nor from his own ego. Rather it is thrust upon him, more or less against his egoistic will and traditional social influences, by the disinterested will to the good that is deeply rooted in his own personality. He is a man who has concerned himself with the moral issues of his day more deeply than the rest of his contemporaries. He is an earnest and sensitive soul. In wrestling with his problem he passes through a period of spiritual culture and psychological preparation that quickens his responsiveness to the subtle influence within of that will to the good which reaches beyond the habitual impulses of the ego. Gradually that growing influence gives new meaning to his problems until, sometimes suddenly, sometimes slowly, he sees them in a new light. A glorious new truth has dawned upon his mind. It is more than the teaching of his fathers; more, he feels sure, than his own sinful heart could devise. It is God who has revealed it to him. Such is his natural conviction. And such, if we agree to give the divine name to the altruistic will within us, we may recognize it to be. It is then God, as immanent in the prophet's soul, that has given him his insight and his commission. Whether God, thus immanent, is but one organic, active part of a spiritual being far transcending his manifestation here is a question into which we have still to inquire.

Upon one feature of the prophet's experience perhaps a further word should be said: the matter of visions, voices and other strange experiences that often accompany his receipt of the revelation. These psychological phenomena are, of course, no proof of any superhuman influence, though they often do much to convince the prophet himself of the superhuman source of his insight. But neither do they suggest that the explanation we have given in terms of normal moral development is unsound. The great prophets have attained their " revelations " out of the travail of their souls. They have been seekers of truth with an intensity that has often put great strain upon them. Or they have struggled with a moral problem that could find a solution only in a revolutionary change of personal attitude and customary thought, against which the ego has naturally fought hard and long. It has been no easy matter to break the moral (or immoral) bonds in which a people has been bound for generations, and the psychological strain has often been enormous. At such times the new insight, quite naturally, comes with a great wave of feeling, creating vivid visual or auditory imagery or other unusual psychological phenomena. Sometimes the prophet may be of a mental type especially susceptible to such experiences, but the fact that he had such experiences does not necessarily indicate that he must have been so. Even a very well balanced, normal personality, undergoing a great revulsion of feeling following a tremendously important discovery (especially after a long period of severe mental strain, and under conditions of strong suggestion due to antecedent beliefs in the supernatural), is likely to experience such abnormal psychological phenomena. Such experiences therefore, when recorded by the prophet, are evidences neither of the reliability nor of the unreliability of his message, but rather of the deep travail of soul through which he has passed to attain it.

THE IDEA OF COMMUNION

(a) *The Sacrifice of Communion.* — There is a form of social experience that we call fellowship or communion. It does not require overt communication. All that is necessary is to be in the presence of some other person or persons, to feel that there is good will between them and you, and to believe that they share your major interests and purposes and that you share theirs. Such fellowship or communion is a subtle source of spiritual strength and comfort among human beings. It is not surprising therefore that when men attained a personalized conception of their gods they should have sought such communion with them. Much of the public ceremonial of religion is designed to cultivate this sense of communion. In any public ceremony there is, of course, a tendency to realize a sense of communion with the other participants. But a religious occasion differentiates itself from one that is merely social and secular by the deeper sense of communion that it generates, an experience that the believer naturally tends to interpret as fellowship with the divine, and one that the unbeliever also may feel and cherish however he explains it.

Among the most dramatic and striking of religious ceremonials are those of sacrifice. In these practices we find chiefly expressed the two ideas of atonement and communion, the one being sometimes much more prominent than the other. For the present let us pay attention to the aspect of communion, usually symbolized by the participants' eating some portion of the sacrifice. From the beginning of human experience the sharing of food has been a real expression of genuine community of life. From time immemorial such sharing has been a recognized symbol of fellowship, and man has found no more eloquent way of expressing his faith in communion with his god, and with his fellow servants of the same god, than in the symbolism of the common meal. Even though the idea of God has been so exalted and spiritualized that he can no longer be thought in any sense to partake of food himself, the Christian religion retains such a ceremony as its most solemn act of worship. The Christian, who sees his ideal of the divine take living shape in the person of Jesus Christ, joins in memorial celebration of Jesus' last meal with his disciples and finds in its eloquent symbolism, replete with stirring memories and lofty ideals, a means of cultivation of a deep and rich sense of communion with God.

In explanation of the sense of value found in such occasions of communion, both social and religious, it has been customary to postulate the satisfaction of a primitive herd instinct or to point to the fact that human beings have been so conditioned as to feel security in union with their fellows. This, however, scarce suffices to explain religious communion, which is independent of numbers and can attain its full richness and reality in solitude as well as in company. Our analysis of religious experience, however, suggests another explanation. The God with whom the religious man communes is within him as the most fundamental feature of his own personality — the disinterested will to the good. With that disinterested will his ego is, at ordinary times, in frequent conflict. But in the period of communion the ego loses its prominence. It surrenders its central place to the thought of a good that is not a good-for-me. The tension between the ego and the disinterested will relaxes, and the mind enjoys a sweet sense of harmony and peace within through union of the familiar egoistic self with something infinitely more worth while. But the value is more than merely that of the solace or bliss of the moment. For the self, always more or less divided, has gained in integration and power. In the moments of communion it has achieved an inner adjustment the influence of which will remain, making it easier thereafter to live in harmony with God and man.

(b)   *The Prayer of Communion.* — In public ceremonial, the cultivation of a sense of communion is undoubtedly aided by the presence of others co-operating in the act of worship. There may be a very deep and real fellowship of kindred minds among those participating, and powerful forces of psychological suggestion may be brought to bear upon the worshipers. But these extraneous influences are not essential to the generation of the experience of communion. It arises also in private prayer and meditation. When prayer consists merely of petitions this subtler subjective effect is probably very little felt. But prayer on that level has little in it that is genuinely religious. It is just one of many ways in which the individual tries to get what he wants. However, a very slight acquaintance with the literature of prayer reveals that the prayer of communion is a thing of far deeper significance. Far more than any acts of public worship, it has been the medium of insight and the source of power to the great religious personalities of history. One cannot study the literature of devotion without realizing that those who practice prayer in this spirit find in it a very precious and sustaining experience. But it is something that is not easily attained, something in which the richer rewards come only to the persistent and zealous practitioner. In the words of Thomas à Kempis, " it is a great art to commune with God."

Why is it that people who believe in a personal God find it difficult to attain a sense of communion with him? This is an interesting and important question for the understanding of religious experience, and the answer proves illuminating. For that answer we may turn to a manual written by Dr. Harry Emerson Fosdick [4] which, for more than a quarter of a century, has enjoyed so wide a popularity among educated religious people that it must be regarded as an accurate expression of their own experience. Dr. Fosdick's answer is not that such experiences are mystical and require a special type of mind, a special spiritual culture or a special saintliness. It is, he says, rather that people tend to begin the practice of prayer with the wrong attitude, and finding it unsatisfactory give up prayer without learning to cultivate the right attitude. The wrong attitude, he says, is the begging attitude, in which prayer is thought to be a means of securing divine favor, even in material things. This is a survival from primitive religion and from childish ideas of God. Disappointed with its results the supplicant loses faith in the practice. Sometimes he keeps it up simply as a " spiritual exercise," but in the absence of the development of the right attitude finds this of little

4 *The Meaning of Prayer* (New York: Abingdon Press, 1915).

value. The right attitude, says Fosdick, involves belief in a
" Presence that disturbs us with the joy of elevated thoughts,"
and the practice of " conversation " with that Presence as a
friend.

To understand the significance of this statement we must
recall what we have already learned of the origin of man's
belief in God — the divided self, the self-conscious ego, and
its discovery, rooted deep within the self, of another and
higher will that seeks in and through each person the good
of all. This is the " Presence that disturbs us with the joy
of elevated thoughts." No one could find it while his mind
was occupied with petitions for divine favor. Neither could
one find it who regarded prayer as a religious exercise to be
performed for self-improvement. And when, with the fading
of belief in a personal God, prayer has become simply meditation, and meditation is pursued for the purpose of spiritual
self-culture, it, too, tends to remain self-centered and so fails
in its purpose. That is probably the reason why people who
give up belief in a personal God usually do not, in spite of
the exhortations of humanists and ethical culture societies,
give much time to any kind of religious exercise. Meditation, if it is to constitute a genuine spiritual exercise broadening the stream of the deeper spiritual life and strengthen-
ing its power over the ego,[5] must bring the ego face to face
with a spiritual reality more fundamental and more worthy
than itself. And it must bring the ego to glad acknowledgment of the existence and worth of that other and higher will
— which means that the ego must in all humility acknowledge
that that disinterested will to the good is indeed both other
and higher than itself.

This may sound as though we have given a naturalistic
psychological explanation of the most sacred and beautiful

[5] The reader should remember the special definition of this term given on
pp. 54–55.

thing in religious experience — the sense of communion with God. Perhaps we have. It all depends upon whether the naturalist can carry the explanation one step farther and give a nontheistic explanation of the origin and activity within man of a will that reaches out, not merely to seek the good of the organism within which it is found nor even of the tribe or race or species to which that organism belongs, but rather to realize the *greater good,* wherever it may be and whatever the cost to the individual within whom that will is found. It is such a will that tends to confront the religious man when he practices what he calls "communion with God." The naturalist may find it through meditation, and without the stimulus that comes from belief in its abiding presence and constant availability in an eternal Spiritual Reality in which he lives and moves and has his being. It must be admitted that, hitherto, not many have learned to find it in that way. But that does not prove that their theory of its ultimate nature is wrong, for people of many creeds have found it and interpreted it differently.

It is only in religious thinking at its clearest and best that the full scope of that will to universal good is recognized. But its factual existence cannot be doubted. Its otherness from the system of appetitive impulses and habits directed to the individual's own welfare and pleasures is obvious. Its superior moral validity is everywhere acknowledged. In the course of man's religious development its persistent presence has increasingly made itself felt; its true nature has gradually been more fully revealed, more adequately understood. In communion with it, when communion is attained, man rightly feels that he has fellowship with a spiritual power that is more than what he ordinarily conceives himself to be — his interests focused on and rooted in his own private organism. Traditionally he calls it God, and has usually believed that it is, in some still more significant way, independent of and greater than himself. Whether he is right in this view we have yet to inquire. But even at this stage we must recognize that there is reason in the traditional view. And we can appreciate also the reason why the religious man has cherished those forms of worship and tradition which have enabled him to set aside the limitations of his narrower and lesser self and enter into communion, within his own soul, with this Presence that he calls divine.

THE IDEA OF ATONEMENT

We have referred to the idea of communion as one of the two most important conceptions underlying the practice of sacrifice. But usually the more prominent of these two concepts is that of atonement. The worshiper believes that he has in some way offended the deity and so cut himself off from communion or favor. The sacrifice is an effort to rectify this situation, to secure an "at-one-ment," a restoration of the proper relationship, "to get right with God." The reason why this belief in the need for atonement plays such a large part in religion becomes obvious when we reflect upon what we have discovered concerning the birth of religion in the individual and the race. Moral experience acquires its religious character in the conflict between the ego and the altruistic will, when the demand of the latter is felt or thought of as more than merely one of the individual's own desires; i.e., as having a distinct authority such as does not belong to the mere expression of one's own will. But this experience becomes impressive only when the conflict is sharp and the cleavage deep. It is when the ideal of disinterested devotion to the good holds its place firmly above and beyond the aims of the ego, and the ego strains against it, that the altruistic will begins to appear as a will that is other and higher than one's own. In brief, it is through conviction of sin that men become convinced that they have found God. Thus the situation in which the religious consciousness becomes primarily and most profoundly impressed with the transcendent reality of the divine being is also one that impresses the individual with his personal separation from and opposition to his God.[6] The same circumstances that produce in the individual the distinctive religious belief in God tend to convince him also of the need of atonement.

This does not mean that it is the person who is in fact most egoistic and whose conduct is most contrary to general moral ideals who becomes most strongly impressed by a belief in a transcendent God. It is not by sinning that people come under conviction of sin, but by hungering and thirsting after righteousness. It is the pure in heart who see God, because the finer and nobler a person's conduct becomes in actual practice, the more sensitive does he tend to become to moral distinctions and the higher grows the reach of his ideal. We do not catch up to our ideals by practicing them. They have a way of growing by geometrical progression while practice advances by arithmetical progression. It is not that way that people become morally smug and self-satisfied, but rather through lowering their ideals to a so-called " practical " level, easily maintained by their socially instilled habits.

Thus there arises an inevitable cleavage within the religious consciousness. It begins with conviction of sin. This is deepened when the moral ideal is interpreted as the expression of a divine will. The religious consciousness thus early develops a sense of separation from God. Yet its satisfaction requires the cultivation of a sense of communion. This is rightly sought in the effort to bring moral practice into harmony with the moral ideal. But the more successful this effort in moving upward toward the ideal, the more does the ideal itself tend to rise beyond the achievement. As the apostle Paul

[6] Note how far this is removed from the theory that belief in a transcendent God is due to wishful thinking.

found, the most meticulous keeping of the law brought no sense of spiritual peace. It only deepened the sensitivity of his conscience and created a profound sense of the insufficiency of the righteousness that is of the law. Paul's experience is not peculiar. It is rather typical of every mind that is really in earnest on moral questions. The more one strives to live up to the moral ideal, the more clearly conscious one becomes of how far short of the highest ideal one falls. Thus, when the ideal is thought of as the will of God and its attainment is thought necessary to true communion with God, that sense of communion becomes a goal that forever eludes the seeker's grasp. The assurance that comes, as William James says, through the firmer grasp of religious realities must therefore be found, if it can be attained at all, in some other way. Atonement (which is an at-one-ment) cannot be achieved through " the works of the law."

It is for this reason that historic religion has always striven to present some other way or ways of atonement; and these, when offered, have usually been readily accepted because so much easier than the hard and unsatisfying way of obedience to the moral law. Commonest of them have been the sacrifices of atonement. The social, commercial and legal analogies of gifts, payments and fines naturally suggested the practice and made it seem rational. Its psychological efficacy depends upon the power of suggestion and is, of course, greatly assisted by elaborate ceremony and mass participation. But wherever religion has attained a high ethical tone some of the finer spirits have seen through the subtle self-deception of such practices and risen up to protest against them. Thus Gautama rejected the elaborate Brahman rituals, and Micah and other of the great Hebrew prophets rose up in protest against the sanguinary ceremonies of the priests. " What doth the Lord require of thee, but to do justly, and to love mercy, and to walk humbly with thy God? " [7]

7 Mic. 6:8.

But this is the kind of ethical purification of religion that takes away a fiction which, though a moral hindrance, has had a certain psychological value. It is moral advance at the cost of mental peace and satisfaction, for it does nothing to meet the need that the fiction formerly supplied. The protests of Micah and his peers therefore went almost unheeded, and the followers of Gautama found new ways of atonement. So long as righteousness is conceived in legalistic terms and God is regarded as a lawgiver, there seems to be no way in which the sensitive religious consciousness can persuade itself that it has made its peace with God save by penances and sacrifices of atonement. The only real escape is to sweep away the whole legalistic conception of righteousness. This, as we shall see later,[8] is what Jesus did. But his followers, while they preserved his teaching, failed to grasp the revolutionary nature of his insight.

The gist of the matter is this: God, as conceived by Jesus, receives and forgives the sinner, not for the purity of heart and life he has actually attained, but for that which he penitently and faithfully strives to attain. Jesus had so profound a conviction of the love of God and so deep a sympathetic understanding of the weakness of sinners that he declared that God receives sinners as sinners, providing that they are aware of their sinfulness and strive against it. The essential insight is that the attitude of penitent faith in itself constitutes a harmonizing of the will of man with the will of God, for the attitude of penitent faith is a will to the good that persistently, though falteringly, pursues an ideal which moves ever ahead of it.

The most influential of the disciples of Jesus was Paul. He was keenly conscious of the futility of the pursuit of spiritual peace by " works of the law," and recognized that in the teaching of Jesus faith had superseded the law. Yet he could not entirely rid his mind of legalism. Conceiving morality as a

[8] Chap. 11.

matter of obedience to a divine law, and religion as a life of penitent faith led by people who, in spite of their best efforts, constantly fall short of the demands of the law, his problem was to see how a divine Lawgiver could justify himself in forgiving sinners merely because they were penitent. Paul solved the problem by seeing in the death of Jesus a paying of the penalty for all mankind.[9] To a legalist in ethics the problem was a real one and the solution ingenious. But when moral worth is interpreted, as it was by Jesus,[10] in terms of personal orientation and effort rather than mere external conformity with a moral law, the problem disappears. But since, through most of human history, morality has been conceived in external and legalistic terms, the theory of a substitutionary atonement has served to mediate the transition of thought from the conception of sin as a breaking of the law that must needs be punished by the Lawgiver, to the conception of the life of faith as the humble effort of an imperfect soul to walk with God. Whether God be conceived as merely immanent or also as transcendent, it is to this latter conception of the religious life that our analysis of religious experience points.

THE PROBLEM OF PHYSICAL EVIL

For all the higher religions the fact of physical evil has always constituted a problem. The higher religions tend to exalt their conceptions of both the goodness and the power of God. But how are these beliefs to be reconciled with the facts of disease and death, storm and drought? The forces of nature mingle so much harshness and niggardliness with their benefits that it is hard to believe them uniformly well disposed toward man. It must be admitted that the belief that they are ordered by an intelligent being for the good of man-

---

[9] The clearest statement of this Pauline theory is in Rom. 3:21–26.

[10] For a further discussion of the teaching of Jesus on sin and righteousness see chap. 11.

kind is a belief held in spite of the facts rather than a natural inference derived from them. Our ignorance is such that it is always possible to argue that every evil may, if only we knew the whole truth, be seen to be a blessing in disguise. But such a contention is an assertion of faith in spite of the evidence, rather than a conclusion validly inferred from experience.

This situation has never been more cogently presented than it was by David Hume. In his *Dialogues Concerning Natural Religion* Hume allows the skeptic, Philo, to be convinced by the argument from the evidences of design in the cosmos "that the cause or causes of order in the universe probably bear some remote analogy to human intelligence." He points to "the uniformity and steadiness of general laws" as refuting the suggestion that this superhuman cause of order may be only "finitely perfect; though far exceeding mankind." Nevertheless, he argues that this "original source of all things . . . has no more regard to good above ill than to heat above cold," citing the manifold physical and moral evil of the world as proof. The conclusion is that the moral qualities of the deity do not even remotely resemble those of man. So the one conclusion of speculative theism, established by the argument from design, is reduced to a proposition of no practical significance, for, as one of the other debaters observes, "to what purpose establish the natural attributes of the deity while the moral are still doubtful and uncertain?"

It may be admitted that, when the question of theism is approached from the purely nonreligious standpoint of metaphysical speculation on the origin and order of the world, Hume's conclusion is reasonable. But these speculations, as we have seen, are not the real source of religious faith. That lies in the moral and religious experience of man's inner self — in the discovery therein of a will that "seeketh not its own." If we call this God then there is no question of His goodness. The only question is whether this good will is operative *only* in man or whether its operation in man is but a part of a larger process of good will. The good will, as manifest in man, is essentially a creative or constructive will. Its essential nature is that of a constructive activity responsive to distinctions of value that enter into experience, and ready to pursue its creative purpose directly, or indirectly through others, as opportunity for the greatest good occurs. And this striving to realize the good is always an effort made in the face of more or less difficulty. It would contradict the very nature of this experience of the divine will as immanent if we were to suggest that, in its character as transcendent, it could accomplish those aims immediately by its own omnipotent fiat. Metaphysical speculations based on inadequate scientific knowledge (such as Hume's form of the argument from design) have been chiefly responsible for exaggerating the notion of divine power to the point where it has created for theism the problem of evil. If the interpretation of the idea of God had been based entirely on the reflective analysis of moral and religious experience, that problem would never have risen. Among religious thinkers of the present day, however, there is a strong tendency to rectify this hoary error by recognizing that the facts of physical evil indicate some limitations upon the power of God to control the physical universe.[11]

If our interpretation of the origin of religion is correct then the divine being was not first thought of as creator or even as controller of the forces of nature, but as the source of the spiritual power felt in religious ceremonies. The trouble began when the idea of this mysterious, intangible and invisible power was used to explain all the mysterious phenomena of nature which were so extraordinary that primitive man felt they called for some special explanation. Thus the sort of

[11] Notable among the leaders of this movement in religious circles are Dr. Hastings Rashdall in England and Professor E. S. Brightman in America.

" Rabbi, who did sin, this man, or his parents, that he should be born blind? " [13]

Jesus repudiated the imputation of the question and denied that the man's blindness was a punishment for any person's sin. In this he was following the teaching of the book of Job, which is a dramatic poem discussing, pro and con, the problem of physical evil and ending with an emphatic repudiation of the notion that it is a form of divine punishment. However, neither Jesus nor the writer of Job was able to offer any positive solution of the problem. Lacking the modern scientific concepts of evolution and natural law they could not but regard the course of nature as controlled in some supernatural way, and being monotheists they had no choice but to attribute this control directly to God. These beliefs set the problem of evil before them in its severest form. Yet, though not seeing any logical way out, neither would surrender his faith in the goodness of God, a faith grounded in the moral consciousness. They and their followers after them gave the only answer that could be given by a monotheist until modern science had shown how the existing order of animate and inanimate nature has come into being and is maintained without direct divine control. They said one must still believe in the goodness of God in spite of all appearances, and that one can be sure that he does the will of God if he seeks to overcome evil with good.[14]

For our analysis of religion this history of thought on the problem of evil is of special significance as pointing to the real grounds of man's belief in the existence of God and of his thought about the divine nature. If man's beliefs about God were chiefly derived from a contemplation of external nature, the logical conclusion would be that pointed out by David

[13] John 9:2.
[14] E.g., Job 13:15: " Though he slay me, yet will I trust in him "; and Rom. 12:21: " Be not overcome of evil, but overcome evil with good."

Hume. He would conclude that " the cause or causes of order in the universe probably bear some remote analogy to human intelligence," but that " the original source of all things has no more regard to good above evil than to heat above cold." Instead of this we find, from earliest times, a conviction that the divine is moral. When, with the rise of monotheism, this conviction presented logical problems to the believer, one explanation after another was offered. If we were to trace the discussion of this problem through the history of religious philosophy we should find extraordinary ingenuity exercised in its solution.

But however difficult the problem became there was one solution that the religious consciousness could never accept: it could never question the conviction of the goodness of God. Obviously this conviction did not rest upon the contemplation of external nature. Nor was it a product of wishful thinking on the part of man, fondly persuading himself of a friendly universe. This latter suggestion is repudiated by the fact that men have believed that God is good and for that very reason have stood in awe of him as one who would punish their sins. The root of the belief lies deeper. It lies in the very nature of the religious consciousness as the discovery within the self of a will to the good that is higher and better than that of the ego [15] and which demands of the ego that it make its own will subservient to the good of others.

TRIBALISM AND UNIVERSALISM

Only three of the world's great religions are genuinely universal in their outlook. They are, in order of antiquity, Buddhism, Christianity and Mohammedanism. The others are content to be hereditary or national in their scope. Primitive religion is merely tribal. The reason for this we have already seen. Religion arose in the concern of the individual for

[15] This term is used in the sense defined on pp. 54–55.

group welfare. It was always altruistic. But in its beginnings it was a narrow altruism. All too often concern for the welfare of the group involved opposition to rival groups. The belief in a superhuman power was molded chiefly by the power that was felt in group ceremonies. It therefore took on the character of those ceremonies. Thus the god of the primitive was necessarily a god of battles and his moral interests were those of the tribal group. Even when tribal gods became identified with objects of nature that, like the sun, are objects for all tribes they did not lose their tribal character. So long as man's ethics were tribal his gods had to remain tribal too. And we must sadly confess that even civilized man has not yet everywhere outgrown tribalism in his ethics and religion.

In India the primitive tribalism of the Hindus passed over into the caste system. The invading light-skinned Hindus strove to maintain their racial distinction from the dark-skinned Dravidian people they had conquered. Thus they persuaded themselves that their gods were interested in maintaining the distinction. In spite of all efforts a considerable fusion of blood and culture took place in the course of centuries, and the distinctions of caste became more a matter of social class and vocation than of race. But the religious emphasis on caste remained and gradually deepened and multiplied the caste divisions. The idea of reincarnation lent itself to the reinforcing of the distinctions, for it suggested that every man's class status at birth was a part of his reward or punishment for his past deeds.

The spiritual genius of Gautama, founder of Buddhism, rejected the distinction. But his teaching was a religion for an order of monks rather than for the common people.[16] It was also unduly pessimistic and impersonal. For a few centuries it made great progress. But these inherent weaknesses eventually undermined it and, in spite of its superior ethic, a re-

[16] He accepted the validity of caste for the laity.

vival of Hinduism swept it out of the country of its birth. Thus India returned to its nationalistic religion and the caste system became more firmly riveted than ever before. Buddhism, with its fine universalistic message, found new homes in lands beyond the borders of India, from Ceylon to Japan. There it has given solace and guidance to millions, though on account of its pessimism and monasticism it can hardly be regarded as a completely satisfactory answer to man's religious needs. It is a way of individual salvation that fails to direct attention to the solution of the pressing social problems of the day. Thus, though it claims to show a way of salvation open to all and teaches kindness toward all, it interests the individual primarily in his own salvation. Though it teaches that all men are brethren, it does not teach that every man is his brother's keeper and can find his personal salvation only in fulfillment of that trust.[17]

Among the early Hebrews, Yahweh (or Jehovah) was at first merely a tribal god who led them in their conquests and thereby showed his superiority over the gods of neighboring countries. Being a simple, pastoral people they were, for some centuries after their settlement in Palestine, frequently attracted by the cults of the more sophisticated peoples whom they had partially displaced. But the fertility rituals and extravagances of the agricultural and city people of Canaan disgusted the best elements among them, and there arose a succession of prophets to plead with the people to be true to their own god and the wholesome and simple mores which, according to the tradition, he endorsed. As the nation acquired unity and power in the days of David and Solomon, they exalted their conception of their god. And as social evils appeared in the days of decline that followed, Amos and other

[17] An excellent and sympathetic account of Hinduism and Buddhism as living religions is to be found in *Faiths Men Live By*, by John Clark Archer (New York: Thomas Nelson & Sons, 1934).

The spirit of that Kingdom was to be "within" its members, dominating their relations with their fellows even while they lived in a world where the political and economic order fell far short of it. It represented the will of God, and the disciples were taught to pray, "Thy Kingdom come. Thy will be done on earth as it is in heaven." They were taught, too, to devote their lives to the extension of that spiritual Kingdom and its realization in the affairs of men. And in that cause they were taught to be ready to pay the price, if need be, of making even the supreme sacrifice as their Master had done.

Of all the lessons that Jesus had to teach, the hardest for his immediate disciples to learn was that of the equality of Jew and Gentile in the Kingdom of God. They sacrificed their possessions when there was need, even to a complete sharing of goods. They recognized the spiritual equality of women and slaves with freemen and, in spite of the difficulties created by a necessary adaptation to the social and economic order of their time, they expressed the spirit of this doctrine to a considerable extent in practice. But they found themselves divided over the admission of the spiritual equality of Gentiles. Their efforts at preaching the doctrine of the Kingdom were at first confined to Jews.

The story of the first preaching to the Gentiles is told in the tenth chapter of the Acts of the Apostles. This writing is so human and psychologically so natural that it can almost certainly be regarded as essentially historical. Peter had apparently been worried over the fact that, hitherto, they had not welcomed Gentiles into the new movement. Prejudices die hard and Peter was repressing the conviction that the attitude of the disciples was contrary to the spirit of Christ. But, as Freud has taught us, repressed convictions have a way of expressing themselves in dreams. Thus Peter had a dream in which he saw a great sheet let down from heaven full of

all sorts of living creatures. A voice said, " Rise, Peter; kill
and eat." But he, seeing no meat there fit for a Jew, replied,
" Not so, Lord; for I have never eaten anything that is common or unclean." This was repeated three times. Shortly
after waking Peter received a request to come and present the
teaching of Christ to a group of Gentiles. He interpreted
the dream as a special injunction to cease treating the Gentiles
as unworthy of the message he had to give. He preached to
them, and baptized them into the Kingdom without demanding any preliminary Jewish ceremony such as circumcision.
The apostolic council at Jerusalem endorsed his action, and
the Christian gospel of the Kingdom entered in practice upon
its program of establishing a brotherhood of all mankind.

Thus there appeared for the first time on earth a religious
movement with an ideal that was a full expression of the disinterested will to the good. Its golden rule taught the individual to devote himself to the good of others equally with
his own. Its concepts of human good cherished the full range
of human values, as expressed in the personality of a leader
who rejected all asceticism,[19] never refused an invitation to a
feast, and is reported to have said, " I am come that they
might have life and that they might have it more abundantly." [20] Its concepts of human relations asserted the spiritual equality of all mankind. There was to be no distinction
of priests and monks from laity, no distinction of caste or race
or sex. All were " kings and priests unto God " [21] and, in the
words of the apostle, " there is neither Jew nor Greek, there
is neither bond nor free, there is neither male nor female: for
ye are all one in Christ Jesus." [22] Even the distinction of
righteous and sinner was broken down, for the saint was
taught in all humility to recognize his shortcomings and the

[19] Matt. 9:14; Luke 7:33–34.
[20] John 10:10.
[21] Rev. 1:6.
[22] Gal. 3:28.

sinner was welcomed in the name of Christ to share the Christian fellowship in penitence and faith.

It is true that the church has, in its teaching and practice, fallen far below its ideal. Yet the ideal has persisted and gained increasing recognition within the church and without. It is the ideal toward which the logic of dispassionate, reflective thought inevitably tends; for it is that disinterested will to the good that is the ultimate source of man's moral and religious life, come to self-conscious realization of its own nature and purpose. If this will is God in man, then this ideal is the culmination of the progressive self-revelation of God to man — a self-revelation made possible as man's intelligence has become able to grasp the greater good, the more distant good and the finer shades of good, and as his will has responded to cast aside, at each successive stage of his development, the individual and racial habits and institutions which have served a more or less useful purpose at the earlier stage, but which at length have come to hamper the movement into a larger and fuller life.

Ancient evils survive and ancient goods become present ills. Habits and institutions there needs must be. But they must change, for life must move and grow. And in difficult times of readjustment, such as that through which we are now passing, it is vitally important that man's consciousness of the ideal in which his religious development has culminated should not be lost. For that ideal is man's self-understanding of his own spiritual nature. To that ideal, therefore, man's habits and institutions must progressively conform if his spirit is to be free to grow.

PART II

INTERPRETATION OF PRACTICE

The Essential Ideal

THE DISINTERESTED WILL

IN OUR ANALYSIS of the processes concerned in the birth of religion in the individual we found the most important factor to be a volitional tendency, operating as a constituent element of the individual self but directed toward the good of other selves. We saw how the resultant conflict within the self led to the conviction that the demands of this altruistic will are demands of some superhuman agency, something divine. And we have seen how reflection on this experience has gradually expanded the concept of duty. From a few negative precepts concerning the avoidance of injury to others it has developed into ideals of positive service involving, if necessary, the ultimate sacrifice.

Equally remarkable has been the expansion of the notion of the extent of the circle of those whose good it is believed the divine being would have us seek. First, it is the narrow social group — my neighbor, so long as he is neighborly. Then there is included the stranger within the camp, the guest who has partaken of our salt. Gradually a broader answer is given to the question, Who is my neighbor? and a more positive answer to the question, Am I my brother's keeper? In the course of time " my neighbors " comes to include the whole tribe, the nation, and neighbor nations; but still with the same proviso, " so long as they are neighborly," and usually also with differentiations concerning race, sex, caste and creed. Then finally, through the life and work of the Galilean teacher, there dawns on the world the ideal that would eliminate the last proviso and break down every barrier. It makes no difference whether my neighbor is neighborly or not. God would have me love even mine enemy. Every man is my neighbor, and I must seek his good equally with my own.

The extraordinary thing is that, though the modern man scarcely does more than lip service to this ideal in its completeness, it yet commends itself to his moral judgment. Nor is this simply acquiescence before the force of tradition or acceptance of a principle on authority, for those who are foremost in criticism of tradition and rejection of its authority still acknowledge the ideal and are often among its strongest supporters. To say that it appeals to their reason is to say that their reflective moral judgment endorses it as a true expression of their own inner experience. The prophets of religion have not simply created an ideal and then persuaded men to adopt it. They have rather, in their progress through the centuries that culminated in Jesus, gradually succeeded in seeing that the true nature of the purposive process that works within the individual is not merely a will to his own good, but rather a disinterested will that seeks, in and through him, to produce the good wherever it may be possible. They expressed this by saying that this type of conduct alone is *right*. When once this doctrine was taught — the fact explicitly pointed out — other people, when they reflected calmly in their best moments, came to see that their own moral consciousness endorsed it. Thus the doctrine spread. It became commonplace — at least as theory. Today it is the most universally accepted principle of moral philosophy, even among those who refuse to follow the prophets in calling the will that demands it divine.

It is when the disinterested will to the good is not reconcilable with egoistic desires that the conflict arises that has issued in the religious interpretation. When it is in harmony with the egoistic impulses the individual naturally accepts it as entirely his own. But the sharp dichotomy that the religious interpretation thus developed between the will of God and the will of man is an error. The altruistic will is not always superior to the egoistic. It is not necessarily right. The intelligent, reflective moral consciousness does not grant it authority over the egoistic desire simply because it is altruistic, but only when the good with which it is concerned is greater than that involved in the goal of the conflicting egoistic desire. The egoistic will is entirely right, and has an equal claim to be called divine, so long as it is pursuing the greatest good that seems, to the individual concerned, to be possible in the circumstances, taking into equal consideration his own good and that of others. If there is to be a distinction here between a human and a divine will it certainly must not be too sharply drawn; for, obviously, the human is in the divine and the divine in the human.

The distinction can be clarified only by the concept of human personality (and this is the typical modern concept) as a system of purposive habits and tendencies, developed in and through a particular organism in the course of its individual and genetic history and directed toward typical situations of positive or negative value. In brief, each particular human self is a bundle of habits and other volitional tendencies. It is a system of specific responses to the values of typical situations. This system is temporal; it has a brief terrestrial life. But in organic relation with it (as a fundamental constituent of it) there is a tendency to seek the good disinterestedly, breaking through the individual system of habits where necessary. The particular habitual tendencies to respond to particular values are particular fixations of this general tendency. It is because of their particular fixity that they constitute the system we call a personality or self. And it is this particular fixity that differentiates them from the general tendency of the disinterested will. This growth of habit contributes the efficiency that makes possible the pursuit of higher and wider values. But its particularity and fixity bring the human system into occasional conflict with the general and disinterested tendency to the good which we have called divine.

Whether this " divine " activity is more than temporal we need not yet decide. But we should note that it is not possible to distinguish between the divine and the human until the individual has developed the capacity to distinguish between the self and other selves, between a good-for-me and a good-for-that-other-but-not-for-me. Prior to that the unified conative drive of the organism simply responds to whatever of value, or good, appears to its limited vision. Will (if at this stage it may be so called) is shortsightedly responsive to the values immediately felt, or envisioned as possibilities of feeling, by the organism in which it is active. At this stage will is neither self-interested [1] nor disinterested. The distinction between human and divine is latent in the creative process and manifests itself only when thought has developed the capacity to see the possibilities of value being realized in other selves. Then, while " habit " responds to the familiar nearer values, " will " shows its essentially disinterested character by responding to this further good. When the good that may be realized in others seems greater than that toward which the particular tendencies of the self are directed, and there is conflict, then the general and disinterested tendency manifests that peculiar kind of constraint over the self that we call the sense of obligation — a constraint that calls for acquiescence but does not compel.

[1] By " self-interest " here is meant an interest *in* the self, i.e., an interest in a good as a good-for-me. All interests, of course, are " self-interests " in the sense that they are interests *of* the self. But some interests are " disinterested " in the sense that the person, though aware of the distinction between good-for-me and good-for-another-but-not-for-me, rejects this reference to self as no valid basis for choice, choosing to pursue the greater good without special concern for self.

REFUTATION OF EGOISM

In naturalistic ethics there is a strong tendency to seek to show that this sense of an obligation to pursue the good of others may be derived from some ultimately egoistic ground.[2] Commonly it is argued that " ought " here can mean only that we ought to consider the welfare of others because it is, in general and in the long run, in our own interest to do so. If, however, the individual is regarded as adequately described in the terms commonly used to account for the organized self, or personality — i.e., those we have recognized as constituting the " ego " — then this position is untenable. Such a self or ego is an organization of tendencies directed toward specific types of situation in which satisfaction has been found; and these are in turn rooted only in the biological drives tending to survival of the individual and perpetuation of the race. Only a few of these tendencies, whether the primary or secondary, are altruistic, and they are directed toward the welfare of limited groups in reaction with which these habits have been developed. If the problem of the development and integration of these tendencies were the *whole* problem of personality, then complete integration could be most easily achieved on a relatively low level of altruism, and personal development could go forward with almost complete inner satisfaction in the expression of the almost unlimited egoistic and very limited altruistic tendencies of the self. Complete personal development of such a self would require only a minimum of attention to the needs of others. Narrow, rather selfish and self-satisfied persons of this type do exist. But even though fairly well integrated they cannot be regarded as well developed personalities. Still more important is the fact that an ethic based on the cultivation of personalities of this type could not logically teach the higher ideals of service

[2] Some specific examples of this theory are discussed in chap. 10.

to the community. For these demand a readiness to serve even to the point of self-sacrifice.

The fact that the moral consciousness of man does, at its best, demand such service reveals the inadequacy of any interpretation of human personality that does not recognize the primary importance of the disinterested will. For this high ideal is not something peculiar to a limited tradition preserved within a single institution, such as the Christian church. It reached its culmination in the teaching of Christ, but this was preceded by a steady growth toward the universalistic ideal in every part of the civilized world. The best ethical teaching of Confucianism, Buddhism, Hinduism and Zoroastrianism is not very different from that of the Hebrew prophetic and wisdom literature. The literature that becomes "classical" is the literature that appeals to what human beings feel to be their own best judgments of value. And the classical literature of the moral and religious life, developing in China, India and around the Levant through a period of several thousand years in which these three centers of civilization exercised very little influence upon one another, manifests in each case the same type of moral development. From primitive notions in which the sense of social responsibility is manifested in little more than a few fundamental prohibitions, such as the Ten Commandments or even less, it grows into positive ideals of high devotion to a broad public good.

Such a development could not possibly have occurred if human beings were merely egoists cannily calculating their own advantage. Nor is it sufficient to point to the fact that such egoism is modified by natural impulses of the type often called instincts of the family and the herd. Altruistic idealism goes far beyond these impulses. And its broad extension is due not so much to *emotional expansion of natural impulses* under the influence of suggestion as it is to calm *reflection on what is morally fitting* and logically implied in the best moral judgments. Emotional extension of natural impulses, and habits inculcated by particular groups to suit the purposes of those groups, are the factors that develop the inconsistencies and prejudices of the moral tradition. Rational reflection breaks them down. But in doing so rational reflection does not take us back to egoism, except in such temporary and decadent movements as Epicureanism. Instead, as is shown by the development of the classical [3] literature of the moral consciousness in all countries, it leads on to a wider vision of the moral horizon, toward universal brotherhood, equity, freedom, and ideals of high devotion.

The fact that human nature, when it has the chance to be intelligent and is not unduly blinded by emotional factors, grows *away* from the egoism with which it necessarily begins, shows that the determining principle of that growth is the disinterested will. Enlightened self-interest and social pressure in the directions the group finds useful can create a solid and respectable citizenry — with the limitations and the tolerance of certain social sores that such citizenry usually manifests. But they could not create the dynamic idealism, ever renewing the revolt against such limitations and tolerance of evil, that is manifested in the classical religious and moral literature of all the world.[4]

These facts indicate that the sense of obligation [5] is rooted, not in the interests of the ego, but in the disinterested will to the good. This will to the good, however, exerts its constraining influence not only on behalf of the greater good of others against the lesser good of the self, but also for the

[3] It should be remembered that the literature that becomes classical is the literature that expresses clearly and well the values that the inarticulate multitude only vaguely feel. It is therefore an excellent indicator of the nature of the deepest human values.

[4] For an account of the earliest known literature of this type, which arose in ancient Egypt, see Breasted: *The Dawn of Conscience*.

[5] For a critical examination of alternative conceptions of obligation see chap. 10.

greater good of the individual (if it is seen) when the particular habits and impulses of the self drive toward some lesser good in the pursuit of which the greater would be lost. Yet there is no omniscience in the judgment as to what constitutes the greater good, either of the self or of others. That judgment is formed out of the experience of the individual, and is influenced not only by immediate experience but also by tradition, precept and example. It is subject to all the fallibilities of memory, the distortions of perspective, and the blindness of passion and prejudice. Yet it gradually disentangles moral truth and error by learning, by experiment and by calm reflection.

This disinterested responsiveness to value is not a mere adventitious accretion to human personality. As our discussion proceeds it will become clear that it is rather its fundamental feature. The particular interests (appetites, impulses, instincts, habits, sentiments, attitudes) are the *subsidiary* developments. The disinterested, unparticularized response to the greatest value presented in experience is the *fundamental* active tendency. This would seem to be the source of its peculiar constraining influence, the sense of obligation. To allow the subsidiary, semiautomatic habits, etc., by their sheer impulsive power to carry the day against the primary tendency to respond to what seems the greatest good, is a disorder in the structure of the self. It is disintegrating, and is felt as such. It is a *wrong* trend in the development of personality. To act in harmony with the most fundamental trend not only tends to realize the greatest good objectively, but it is integrative and constructive, advancing the upbuilding of that system of will and habit we call personality — the system whereby greater efficiency, scope and power are achieved for the continued pursuit of further values. It is a right trend in the development of personality. And this is the most fundamental sense in which anything can be right or wrong.

MORAL GOOD AND NATURAL GOOD

Here we must point out the important distinction between moral goodness and other forms of good.[6] Morally, the disinterested pursuit of the good is always good, and the degree of its goodness depends only upon the energy with which all the resources of the personality (especially its intelligence) are utilized in the pursuit. The degree of moral goodness does not depend upon the success of the pursuit, or upon the correctness of the judgment as to what objective situations constitute the greatest good and therefore ought to be produced or maintained; lack of success and incorrectness of ethical judgment are occasion for moral blame only when they are due to lack of vigor and completeness in the disinterested pursuit of the good. Nevertheless (the point needs emphasizing) intelligent inquiry, with whatever resources of intellect and information we can command, is a vitally important part of the activity of the disinterested will to good. For the dull, prejudiced or lazy adherence to first impressions, traditional principles and accepted institutions is the commonest source of error in ethical judgment.

If moral good is found in the disinterested pursuit of the good, then what is this latter " good," the good pursued? For convenience we may call it " natural good " or, following Professor Nicolai Hartmann, the " situational value." It would take us too far into the general field of ethics to enter on an adequate discussion of this question, but a few points must, even at the danger of appearing dogmatic, be made clear. In the first place, the will aims primarily at physical and psychological situations, not at pleasure.[7] The situations aimed

---

[6] Compare the distinction between moral values and situational values in Hartmann's *Ethics*.

[7] For a critique of the theory, known as " psychological hedonism," that the will aims primarily at pleasure, cf. Hastings Rashdall: *Theory of Good and Evil* (2nd ed., 2 vols.; New York: Oxford University Press, 1924), Vol. I, chap. 2.

at, or wanted, seem pleasing or satisfying in prospect simply because we want them; and for the same reason the progressive pursuit of them is pleasant. In the second place, those objectives that involve intellectual, aesthetic and moral satisfaction have, we generally recognize, a satisfying *quality* that cannot be compared with ordinary pleasure. John Stuart Mill recognized this difference of quality among what he still uniformly called " pleasures "; [8] but in doing so, it is generally admitted, he surrendered the essential principle of hedonism — the theory that the good is simply a matter of pleasure. Nicolai Hartmann calls these distinctions of quality in our experience of values, differences of " scale "; [9] there is a " value scale " in which some values are seen as " higher " and so as values that *ought* to be preferred. In the third place, these value qualities actually exist only in the experience of individual human beings; there is no other good at which we may aim, save that which is enjoyed by ourselves and our fellows; there is no good of the state or of God that we can pursue, save the good of the individuals who have their being in the state and (it may be) in God.

The " natural good " at which the disinterested will aims is, as we have seen, a physical or psychological situation (e.g., food, knowledge, the erection of a building, the organization of a club, the winning of a game) in which value qualities are realized in the immediate experience of individuals. And in aiming at the greatest good this will aims at the situations in which, for all concerned, there is the greatest experience of such values. In the measuring of the greatest value the distinctions of scale are, for the developed moral consciousness, of primary importance. But the values that pertain to situations are very complex; every situation has consequences beyond itself that contain values and disvalues; and the attain-

---

[8] *Utilitarianism*, chap. 2.
[9] *Ethics*, especially Vol. II, chaps. 3, 4, 5.

ment of the situation requires the adoption of means that
entail other values. So the values of the total situation, inclusive of means and consequences, have to be considered. Of
these values some are positive and some negative (e.g., pleasures and pains), and they differ in intensity and in longevity
and in certainty as well as in quantity and scale. Thus the task
of estimating the greatest value is often very difficult, although
commonly very plain.

THE GOOD AS PERSONAL DEVELOPMENT

The problem of evaluation is enormously complicated by
the facts that people differ so from each other and that the
realization of most values (and especially the highest, the intellectual, aesthetic and moral) depends upon the active response of the persons concerned in the situation. We cannot spoon-feed the higher values into the lives of others. All
we can do, in most cases, is help to create the conditions and
the stimuli which give them the opportunity to realize those
values.

Here there is a broad principle that comes to our aid. The
higher values (and the realization of these requires and tends
toward the realization of most that is important among the
lower) are realized in activity that involves personal development, physical, intellectual, aesthetic and moral. So our task
resolves itself into creating for others the conditions helpful to
personal development, such as economic opportunity, education, freedom, wholesome social restraint and inspiring example. The natural good which is the objective goal of the
disinterested will can thus be broadly stated as *the conditions
of personal development of all concerned*. And, since personal development needs must be in harmony with, and involve the expansion of, the disinterested will to the good, the
achievement of natural good is seen to involve the achievement of moral good also.

If we recognize the primary importance of the disinterested will, in the sense that it occupies so fundamental a place in human nature that continuous personal development and complete integration of personality require that personal development shall always occur in harmony with it, then there will, in general, arise no conflict between our efforts to secure the good (personal development) of an individual and our efforts to secure the good of all other individuals in the group to which he belongs. Similarly there will, in general, be no conflict between our pursuit of the good of our own group and of other groups. For any contribution to the development of a personality dominated by the disinterested will must tend to work through him to the good of the group; and no contribution to the seeming good of an individual that would be unfair to the group can, in the last analysis, be a contribution to his *true* good, since it must tend to encourage him to accept and pursue advantages contrary to the good of the group, and thus hamper the growth and integration of that personality under control of the disinterested will.

It must be admitted, however, that this general tendency to harmony of the true good of the individual (which includes his moral good, or harmony with the disinterested will) with the true good of the group and of human society as a whole, is no more than a general tendency. Specific cases will arise when the good of society, or of the greater number, can be achieved only by measures that deprive some individuals of important opportunities of self-development — and opportunities that would seem in no way to discourage their moral development. In such cases we must seek to achieve the greatest balance of good over evil for all concerned, giving due weight to the more fundamental considerations, such as life itself. In those cases, however, where the individuals who suffer for the larger good of others do so of their own free moral will, the loss they suffer is often, perhaps always, offset by the gain to the inner strength, growth and integration of personality achieved in their self-sacrificing action.

Once it is clearly recognized that the disinterested will to the good is the ultimate determining principle [10] of the growth of human personality, it becomes evident that not only the natural good of the individual, but also his moral good, may be expressed in terms of personal development. Personal development involves living activity, and all living activity is a natural good for the individual so far as it constitutes a constructive contribution to his further living activity, toward the complete or abundant life. In so far as it has the reverse effect it is a natural evil. And, in that the effect of most of our activities is mixed, they (and the factors instrumental to them) are to be accounted as good or evil according to the major tendency of their effects. It is at the production of such natural good, wherever opportunity affords, that the enlightened and disinterested will aims. Since the complete and abundant life or full and true personal development must grow under the increasing dominance of the disinterested will, to aim at the natural good of an individual is, in general, to aim at his moral good also.

The only exception is the case where the disinterested will of that individual would demand of him his life or, perhaps, some other very great personal sacrifice; for it can scarcely be contended that *every* act of personal sacrifice for the greater good of others means so much to the moral development of the individual as to tend on the whole to produce that capacity for the more abundant life in which personal development, as a natural good, consists. Certainly this is not the case in the sacrifice of life itself, unless man is immortal. However, since the disinterested will seeks the good of all individuals concerned, it does not have to attain the sometimes impossible

---

[10] I.e., developments that are out of harmony with it ultimately lead to disintegration and stultification of personality.

feat of achieving a result in which none shall suffer loss.   But in seeking to produce the greatest possible good it seeks to induce all concerned to contribute their utmost to that same goal in the same disinterested manner.   Thus the pursuit of the natural good of the social whole involves the pursuit of the moral good of its members also.

While the natural good of the individual then consists in that personal development which makes for the more abundant life, his moral good consists in that kind of personal development which alone can be continuous and perfectly integrated because in harmony with the most fundamental element in personality — the disinterested will to good.   In general, the natural good is, in the long run, achieved most fully by adhering to what is morally good also, for departures from the fundamental principle of personality must in the end lead to self-stultifying conflict which inhibits further development until rectified.   So, if the "long run" of life were eternal, to be true to the morally good would also entail the greatest natural good, not only for others but for the performer of the moral action also.   It is this faith that lies behind the concept involved in the paradoxical saying of Jesus: "For whosoever will save his life shall lose it: and whosoever will lose his life for my sake shall find it." [11]   The "salvation" of the individual consists in the fullest possible realization of all the potentialities of his personality; and the way to that self-realization lies, not in the careful preservation of all his capacities and resources for his own needs, but in selfless devotion to the ideal of human service as presented in the person of Christ.

MORAL GOOD AND FAITH IN IMMORTALITY

Moral goodness, as our analysis has revealed it, involves active growth of personality in harmony with the disinterested

[11] Matt. 16:25.

will. Its activity is directed toward that constructive modification of the environment which makes possible " the completest life for all." [12] Moral goodness is thus not a static but
an active condition. And personality, as we have seen, is a
system of will. Thus moral personality, if it is to survive,
must survive not as a mere passive consciousness — not even
as a passive contemplation of divine perfection — but as a
system of constructive activity.

The concept of an immortality of static perfection is the
product of an inadequate analysis of the nature of personality
and its moral good. It is, unfortunately, a very serious error,
for it presupposes the sudden and miraculous transition of
personality from a state of imperfection to one of perfection.
Or, even if it rejects this hope, it looks for the process of perfecting to come through external influences, such as a course
of purgatorial purging. Such conceptions are fundamentally
immoral if morality is, as we have contended, a process of
active and disinterested seeking of the good. They suggest,
as Marx, Dewey and many other critics have pointed out, that
the realization of the complete moral good of mankind can
be divorced from the pursuit of his natural good in this life.
Such a belief can be used, and has been used, as an " opiate of
the proletariat " and an excuse for the toleration of social ills.

The situation is very different if the survival of personality
after death is looked upon as the continuation, in a new set
of circumstances, of a process of personal development begun here.[13] The " saving of souls " then no longer presents
the alternatives between a sudden and unearned static per-

---

[12] M. C. Otto: *Things and Ideals* (New York: Henry Holt & Co., 1924).

[13] This view has been very widely adopted by religious thinkers in recent
decades. See A. S. Pringle-Pattison: *The Idea of Immortality* (New York:
Oxford University Press, 1923); J. Y. Simpson: *Man and the Attainment of
Immortality* (3rd ed.; London: Hodder & Stoughton, 1923); and William
Adams Brown: *The Christian Hope* (New York: Charles Scribner's Sons,
1912).

fection and an absolute loss or a loss only retrieved through external influences or purgings. It becomes instead a matter of degree. It is the potentialities of personality that are "saved," and they are saved by being actively developed. The faith in immortality then becomes the faith that this process of personal development begun in this life does not necessarily cease with death, but goes on to the realization of further goals, making good its deficiencies so far as it is willing to learn from past experience. And it means that both the natural and the moral good attained in this life — the whole personal development — contribute to the initial stages of the life beyond.

We shall not yet pause to inquire whether such a hope is reasonable or probable; what we are here concerned to show is that it is socially valuable — a stimulus to every good work rather than a distraction from the serious problems of life. Also it is morally helpful in our view of the moral life, since, as already shown, it would imply that the natural and the moral good of the individual are in all cases ultimately one. These conclusions it is important to establish before commencing the inquiry, which we shall later undertake,[14] into the possibility of immortality; for there has been a strong tendency in recent decades to decry all attention to the possibilities of the next life as a fruitless distraction from the facing of the stern realities of this. This criticism is valid as against many of the traditional interpretations of the doctrine of immortality and has been useful in exposing their unfortunate influence, though it has probably greatly exaggerated their bad effects. However, to such an interpretation of the hope of immortality as grows most naturally out of the analysis of personality and morality developed here, such criticism does not apply. An immortality that is but a continuation of the progress of personality made here only makes that progress more important

[14] Chap. 8.

to attain. It offers a hope that stimulates every effort to make the most of every opportunity; and when progress proves difficult and slow, and when losses are endured, its larger vision sustains the spirit that might otherwise surrender in despair.

MORAL GOOD AND FAITH IN THE DIVINE TRANSCENDENCE

(a) *John Dewey.* — As with the doctrine of immortality, so with that of the divine transcendence — its practical value as well as its truth has in recent decades been strongly called in question. This is almost entirely a modern argument against religion. Before the later days of the nineteenth century even the opponents of religious belief recognized its moral value as a support of the social order, and many expressed concern at what would be the effect upon society should there ever occur a general abandonment of religion. The new line of attack has developed in part because religion had been too much conceived as supporting morality merely with a system of supernatural sanctions, such as the fires of hell, and these conceptions have rapidly been losing their grip on the modern mind. A deeper reason, however, lies in the fact that religious support of the moral order, on account of traditional forms of religious belief and expression, has tended to be conservative and has stood in the way of the zeal of modern reformers. This is certainly one reason why Marxian socialism has set itself against theism, and it is also one of the strong objections raised by Professor Dewey.

A contributing factor in the development of this attitude has been the optimistic faith in the continuing " ascent of man " generated by the theory of evolution. This faith in human sufficiency has received some severe shocks through the war, the depression and the rise of totalitarianism, and there has been a tendency among many religious thinkers to reassert man's dependence upon some special aid from a transcendent deity.[15]   In spite of the sorry exhibition made by human nature in recent decades Dewey's faith, however, has undergone little change.   His Terry Lectures at Yale, published in 1934, reiterate the charge that the search for evidence for the existence of what he calls " the supernatural " is something that " diverts attention and energy from ideal values and from the exploration of actual conditions by means of which they may be promoted."   In place of this he urges that men and women should be " actuated throughout the length and breadth of human relations with the faith and ardor that have at times marked historic religions," though he admits that " to achieve this faith and *élan* is no easy task." And again, he admits the novelty and difficulty of his naturalistic program when he says: " One of the few experiments in the attachment of emotion to ends that mankind has not tried is that of devotion, so intense as to be religious, to intelligence as a force in social action." [16]

So far as Dewey's protest is directed against those types of theology which deprecate human effort and intelligence and teach a reliance upon divine interposition, and those which exaggerate human sinfulness to such an extent as to destroy the hope of improvement through reform of human institutions, his position is justified by our own analysis.   Human nature cannot be hopeless if its fundamental feature is a disinterested will to the good of all.   But Dewey himself recognizes, in the passages quoted, that the supreme historic manifestations of human idealism have occurred in the lives of those who have believed their own ideals to have their source in some tran-

[15] This has been especially the case among those influenced by the Swiss theologian, Karl Barth.   A moderate and stimulating presentation of this point of view is to be found in the writings of Professor Reinhold Niebuhr, e.g., *Moral Man and Immoral Society* (New York: Charles Scribner's Sons, 1932) and *The Nature and Destiny of Man* (Scribner's, 1941) .

[16] Dewey: *A Common Faith* (New Haven, Conn.: Yale University Press, 1934) , pp. 46, 79, 80–81.

scendent moral personality. The virtues of urbanity, tolerance, generosity and zeal for the *common* good are not difficult for the intelligent modern man to cultivate. But high
devotion, self-sacrifice and zeal for a good we can never share
in, call for a rare loftiness of spirit. In particular it is hard
to stir the masses of men to have faith in an ideal which experience seems to brand as " impractical " if they believe that
it has no deeper authority than the sweetness and fond aspiration of some kindly human spirit. Yet the chains of harsh
custom, prejudice and fear are riveted so firmly upon the
popular consciousness that without high courage and faith
we can never break them. Those who lead in that great human enterprise must be able to believe in the possibility of
the apparently impractical and in the validity of an ideal that
seems too good to be true.

If a man believes that his ideals are merely the effects upon
him of a process of social conditioning he is likely to deem it
the path of wisdom to shake off those effects when they impel
him toward a line of action that is very inconvenient. If he
believes that they are merely the effect of some sympathetic
tendencies and herd impulses of his nature which are of no
deeper significance than many other natural tendencies within
him, then the rational thing for him to do is to seek to control
all these natural tendencies in what seems to be his own self-
interest. But if he believes that the disinterested will to the
good of all is the most fundamental tendency of his nature,
that it is the expression of that which is eternal within him,
the link of his own spiritual life with a wider spiritual activity
which is the ultimate source of his being and in harmony with
which his personality can alone attain its utmost fulfillment,
then the ideals toward which that disinterested will aspires
become the most significant features of his whole world. They
then define the goal of his most rational endeavor, his " reasonable service." They help to give him courage, assurance,

and a zeal that will not be denied.   One must not exaggerate
their effect, of course, for he is still a creature of habits, passions and traditions.   But he has a weapon of reason against
these fettering conditions that no nontheistic philosophy
could give him.   This does not prove that the doctrine of
transcendence is true, but it does show that, thus interpreted,
it is morally wholesome.   And the effort to justify faith in
the superhuman origin of our ideals of disinterested service,
far from being a waste of time and useless distraction, as urged
by Dewey, is a much needed contribution to the support of
the human spirit in the pursuit of those ideals.

The reason why a belief in their superhuman source gives
power to human ideals may be seen from Dewey's own analysis of religious experience.[17]   The term religious, applied to
modes of human behavior, means, as he says, much more than
belief in supernatural sanctions of the moral law.   It refers
to " changes in ourselves in relation to the world " that are
" inclusive and deep seated."   These " pertain to our being
in its entirety," are " enduring, . . . a composing and har-
monising of the various elements of our being."   The religious " includes a note of submission.   But it is voluntary,
not externally imposed."   It is " outgoing," " ready and glad."
" It is a change *of* will conceived as the organic plenitude of
our being, rather than any special change *in* will."   These
phrases very aptly describe the experience normally involved
in that breaking forth into conscious prominence of the disinterested will, and the reorientation of life under its influence, which we have described as the birth of religion in the
individual.   Its effect Dewey describes equally well.   Moral
faith, he says, is religious in quality " only when the ends of
moral conviction arouse emotions that are not only intense
but are actuated and supported by ends so inclusive that they
unify the self." [18]   " There is such a thing," he claims, " as

17 *Ibid.,* pp. 16, 17.   18 *Ibid.,* p. 22.

faith in intelligence becoming religious in quality." Yet the admission follows: "Lives that are consciously inspired by loyalty to such ideals . . . are still comparatively infrequent to the extent of that comprehensiveness and intensity which arouse an ardour religious in function." [19]

Here it is frankly admitted that belief in the superhuman source of our ideals is so commonly accompanied by a far-reaching inner change of will and unification of personality under their influence, resulting in the intensification of those ideals and their growth in comprehensiveness, that these changes are commonly regarded as the *effects* of such belief. However, Dewey denies this conclusion and points out that such personal adjustment is sometimes attained without such a belief. Nevertheless, he admits that in that case it rarely reaches the same "comprehensiveness and intensity." Now this distinctively "religious" development of character is certainly not due to fear of supernatural sanctions, hope of eternal rewards, or belief that the ideal is eternally accomplished without our efforts. But it is too distinctively associated with faith in the suprahuman source of our ideals not to be causally related to that faith.

The psychological reason for this development is not difficult to detect. Wholehearted loyalty [20] and devotion depend upon the expansion of what William James called the "empirical self" [21] to include the larger group so that we make its cause our own. It is fairly easily achieved in small group loyalties and national patriotism, but it is difficult for it to transcend the divisions of class, creed, party, race and nation. The loyalties of the rational man grow out of the *factual* unities of life and their logical implications, and they

[19] *Ibid.*, p. 27.

[20] For an analysis of love and loyalty see my earlier work, *The Mind in Action: A Study of Motives and Values* (New York: D. Appleton & Co., 1931), pp. 123–44.

[21] *Principles of Psychology* (New York: Longmans, Green & Co.).

tend to be limited by the factual divisions. In what sense is the brotherhood of man a fact if his groupings are merely assemblies for mutual advantage in the struggle for existence against neighboring groups? Even the growing mutual economic and cultural dependence of classes and nations is too much shot through with rivalry and exceptions, too tardy and remote, to develop a widespread and living sense of unity that can overcome narrow interests and traditional prejudices. Mankind today, as in every age, deeply needs that sense of human brotherhood which comes from a faith that we are all, in some very real sense, children of one Father. And man has within him a persistent witness to the reality of that bond in the disinterested will that seeks in and through each the good of all.

Ideals that are merely ideal — the product of human imagination — have small power to mold personality in opposition to the brutal facts of man's inhumanity to man. But an ideal that is the logical implication of the persistent and inescapable promptings of a man's own heart is a different matter. Loyalty is an identification of the self with others. As such it must be more than a figure of speech. Only when it is felt as a living reality can it attain that intensity and comprehensiveness which Dewey rightly calls "religious." And nothing contributes so much to such an inner adjustment of personality as the conviction that our unity of spirit with all the human race is the deepest of realities through our sharing in the universal life of God, who is over us and in us all, the source of all our ideals, and the pledge of their fulfillment if we understand them truly and seek them earnestly.

(b)   *Nicolai Hartmann.* — Another type of moral objection to faith in the divine transcendence is urged by Professor Nicolai Hartmann. His *Ethics,* first published in Germany in 1926, has received wide recognition as one of the most significant contributions to the subject in the twentieth century.

It categorically rejects formalism, utilitarianism and subjectivism and presents a realistic theory of an order of moral values inherent in the structure of reality and open to human discernment in and through unbiased reflective analysis. But although the universe is thus recognized as a moral, as well as a physical, order Hartmann refuses to regard that superhuman moral order as personal. He rightly recognizes that personality is essentially free in relation to the objective values presented in its experience, and that it acquires its own distinctive moral value or disvalue according to its selective, purposive response to these values. In a word, personality is "teleological," and this freedom and responsibility inherent in genuinely purposive behavior are essential to the moral nature of man. Without them he would not be a moral being and our whole moral experience would be a tragic illusion. But this freedom and responsibility of man, argues Hartmann, imply the negation of any theory of cosmic teleology, and therefore of any superhuman personality as the source of our moral ideals. " The Aristotelian philosophy," he writes,

which gave to cosmic teleology its classic form, was rooted in a metaphysic of organic nature. From that it transferred the thought to the whole of inorganic nature, to motion itself; and it ultimately included everything in one single teleological cosmic principle, in the pure energy of the " first mover." . . . But [he objects] such a metaphysical primacy of axiological determination means a perfect determination, in which man is deprived of all range for any determination emanating from himself. . . . He is handed over unconditionally, in a bondage not of his choosing, to fixed cosmic ends. . . . For ethics this view . . . is nothing short of catastrophic.[22]

We must, I think, admit that this or any other form of thoroughgoing determinism, which denies the reality of all

[22] *Ethics*, I, 283, 287.

human freedom and responsibility, involves a flat denial of the essential features of our moral experience and should therefore be rejected; for our moral experience has as much claim to validity as our sensory experience. Fortunately, both theological and materialistic determinism have largely disappeared from modern philosophy.

But Hartmann is certainly not justified in assuming that there is no middle ground between such an assertion of the sovereignty of God as robs man of all true freedom and responsibility, and a complete abandonment of all superhuman, or cosmic, teleology. In our analysis we have found that God is primarily known to man as the altruistic will that seeks, in and through each individual, the good of all. If this purposive agency within us is regarded as a manifestation of a greater purposive agent beyond us, it would be contradictory to suppose that greater agent to have all the universe so much in his control that the very ego which opposes the altruistic will is also completely controlled by the external agent. That, and any denial of human freedom, would be a contradiction of religious experience rather than an interpretation of it. Indeed, as Hartmann shows, it is not as an interpretation of our moral and religious experience that the notion of an all-encompassing cosmic teleology arises, but from metaphysical speculation upon external nature, seeking prematurely to fill the gaps in our scientific knowledge. What religious experience suggests is that God, as found in man striving toward the good, is not a product of human striving but rather the source of all that is good in it; that his being therefore transcends the human and may guide and sustain ours. But the relation of God, so far as he transcends man, to the rest of nature remains a question to be decided in the light of all the rest of our experience; and it is only the premature, partly scientific speculations of certain philosophers, and the emotional but uncritical exaltation of their God by certain prophets, priests and theologians, that have led to the extension of the principle of superhuman teleology to the extreme which Hartmann so rightly condemns.

THE SIGNIFICANCE OF FREEDOM

Our analysis of the nature of the good as found essentially in personal development emphasizes the importance of freedom. There is no *development* of personality that does not spring spontaneously from within in response to values felt or anticipated. External pressures do not develop personality, though they may deform it. Pressure would have no place at all in the educative process were it not that the natural and social world inevitably exerts certain pressures to which the person must adapt himself or be seriously injured. Educative pressure is a pressure applied with good will, discrimination and understanding, which prepares the person to make these adjustments to nature and society. It does not contribute directly to personal development, but only indirectly in that it saves from disaster. Actual personal development comes through the positive response from within. It flourishes most, therefore, where pressure is least.

Now the social groupings of mankind always involve a certain amount of pressure. The family, the local community, the church and the state all set limits to the freedom of the individual and make demands upon him. This raises the question of the value of the religious group, the church. The local community is inevitable, and few question the necessity of the family and the state. But there are many who believe that religion might well become a purely individual matter and so would remove the church as an unnecessary restriction upon freedom. It becomes a matter of great importance, therefore, to consider the place of the church in the religious life of the individual and in the social life of the community. To these questions we turn in the next two chapters. We must inquire why the church exists as a distinct grouping within the complex modern community. We shall see that it constitutes a natural and inevitable group so long as man gives any expression to religious feeling. We must consider its function in relation to the individual and the state. In particular, we must consider the significance of the insight into the nature of man's religious life that we have gained in our analysis, for the interpretation of the church's proper attitude to the problems of modern society. We shall see that the weight of the church's influence must be placed on the side of freedom and shall inquire how this is to be done.

With regard to the relation of the church to the individuals within it, we shall see that the emphasis on freedom becomes of still greater importance. The greatest mistakes of well meaning religious people have been made in the worse than futile effort to do good by shaping personality under pressure. In no sphere of religious activity is this more disastrous than in that of thought. We can conform our conduct deliberately to social demands, and usually it is best to do so. But we cannot deliberately conform our thought. It may conform naturally through the influence of suggestion. But if it does not we do ourselves injury if we try to believe what does not seem to us to be true. And we do ourselves and others injury by pretending to believe what we do not. And society does injury by putting pressure on anyone to believe or to pretend to believe (as one does when he hides his belief) what he cannot honestly believe. For this reason, probably the greatest wrong that the church has done to society, and to its own members, is in the establishment of creeds, and in the effort to enforce them by attaching to them the threats of religious penalties, social sanctions and, even worse, the sanctions of law and economic disability.

Complete religious freedom means more than the absence of legal and economic pressure. It means the absence of social and religious pressure. This means that religious people must attach no moral stigma or religious disability to any form of belief. The real moral stigma and religious disability attach to simulated beliefs and to the efforts to force others to hide and simulate beliefs. The churches, undoubtedly, have done much good. But in this respect, unfortunately, they have certainly done much harm; they have blighted the free personal development (the truest good) of their own members and of many outside. They have done this in part because of a belief that correctness of doctrine is essential to personal salvation, and in part because unanimity on doctrine seemed necessary to the unity and efficiency of the church in all its work, so that the exclusion of the dissenter and unbeliever seemed the lesser of two evils.

If our analysis of the essential nature of religion is accepted as sound then I believe that both these assumptions can be shown to be false. This will involve us in an examination of the relation of the church to society and to the individual. In that inquiry we shall see that the church can and, if it is best to fulfill its function, must, be a free-thinking community.

This does not mean that it must be a community of " freethinkers " in the current negative sense of the term. But it does mean that it must have room in full fellowship for all people, whatever their opinions on theological questions. We shall examine the essential nature of the church, its psychological structure, its ethical function and (for Christianity) its historical roots. And we shall see that such a free religious community is the logical outcome of its nature and origin, the true way to restore its lost unity and its waning influence. Our examination will show the world's need of such a church and its value for the personal development of people of all creeds and none. It will, I think, show too that, by the exercise of a wise mutual tolerance, persons of all shades of belief may share the spiritual helpfulness of such a church, and that all persons of genuine good will could find in it an instrument and a sphere of work for the good of mankind.

This further interpretation of the practical religious life constitutes, then, the theme of our next two chapters. In the remainder of the book we turn our attention to the two most important questions concerning the theoretical significance of religious experience for the whole meaning of life. These problems — of God and immortality — are of tremendous importance even for the practical religious life. Yet it is plain that that life must go on without first reaching certainty and unanimity on such ultimate questions of belief. We leave the discussion of them to the last because we wish to show how far the practical religious life can go forward with unity and value without attaining reasoned certainty on these matters and without seeking to impose uniformity of opinion where no obvious objective ground for it exists.

The Great Society

RELIGION AS INDIVIDUAL AND AS SOCIAL PHENOMENON

IF OUR ANALYSIS of religious experience is correct then religion is primarily neither an exclusively social nor an exclusively individual fact. Its problem is one of a personal adaptation which involves both an adjustment within the individual and an adjustment of his relations with his fellows. It is an effort of man to " get right with God," as the evangelical theologians have so emphatically said; but " God " is the name for something felt within the self as a desire and a duty to " get right with man." We need not repeat nor add to what has already been said as to the inadequacy of merely social theories of religion, such as that of Durkheim. But it becomes necessary to point out the equal inadequacy of such individualistic statements as that of Whitehead, that " religion is what we do with our solitariness " or that " religion is force of belief cleansing the inward parts." [1] The element of belief in religion is important; and so is that solitary meditation whereby our values fall into true perspective, resulting in inner personal adjustment in harmony with the disinterested will to the good. But this means that it is chiefly the social attitudes of the individual that need adjusting. And this cannot be done without social effects.

Simply because the religious adjustment involves an adjustment of attitude toward other people, other people are interested in it. Even though it is an inner adjustment in the depths of the inner personality it involves feelings that

[1] *Religion in the Making*, pp. 16, 15.

151

cannot be hidden. And the feelings involved, and the satisfactions found, are of a kind that others share. Thus mutual
expression and mutual understanding of common feelings,
interests and attitudes is the inevitable result of any extended
process of religious thought and activity. And when a number of people discover that they have feelings, interests and
attitudes in common they *become* a group whether they deliberately will it or not. There is then already a psychological cohesion which can scarcely be restrained from developing further. For its further development it needs that the
common interests shall be so communicated that each may
recognize the other as a person with whom he has that interest
in common. With such mutual recognition the group is con-
summated as a psychological unit. The degree of its cohesion
depends primarily upon the strength of the common interests
that bind this group together, relative to that of other interests that might divide it. The rest is a matter of organization, which depends chiefly upon the nature of the goals
involved in the common interests and the capacity of the
group to develop intelligent leaders.

Now the primary religious interest is an interest in the welfare of others. But it is not felt, and does not at first manifest
itself, merely in general or abstract terms. It is always directed toward specific goods of specific persons. Thus the
group formed by expression of these specific interests is always limited and distinguished from others by common possession of these specific interests. In the small primitive community these interests are simply those concerned with the
ordinary welfare of the contiguous group. Thus the religious unit tends to be one with the political, economic and
military unit. The group has but one religion and there is
no distinction between church and state. Each person's religious feelings impel him to participate in all common interests. Yet his religion is more than the sum of those inter-

ests, for it concerns the inner adjustment of the ego to the common interests. And, since each person finds the need of this inner adjustment, and since the small primitive community allows so little room for personal idiosyncrasy, each tends to find help toward satisfying inner adjustment in the same ceremonies. Thus these become a further common interest — the interest in the common religious ceremony — an interest that is enhanced by the belief in its effective, largely magical contribution to material common interests. Because of these magical beliefs the group interest in religion is enormously strengthened. But it is important to recognize that they are not the sole reason why religion becomes a group phenomenon. It is a group phenomenon primarily because it is rooted in a natural human concern for the common good.

RELIGION AS CONSERVER OF THE SOCIAL ORDER

We have already seen how well recognized among anthropologists is the fact that the social stability of primitive and simple communities rests upon religion. Traditional religion supports the traditional mores. The reason for this is plain. Children learn their moral principles from their elders, and in primitive and simple societies find very little reason for questioning them. The mores are accepted as good. If any moral conflict is experienced it is almost entirely that of the ego asserting its private desires against principles recognized as of social value. Religion, in the inner experience of the individual, supports the mores so long as they are regarded as good. And the religious endorsement of the mores becomes a part of the body of religious teaching accepted as having divine authority.

Until very recent decades this religious support of the mores was recognized, even by naturalistic thinkers, as its chief or only recommendation. But liberal religious thought itself has today almost given up the belief in religious sanctions of the moral code, so that in our modern civilization this dubious utility of religion is rapidly being lost. Yet religion still continues to bolster up our traditional moral principles, laws and institutions. In so far as this is due to a belief that these, in any specific present form, are endorsed by a specific divine revelation the belief is, of course, without foundation, and does harm in its tendency to remove these principles and institutions beyond criticism. For this reason many naturalists of the present day question the whole social value of religion, regarding it as a drag on the wheels of progress and as entirely unnecessary, in an intelligent and educated modern society, as a buttress of the social order. Thus we have, in the past hundred years, a new phenomenon in the history of civilization — a crusade against all religion carried on in the name of morality. In Europe the great revolutionary originator of this crusade was Karl Marx. In America it has been vigorously prosecuted in the interests of a much milder program of reforms by John Dewey.

There can be little doubt that the twentieth century has witnessed a widespread decline of religious faith, such as has not occurred among the masses of the community since the days of the twilight of the gods in ancient Greece. But a review of the course of social history during the same period scarcely bears out the hopes of its apostles that it would be accompanied by the development of a higher and finer type of moral social consciousness in theory and practice. There are many causes, of course, for the serious modern development of political tyranny, race antagonisms, crime, divorce, and other evils that have seemed to put the clock back in the last three decades. But there can be little doubt that the downward grade has to some extent been made easier by the decline of religious faith. This does not mean, we may hope, that world civilization cannot survive without the support of certain false elements of religious belief. But it does mean that we should recognize the part that religion has always played in the preservation of the social order, and concern ourselves deeply and actively for the discovery and maintenance of those religious beliefs that have reasonable claim to be true and valuable.

In what way then, we may ask, can an intelligent and reasonable minimum of religious belief bolster the moral life of the community? Certainly not by threats of hell or any other sanctions, nor by promise of eternal rewards. Nor can we turn to an argument regarding the special revelation of specific moral laws. It must be recognized that this approach is too dubious to be effective and is inimical to the highest morality because it places it on relatively low grounds. But if we can believe that the will to the general good, which we find within us, is something more than just another of the specific emotional tendencies generated by social pressures or developed by nature in the interests of the race with her typical carelessness of the individual, then that higher will acquires a greater significance. If we call it by the name of God and recognize that it is the central principle of life — a cosmic principle and not just another habit or an evolutionary accident — then it becomes essentially reasonable to give it first place in our lives. If we can believe that it transcends our little lives, feels with us, gathers our lives into that of its own greater personality, so that we can find our truest and surest good in its service, then the religious life will take on a sense of assurance that will make possible a higher devotion. And yet such a belief calls for that critical examination of the value of every principle, law and institution which makes impossible an obscurantist conservatism. It shows how the larger religious faith can conserve social values without becoming an obstacle to useful social change. It shows, too, how one may believe in the divine endorsement of the central principle of the moral life — the disinterested pursuit of the good — without parting company with one who religiously pursues the same goal and yet cannot give to the principle the same metaphysical interpretation.

RELIGION AS DYNAMIC OF SOCIAL CHANGE

It must however not be supposed that religion, even in the past, has been no more than a conserver of existing social values, a rigid upholder of things as they are. The fact must not be overlooked that, historically, it has also been one of the greatest dynamics of social change. In such cases we usually find religion arrayed against religion, one dynamic and the other conservative, one appealing to new prophetic insights or revelations and the other to traditional principles, or one appealing to a new deduction from some general principles and the other to specific endorsements of the existing order. In the history of Christianity these revolutionary movements have always found the ammunition they required in the teachings of Jesus, though many leaders have not hesitated to claim direct divine guidance. In the pre-Christian era the Hebrew prophets proclaimed their radical social teaching with a "Thus saith the Lord." In Arabia Mohammed carried through a sweeping program of social change based upon similar claims to specific revelations. But, in general, the power that religious conviction gives to movements for political and social reform is due to the assurance of the religious person that his cause is productive of good, is objectively right, and that therefore it is the will of God. This assurance rests, in the last instance, upon the foundation stone of all religion, the experience of the disinterested will to the good, resulting in the sense of a religious obligation to do what seems to be best.

What seems to the religious person to be best will, of course, be affected by many circumstances, including those of his traditional beliefs and special personal, class, racial or other sectional interests. But on the whole, it must be recognized, the dynamic force of religion is directed toward the ideal, whatever it may seem to be, rather than simply toward the preservation of traditions for their own sake or the mere continuity of established personal and social habits. Thus it requires only the growth of the conviction that something in a present law, tradition or institution is not in accord with the ideal, and a religious demand is aroused that it be changed. If the condition recognized as wrong is one that has had specific endorsement from the traditional religion, a crisis is created within that religion. Either the notion of a special divine endorsement in this case is given up, or it must be reinterpreted in harmony with the requirements of the ideal. In order that religion may cease to be a source of support for inadequate moral principles and for institutions that have outlived their usefulness, it is necessary that the belief in the specific establishment or endorsement of these by special revelation be given up. And, if religion is nevertheless to continue to be a buttress of social order and a dynamic of social progress, it must assert a significant divine endorsement of the *general principle* of the disinterested pursuit of the good, so that egoism and every narrow sectionalism or nationalism may be recognized as contrary to the divine will.

In Christianity this condition is practically achieved in the teaching of Jesus himself, for he divests the rigid and specific Old Testament law of all authority and founds his ethics on sweeping principles of disinterested good will, such as the Golden Rule and the principle of love to one's neighbor. These are supported and interpreted in parables, paradoxes and hyperboles, which cannot be taken literally, but all serve to emphasize the sweeping breadth and intensity of his ideal of human service. Thus the parable of the Good Samaritan abolishes all limits from the concept of " neighbor "; the paradox, " He that saveth his life shall lose it," sets the ideal of service above all self-interest; the hyperbole of the camel and the needle's eye emphasizes the psychological antagonism between the spiritual life and the problems of care for an accumulation of material things.   As is also the case with Socrates, we have his teaching only at second hand, so that we are never sure that we have his exact statements anywhere. But the whole tenor of what is preserved indicates that it was the reverse of formalism and legalism, and constituted, both in precept and in example, a magnificent expression of the disinterested will to the good of all.   The difficulty that human beings find in maintaining an attitude of critical intelligence in the realm of morals is tragically manifested in the fact that so high and free an expression of the ideal should have been so much legalized and formalized by subsequent disciples.

INDIVIDUAL AND SOCIAL IMPLEMENTATION
OF THE RELIGIOUS IDEAL

The adoption of the right ideal is one thing.   Its implementation is another.   In general, social ideals require social (and usually legal) implementation, not mere individual action.   Where the religious group is one with the political (the tribe, state or nation), social implementation naturally follows from the adoption of a religious principle.   But the principles tend to become highly formalized and rigid, and individuality is crushed.   In complex societies, where there is sufficient religious freedom, the religious groups tend to be more or less completely differentiated from the state.   Some individuals stand outside the religious group; and the religious group itself tends to be divided into groups differing in beliefs, ideals and methods.   When a religious group constitutes a minority devoid of political power, the social implementation of its ideals is very difficult or impossible. When it is a majority and possesses political power it is often a difficult question how far it should use that power to give social implementation to its ideals against the will of a minority; for example, should it prohibit the slave trade or the liquor trade? Only a weighing of the good and evil involved in social or legal action, in each case, can decide such questions; and mistakes are sure to be made.

Because of the sweeping nature of its ideal of the good, Christianity needs must face this question. Jesus himself seems to have made no effort to secure a social implementation of his ideals in his own day, and stood aside from the only significant movement of that kind in his own country — the movement for Jewish independence, which subsequently culminated in futile rebellion and the destruction of Jerusalem. He sought instead to build the " Kingdom of God " as a religious society which might work like a leaven to leaven the whole lump. Considering the political impotence of the people to whom he preached it is obvious that there was no other way. Thus the first Christian centuries placed the emphasis upon the cultivation of personal character and the attainment of individual salvation.

When, in the later Roman Empire, the church acquired numbers and political influence it turned its attention to the social implementation of its ideals. It brought about reforms in the treatment of slaves, of infants and of the poor. It secured the abolition of the gladiatorial games and the adoption of its ideal of marriage, which involved a great improvement in the status of women. It emphasized the moral responsibility of rulers and officials. But the church came to power in a period of political decline, social disintegration and barbarian invasion; and at the same time it was corrupted by the influx of masses who did not understand or share its ideals. So far as civilization was saved in the Dark Ages that followed, it was the church that saved it, for the church retained a strong sense of social values in spite of its corruption. But the long period of political impotence had turned its thoughts chiefly inward upon the problems of the individual soul. Its many sins and failures, in its period of great political influence amidst terrific difficulties, intensified this tendency. So the revival of Christianity in the Reformation era saw a revulsion of feeling against the influence of the church in the state. It was not until the nineteenth century that the thoughts of Christian leaders turned again to the social implementation of their gospel of good will.

The "social gospel," under the stimulus of leaders such as Walter Rauschenbusch,[2] has today become a commonplace and is the chief interest of many religious groups. Like every vigorous movement it has sometimes gone to extremes, neglecting the vital but less spectacular task of cultivating the individual spiritual life; and sometimes it has lent its support to political movements of dubious wisdom. But its central idea is unquestionably right, and in a democracy it becomes of pressing moral importance. Where a citizen plays a part in government, and can influence by his voice or vote the laws and administrative measures that affect the welfare of the community, the principle of universal good will must determine his use of that power if he is to be true to the deepest insight of ethics and religion.

In our complex modern civilization it is becoming increasingly evident that the attainment of the ideal of the more abundant life for all cannot be left to individual good will, but requires social and often legal measures. Our modern economic order, supported by our law of property, deprives millions of access to the means of production, shuts off others from the educational opportunities necessary for full development of their mental capacities, leaves large numbers in want, encourages vice and crime, works injustice on individuals, classes and nations, thus leading to revolution and war.

[2] Author of *Christianity and the Social Crisis* and numerous other works.

These facts present problems that are beyond remedy by individual morality, for they destroy personality faster than the means at the disposal of religion can remake it. Consequently they call imperiously for the social implementation of the moral and religious ideal. And in spite of the difficulties and dangers of carrying the religious motivation into political activity the thing must be done.

It must be recognized, however, that here good will alone does not suffice. Intelligence and expert knowledge are also necessary. Even the experts honestly differ on the wisdom of many proposed solutions of the various problems. It would be presumptuous of religious leaders to claim superior ability to decide the right and wrong of many complicated issues. However, they need not regard themselves as therefore powerless to act and exonerated from responsibility. There are three things that they can do.

In the first place, the issue is often sufficiently clear as merely one of the retention or nonretention by one group or another of privileges which are injurious to others and have no justification in social utility or past service; and sometimes it is simply a matter of whether a necessary burden shall be borne by the strong or by the weak. In the second place, where the means of remedy is doubtful or unknown, a great service can be done simply by keeping the need before the attention of the community. The church should be the most sensitive part of the community conscience, recognizing and declaring injustice where it exists, and insisting that evils be not hidden by those whose interests might be at stake or simply forgotten by a careless majority which is not itself affected. In the third place, religion should be able to discover, within the essential feature of its own experience, an insight into the nature of man which illuminates many of the social problems of our day and shows the real wisdom of the more liberal modes of dealing with them. To show the meaning and the truth of this last point will occupy us for the remainder of this chapter.

THE LIBERAL FAITH IN HUMAN NATURE

Liberalism in social affairs, like religion itself, has suffered from an unwarranted identification with certain temporary beliefs and programs that it has at times adopted and that have been outgrown (e.g., the economic doctrine of laissez faire). But liberalism is really something more complex and subtle than any specific set of principles. Because human motives are always so complex, no party that has ever worn the name has ever exemplified in its purity the liberal spirit. Nor has any party a monopoly of it. It is a typical attitude to human problems that defines itself differently from time to time and yet always retains its own distinctively recognizable character. Its difficulty is that it is not always sure of itself. The fundamental faith on which it rests has not been made explicitly conscious. Consequently, in times of crisis it has too often become hesitant and flaccid. It is for that reason that, in many circles, it has fallen today into some disrepute. Yet the world is suffering from an illiberalism that threatens to lay it in ruins. What is needed is that liberalism should find its feet by acquiring a truer insight into its own foundation. That foundation, I think it can be shown, is a certain faith in human nature which may find enlightenment and support in the analysis of the religious consciousness of man that has been developed in these pages.

In recent decades both liberalism and democracy have been challenged by movements, such as fascism and communism, claiming to be more vigorous and direct means of securing socially desirable goals. The reason for the widespread loss of faith in liberal and democratic procedure is the loss of faith in man himself that has come over the world in the mood of disillusionment following the First World War, the collapse of the postwar settlement, and the failure of economic individualism. It is true that the rapid overcoming of many of man's physical problems, which has come as the suddenly ripened fruit of three centuries of scientific work, has called for a series of far-reaching social adjustments, which lack of understanding and the rigidity of habit and prejudice have prevented us from achieving. But the failures of these few decades in the face of extremely difficult problems constitute no reason for despair. The problems are not beyond the intelligence of the best minds. If they were, the opponents of liberalism and democracy would be in no better position than others. Their contention is that the masses of mankind cannot be persuaded by the methods of liberalism and democracy to adopt the solutions that the best minds find. This means, not that they are not sufficiently intelligent, but that, so long as they are free to pursue their own petty interests, they do not have the mutual good will to adopt the necessary measures by collective action. Thus it is argued that power must be retained in the hands of the few, and that the multitude must be constantly subjected to checks and controls and ultimately be directed by force.

It is here that a liberal political philosophy must take up the issue. It must be admitted that there are many things which the masses and the layman do not understand and that these must be left to the expert and the leader. But it must be asserted that the ultimate power can be safely left with the people when they have enlightened leadership, because it is possible to trust in their good will. The liberal philosophy of human nature might be succinctly stated as *a faith in the good will of the normal human being.* A little more exactly stated, it is the conviction that normal human beings are naturally animated by good will toward each other so that, unless specifically and strongly stirred by such feelings as anger, fear, jealousy and greed, they will adopt attitudes manifesting interest in the common good; and, in the absence of circumstances arousing such special antipathies, they will tend to seek each other's good even without special egoistic incentives to do so. In brief, it embodies the essential insight of religion, as brought out in our analysis, that the disinterested will to the good of all is the deepest-rooted principle of human personality and may become its dominant principle.

This faith does not ignore the obvious facts of criminality and indifference, both of individuals and of groups, but it does deny that such conditions are necessary and incurable. It holds that an interest in the welfare of others is as natural to human beings as is the interest in self. It maintains that human good will needs only opportunity and stimulus, and the absence of overstimulation of the opposing impulses to rivalry, greed and fear, for it to blossom forth into the dominant attitude of life. It believes that human beings naturally tend to be kindly and co-operative, so that institutions based upon these motives, when properly understood, may be expected to succeed, providing circumstances arousing strong antagonistic tendencies are absent. It asserts that the bribing and dragooning of the individual is not the only way to get him to do his duty, but that another possible motive is that of an appeal to him to co-operate in the common good.

This connection of liberalism with such an optimistic faith in human nature has been expressed by many of its twentieth century apostles. Thus Professor L. T. Hobhouse wrote:

Liberalism is the belief that society can safely be founded on this self-directing power of personality, that it is only on this foundation that a true community can be built, and that so established its foundations are so deep and wide that there is no limit we can place to the extent of the building.[3]

[3] L. T. Hobhouse: *Liberalism* (London: Williams & Norgate, 1911; now published by Oxford University Press), p. 123.

Again, we find Professor W. E. Hocking saying:

Liberalism maintains that the greatest natural resource of any community is the latent intelligence and good will of its members; and it seeks those forms of society which run a certain risk of preliminary disorder in order to elicit that resource. Since such individuals can be developed only by being trusted with somewhat more than they can, at the moment, do well, liberalism is a sort of honor system. Its liberality toward individuals will only be justified if those individuals are in turn liberal toward their groups.[4]

THE FASCIST THEORY OF HUMAN NATURE

This favorable view of human nature stands in striking contrast to the fascist estimate as that is interpreted even by so idealistic a representative as Major Barnes:

The general will . . . can be no more than the life instinct of the herd, a reflection of its vital solidarity. But this is not apparently a rational force at all. . . . Normally it is a relatively dormant force, negative rather than positive, so that in the absence of any acute crisis it is very feebly manifested, if at all. . . . And since it is strong in proportion to a society's cohesion, it must be recognised as pre-eminently selfish. . . . *The sum of the individual wills of a community is never the same thing, even if unanimous, as the general will,* for the same reason that the sum of individual interests of the members of a community does not amount to the general interest. . . . Education . . . placed the predominantly selfish in a better position to pursue their selfish aims than before, however much it placed the predominantly unselfish in a better position to pursue unselfish aims. And unfortunately the predominantly selfish remained the overwhelming majority.[5]

Mussolini himself, the fountainhead of fascism, declares:

[4] W. E. Hocking: *The Lasting Elements of Individualism* (New Haven, Conn.: Yale University Press, 1937) , p. 5.

[5] J. S. Barnes: *Fascism* (London: T. Butterworth, Ltd., 1931; now published by Oxford University Press) , pp. 92-99.

Struggle is the origin of all things, for life is full of contrasts; there is love and hatred, white and black, day and night, good and evil; and until these contrasts achieve balance struggle fatefully remains at the root of human nature. However it is good for it to be so.[6] . . . Men are not brothers, neither do they want to be, and evidently they cannot be. Peace is hence absurd, or, rather, is a necessary pause in the process of war. There is something that binds man to his destiny of struggling either against his fellows or against himself. . . . I see the world as it actually is; that is a world of unbridled egoism.[7]

This is the general tone of fascist [8] analyses of human nature, and the ground of the fascist conviction as to the necessity of authoritarianism and its disdain of the plea for personal liberty. Morality is conceived as consisting in obedience to a law higher than anything to be found within human personality — a law of a transcendent God or of the state. Conscience is regarded as expressing itself as a recognition of the stern voice of duty — a duty imposed from without — not as the expression of the best that is *within*. This being the view held of human nature and of the roots of the moral life, the conclusion becomes almost inevitable that government must " tend to become the prerogative of a class of *optimi,* of those persons whose egoisms are habitually overridden by their social sense, by a well-informed patriotism, by a high moral purpose." [9] One only wonders how such individuals are to be found and given power, and how they are to be saved from the corrupting effects of possession of power. Indeed, if general human nature is naturally so self-

---

[6] B. Mussolini: *The Doctrine of Fascism* (Rome: Ardita, 1935) , p. 35.

[7] Quoted by Mario Palmieri: *The Philosophy of Fascism* (Chicago: Fortune Press, Inc., 1936) , pp. 81, 82.

[8] The nazi philosophy builds on the same basis, developing its more extreme views by addition of the racial doctrines of Nordic superiority and anti-Semitism.

[9] Palmieri, *op. cit.,* p. 109.

ish, it is remarkable that the higher moral type is to be found at all.

It is not merely the reactionary fascist movement, however, that is characterized by this low view of human nature. It is instead typical, in greater or lesser degree, of conservatism generally. As instancing this we may point to what is acknowledgedly an expression of the finer ideals of English political Conservatism, made by one of the most noble-minded Conservatives:

Conservatives defend the Constitution, property, and the existing social order, partly from the natural conservative love of what exists, partly from a dread of injustice threatened to individuals by advocates of revolutionary change. . . . Conservatism is certainly not opposed to liberty. . . . The liberty of the subject has been so largely the purpose of our constitutional system that no party can champion the traditional Constitution without also defending the principles of liberty. . . . But it may be claimed for Conservatism that it has achieved under happier auspices than Liberalism a compromise between liberty and authority . . . in its reverence for the sanctions of religion. . . . The religious sentiment which is hostile to injustice is also unwilling to acquiesce in the sufferings of people from poverty and its attendant evils. Hence Conservatism comes also to be identified with measures of social improvement designed to raise the condition of the poor. . . . Conservatism arose to resist Jacobinism [of the French Revolution], and that is to this day its most essential and fundamental character. . . . In the Socialist movement . . . we seem sometimes to catch the Jacobin accents of reckless disregard of private rights; of merciless hatred toward those who, perhaps through no fault of their own, have become associated with some real or fancied abuse; of that disposition, not gradually to develop one state of society out of another, but to make a clean sweep of institutions in the interest of a half-thought-out reform. It is in so far as these elements are present in the Socialist movement that Conservatism is opposed to it.[10]

Thus Conservatism seeks the common good, favors reform, upholds the democratic institutions wrought into the constitution, and stands for at least that measure of liberty guaranteed by the constitution and tested for its safety in experience of its working.   No one familiar with the history of the nineteenth century in Britain will deny this claim that Conservatives have favored and introduced many valuable social and economic reforms.   But there are phrases in Lord Cecil's statement of his ideals which show a conception of the nature of the social problem, and an attitude of mind, which distinguish his approach to the goal of the common good from that of the man of genuinely liberal political philosophy. His references to the motives of Conservatism — the dread of injustice, the reverence for authoritative sanctions, the suspicion of possible Jacobin excesses on the part of modern British Socialists — all show the distinction of spirit and outlook between conservative and liberal.

Conservatism is cautious, suspicious of radical change, hesitant to make reforms.   (Cecil admits it has often been too hesitant.)   It upholds established authority in church and state.   It dreads injustice at the hands of reformers.   It remembers the French Revolution for the excesses of Jacobinism rather than for its ideals of liberty, equality and fraternity. It fears that these excesses would again manifest themselves in a successful Socialist party.   It insists that the competitive system alone can extract from the worker his best efforts.   All these elements in its attitude are evidence of its relatively small confidence in the natural good will of the normal human being.   Thus, in despite of its admiration of the present relatively liberal institutions of Western democracies, of its

[10] Lord Hugh Cecil: *Conservatism* (London: Williams & Norgate, 1927; now published by Oxford University Press), pp. 244–49 *passim*.

desire to eliminate obvious and excessive injustices, and of its ideal of the common good, it often hesitates to make reforms until it is too late; and its opposition to needed change today is placing civilization in jeopardy.

Most of the typical clashes between liberal and conservative policies in Britain and America in the past few decades illustrate this diversity of attitude. Conservatism tends to be imperialistic. It lays to its soul the flattering unction of the " white man's burden " because it distrusts the moral and intellectual capacities of the colored man. For the same reason it has opposed self-government in India. Distrusting the intentions of the Irish Catholics and the South African Dutch it opposed the grant of dominion status in both cases. It wrote the oppressive clauses in the Versailles treaty because it distrusted the new German republic's intention to become a good European, and it maintained that distrust and consequent oppression until it goaded the Germans into reaction and revolt. On all these questions men of liberal political philosophy in all parties were on the other side. And the ground of the difference was not one of economic interests, for the economic interests of all parties, so far as they were affected at all by these issues, have been practically the same. It is rather that most of the leaders of the other parties have believed that policies of good will and generosity would call forth a favorable response from the foreign peoples concerned, but the Conservatives, with a more limited faith in human nature, feared that they would not, and so put their trust in the policy of the strong arm and the heavy hand.

In America, conservative members of both parties defeated the League of Nations and the World Court proposal, passed the Japanese exclusion act, erected the Smoot-Hawley tariff, opposed collective bargaining and the organization of industrial unions, organized the Ku Klux Klan, maintained discrimination against the Negro, opposed the recognition of

Russia, and resisted experimentation in dealing with the depression. And they still exploit the fear of communism. In some of these matters economic considerations enter in to motivate the different policy of the liberals, but by no means in all; and in few if any of them are economic considerations paramount, for American liberalism is by no means identified with the proletariat. Nor is the difference really a moral one. The ordinary American conservative citizen is personally just as generous and goodhearted a person as his liberal neighbor, and the old guard Democrats and Republicans number just as many genuine humanitarians among their leaders as there are among the New Dealers and Progressives. The difference is not in their desire for the good of the other person, but in their faith in his good will. The root of the difference does not lie in the strength of the desire for the common good, and is only partly due to a calculation of personal economic interests. Fundamentally, and most important, the root of the difference lies in different theories of human nature.

THE POLITICAL TREND OF LIBERALISM

This definition of liberalism as fundamentally a theory of human nature — a faith in the good will of the normal human being — has the advantage of obviating the necessity of attempting to define it in terms of a specific political program. The liberalism of yesterday is already, to a great extent, the conservatism of today. This is a general principle which applies to much more than the obvious case of laissez faire. On the other hand, what would be a sound liberal policy in one country, at a certain stage of development, may not be a sound policy for another country at a different stage of development. A striking example of this is to be found in the failure of the liberal leaders of the Chinese revolution of 1911 to establish in China a liberal democratic form of gov-

ernment. Because of the lack of psychological preparation
and general education, their movement collapsed into chaos
for a quarter of a century. A wiser liberalism would not, at
that stage, have completely destroyed the monarchy on which
the unity of the country depended.

Thus neither laissez faire, nor even democracy, necessarily
constitutes liberalism. Liberalism must define its policy in
accordance with its own spirit to meet the exigencies of each
new situation. Each age presents its problems. Liberalism
will always distinguish itself from conservatism by its readiness to experiment with those solutions which require some
additional reliance upon the good will of the normal human
being; and where such good will seems lacking, liberalism
will seek to find and remove the causes of distrust and antagonism and to cultivate the necessary good will. It will
do this because it believes in the possibility of success in such
efforts.

Thus liberalism will move in the direction of co-operative
solutions of both economic and international problems and,
in general, toward democratic solutions also. It will seek to
extend those forms of co-operative and government action
in the economic field which have already, in various places,
been found successful, and to prepare the psychological basis
necessary for their further extension. In international affairs
it will mean an abandonment of American isolationism, not
merely and blindly to "take the side of the democracies,"
but to work and press for a fundamentally just solution of
world problems through some such instrumentalities as the
World Court and a new League of Nations, enforcing international law though giving no sanction to treaties dictated
by force, and guaranteeing to all peoples adequate economic
opportunity and freedom from external aggression.

The solutions eventually reached by liberalism may, in the
long run, not greatly differ from those envisaged by com-

munism as its ultimate goal. But the difference in method is due to the different theories of human nature. Dialectical materialism issues in economic determinism, the theory of the class war and the belief in a necessary period of dictatorship for the forcible shaping of a popular mentality conducive to a co-operative social order. It therefore refuses to believe in the possibility of a gradual redistribution of wealth without a resort to violence on the part of the wealthy in defense of their status. Because it expects to have to use force, in the long run, to meet force, it is ready to hasten its goal by use of force when opportunity offers, as in Russia in 1917, when it overthrew an incipient democracy, and more recently when it attacked Finland and other countries. Because of this belief in the necessity of force, and readiness to get its blow in first when it can, communism has stimulated the violent counteraction of fascism. Thus the refusal to believe in the good will of the normal human being has brought about its own nemesis and has forced upon communists the remarkable changes in tactics manifested in recent years. Yet, in spite of their occasional role as apostles of peace and democracy, communists can never be true liberals because of their fundamentally different theory of human nature. The purges, oppression and aggressions of Russia under Stalin are not due to a double dose of original sin in the souls of the party leaders, but are the logical result of the application of the Marxist philosophy of human nature to the problems those leaders have had to face.

In general, as has already been said, liberalism will tend toward democratic procedures. Such procedures give scope for personality, and the free development of personality is the essential medium of all value. But it is a mistake simply to *identify* political liberalism with democracy. Liberalism is a faith in the *good will* of the normal human being. But the successful working of democracy requires also that he possess *intelligence* and *knowledge* adequate to the tasks entrusted to him. Democratic procedure can be successful only if those who vote on a question adequately understand the issues involved. A vote without understanding is either an expression of prejudice, a response to propaganda, a reliance on authorities, or mere guesswork. Good will in a man's heart without understanding in his head does not make it safe to put a ballot-paper into his hands. Liberalism is a faith in the good will of the normal human being. But it is not, or should not be, a naïve belief in the competence of the average citizen to solve complex problems of economics or foreign policy on which he has only the scantiest information, or to make wise choices of personnel among candidates he does not know, who are seeking positions the qualifications necessary for which he does not understand.

It is important, therefore, to be quite clear as to what is implied by our statement that religion, when it becomes conscious of its own roots in a disinterested will to the good that is fundamental to the structure of human personality, will tend to support social policies that are characteristically liberal. It does not mean that political liberals are always right and their opponents wrong. It does not mean that the most democratic procedure is always necessarily the best. It does not mean *vox populi, vox dei*. But it does mean that public policy should be shaped on the assumption that the normal human being, when convinced that others are acting toward him with good will, can, in general, be trusted to respond with good will. It will therefore encourage every effort at the creation of good will. It will ease the fears that motivate so many repressive measures. It will encourage experimentation in the direction of wider and closer political organization. It will facilitate the substitution of co-operation for competition in the economic sphere. It will reduce the suspicion that hampers the work of even well tried leaders. It will work toward the emancipation of repressed and segregated sections of the community. It will ease the tensions that lead to national rivalry and war. It will facilitate the organization of peace and security.

THEOLOGY AND THE THEORY OF HUMAN NATURE

For the most part a man's theory of human nature is an expression of his experience and temperament. For this reason few people are consistently liberal or conservative, but are more liberal toward some groups, and on some questions, and at some times, than others. But a general trend in one direction or another is often determined by a general philosophical and theological viewpoint. At first thought it might be expected that, if our analysis is sound and religion arises from man's experience of the disinterested will within himself, religion would always tend to cultivate a faith in human good will. But this is not in fact the case. As we have seen, the more intense forms of religious experience tend to arise when there is a decided element of conflict within the self, resulting in a severe sense of sin. Thus there has been a strong tendency, among the more vivid religious personalities, to confess aloud their own sinfulness and declare emphatically the sinfulness of the race.

In Christianity this type of theology came into the ascendant through the tremendous influence of Augustine. It found support in much of the writing of Paul, who appears to have been of a similar semineurotic temperament, deeply impressed with his own shortcomings. Both preached love toward their fellow men, but both were so impressed by their own need of a special divine aid that they could not believe there was enough natural goodness in the common man to see any hope for human society apart from a special divine intervention. This outlook culminated in the doctrine of the total depravity of man — a doctrine which for centuries has perverted and distorted Christian efforts to be of use to society. It has created the harsh type of Christian moralist whose chief thought of how to do good was to make people afraid to do ill. And it has taught Christians to despair of doing any permanent good by seeking to improve the social order on earth, directing them to make all human charity merely a means to prepare themselves and others for the next world.

But this despair of the conduct of men in their practical affairs is the very antithesis of the conclusion which ought to be drawn from religious experience. It is certainly not the conclusion that Jesus drew. The remarkable wholesomeness of his teaching is largely due to the fact that he differs from other great religious personalities in being driven not by a consciousness of sin, but simply by a tremendous zeal for human moral welfare, to be manifested in righteousness and love. To Jesus all men were children of God; that was to him the most important of all truths and the ground of a lively hope and faith for this world and the next. The earliest Christian statement of a philosophical theology is in the same tone: " In the beginning was the *Logos,* and the *Logos* was with God, and the *Logos* was God. . . . In him was life and the life was the light of men. . . . There was the true light, even the light which lighteth every man, coming into the world." [11] Here the immanence of God in man is taught as the cardinal fact, the source of the life and light, the reason and moral insight of man. The Greek theologians, from Clement of Alexandria in the second century to Theodore of Mopsuestia in the fifth, continued to give prominence to this doctrine of immanence and, on the whole, did not exaggerate the sinfulness of man. It was the Latin theology, under the influence of Augustine, and facing the collapse of its civi-

[11] John 1:1–9.

lization amid corruption and defeat, that imposed this tragic misrepresentation upon Christian thought.[12]

In spite of a certain revival of this type of thinking in the Barthian movement, due to the present-day reaction from the optimism of thirty years ago, the general trend of Christian thought today is with the Greek rather than the Latin theology. The chief emphasis in the religious thought of this century has been on the doctrine of immanence — an emphasis which, it is now fairly clear, will not be allowed to pass over into mere pantheism. In spite of the new pessimism of the last decade, it seems evident that Christian thought has thoroughly shaken off its exaggerated sense of sin. It is a problem on which the age has hardly yet found its balance. But if our analysis of religious experience is sound it should be possible to obtain a sober yet hopeful view. The very fact of the consciousness of sin is due to that in man which we have recognized as divine — the disinterested will to the good. And because this element of human personality is fundamental — no mere occasional and superficial growth — man finds no complete satisfaction until he makes his peace with it.

Thus there is always in man an element of good will to which appeal can be made. Human nature is on the side of human progress. The problem is to set aside the *damnosa hereditas* of prejudice, false tradition, superstition, fear, hatred, that survives from the childhood of the race, and to develop institutions adequate to its maturity. There is in the human heart enough of natural good will. It remains for intelligence to enable it to find its way.

Now this liberal faith that human beings are fundamentally creatures of good will, while it is an implication of our analysis of religious experience, is not a conclusion drawn from a religious metaphysic. Its basis is empirical; and it is often rec-

[12] These trends in early church history are well portrayed by F. D. Kershner: *Pioneers of Christian Thought* (Indianapolis: Bobbs-Merrill Co., 1930) .

ognized as factual even by those who cannot accept metaphysical views of a theistic character.   It is, for example, emphatically proclaimed by John Dewey.[13]   It offers, therefore, the basis of a practical program of social progress which is independent of further details of creed.   Men of good will, who believe in the good will of others, may work together in spite of differences of theological opinion.   That faith in the good will of others may for some be simply a " hunch," for others an expression of temperament, for yet others an induction from experience or a deduction from a philosophical theory. For the religious man it may be any or all of these.   But it should also be a conviction arising from an intelligent analysis of his own religious experience.   Let that clearsighted conviction, with all the dynamic zeal that flows from a deep religious experience, be thrust into the movement for a liberal social implementation of the ideal of the common good, and the present dark outlook of civilization should rapidly be changed.

[13] Conspicuous examples among naturalistic thinkers on the other side are E. B. Holt, especially in his article, " The Whimsical Condition of Social Psychology, and of Mankind," in *American Philosophy of Today and Tomorrow,* edited by H. M. Kallen and S. Hook (New York: Lee Furman, Inc., 1935) ; and J. W. Krutch: *The Modern Temper* (New York: Harcourt, Brace & Co., 1932) and *Experience and Art* (New York: H. Smith, 1933) .

The Religious Community

INDIVIDUAL BELIEF AND SOCIAL INTERACTION

EVEN our most private beliefs are not devoid of social effects, for if the belief has any importance at all it affects our behavior; and if it is not communicated to others it either fades away or else creates a sense of isolation from our fellows which is psychologically and socially unhealthy. Further, as was pointed out at the beginning of the previous chapter, beliefs that are shared, if they concern matters of common interest, tend to create psychological groups. The chief characteristic of the psychological group is that it tends to co-operate in the pursuit of certain common ends. A church, a nation, a political party, a football team, a street corner gang and a trade union are examples of such groups. It is not necessary that they should come together in one place to form a crowd, though they tend to do so as opportunity and need arise. All that is necessary is that they should *have* a common purpose, and have succeeded in *communicating* this fact to each other so that they *recognize* each other as persons animated by a common purpose. The result will be a tendency to co-operative action. Such action may be more or less co-ordinated, the degree of co-ordination depending chiefly on the recognition of common leaders, upon the clarity and unity with which the end and the means to it are grasped, and upon the efficiency of communication.

The problem into which we must now inquire is how far certain differences in religious belief need affect the unity and co-ordination of effort of those who hold to the same religious ideal. In particular, if, in the terms of our analysis, it is agreed that it is the will of God that the fullest possible measure of value should be realized in the lives of all mankind, and that it is the religious duty and privilege of each of us to devote the self to that ideal, then is it necessary that we should be agreed on the questions of the transcendence of God and the ultimate destiny of human personality? Must the church excommunicate as heretics all who cannot accept its majority beliefs upon these great questions? Must those who do not accept these majority beliefs of the church feel themselves obliged to withdraw from membership and co-operation with it and pursue the realization of the same ideal alone or in separate groups?

We have been so accustomed to thinking of religion in terms of doctrinal beliefs, and of the distinctions between religious groups in terms of creed, that it may at first seem strange to consider the unity of religious groups in any other terms. But it is really the unity of ideal or purpose that matters most for the creation of a psychological unity among people. And this unity exists over a wide range of people inside and outside of the present churches. Yet this great number of people who possess this common ideal fail to achieve co-operation, and thus they also fail to give to the ideal the power it would have if it were recognized as the ideal of so great a number. Thus there already exists a real religious unity which fails of being implemented because intellectual disunity is given the greater prominence. What is needed is to give the greater prominence to the real element of religious unity, the common ideal, that it may have the power that comes from such demonstration of support. This means that those who hold this ideal must succeed in *communicating* the fact to each other, in recognizable and convincing terms, so that all may feel the fact that they are animated by this common purpose. From that communication and recognition, tendencies to co-operative implementation of the ideal will inevitably grow. The rest becomes a matter of developing and recognizing common leaders and finding agreed means to the common ends.

Differences of belief inevitably involve differences in choice of leaders and of means. So if the religious society (the church) is able to recognize itself as one (one body, a psychological, or spiritual, unity) in spite of great differences of opinion, it must allow of much liberty to individuals and sub-groups within the larger whole in the choice of leaders and means of work. Co-ordination of effort in any co-operative enterprise can never be made complete in every detail except at the cost of a surrender of freedom and initiative which is injurious to the finer flowers of personality. Yet where there *is* a common ideal, a large measure of unity, common recognition and co-operation is possible; and the power of that ideal is enhanced in the degree to which this is achieved. Religion suffers much from the petty divisions that are due to relatively minor differences of belief. But it suffers more from branding as irreligious those persons and organizations which, though they pursue the religious ideal, do not share the typical metaphysical convictions of the church concerning God and the soul. The question for the more orthodox Christians therefore is whether the church cannot extend its fellowship to include all those who share its ultimate ideal, and do this without departure from the essential character of historic Christianity. The question for those who share the church's ideal, but not its metaphysical beliefs, is whether they should welcome such an invitation where and when it comes, asserting the common character of the religious ideal, joining in one great religious body that holds that ideal and allows freedom of belief and action, and co-operating so far as possible in the attainment of that ideal.

TRUTH AND FREEDOM OF THOUGHT

Ought not the unity of the Christian faith to be conceived as a unity of purposes and ideals rather than as a unity of beliefs on questions of history and metaphysics? Faith is a believing *in* something, and only incidentally a believing *about* something. It is primarily an acceptance of certain evaluations and only secondarily, if at all, an acceptance of alleged cold facts. And one of the primary evaluations of the Christian faith is the evaluation of truth itself. This evaluation was never put into the creeds. It was accepted unquestioningly, and the church never seems to have thought it necessary to put into its formal creeds the things that nobody doubted. Even the Old Roman Symbol, from which the so-called Apostles' Creed developed, was drawn up primarily to keep Marcion and his followers out of the church,[1] and each addition was made to refute some heresy. In all this the church thought it was defending truth. To maintain its primary faith in the value of truth it sought to make final decisions and exclude error. But the sad history of succeeding centuries has shown that this is not the way to attain the primary end, that the only way to attain and maintain truth is by the completest freedom of thought and discussion. Thus loyalty to truth calls for the relegation of creeds to the student's study and the opening up of the forum of free discussion. A church that is truly Christian must adopt the best method to attain and disseminate truth. That means that it must open its doors to all who adopt its own ideal, of which one part is the love of truth; so it must place no barriers in the way of seeking truth.

It is remarkable how far the churches have advanced in recent decades toward this bold attitude.[2] But there will still

[1] A. C. McGiffert: *The Apostles' Creed* (New York: Charles Scribner's Sons, 1902).

[2] For an excellent account of this movement see W. M. Horton: *Theism and the Modern Mood* (New York: Harper & Brothers, 1930).

be many who hesitate to admit into the circle of optional opinions even the ideas of God and immortality, which have so often been regarded as the essential minimum of all religion. So we must recall that our analysis, if sound, has shown that no specific beliefs constitute the essential minimum of religion. The essential minimum, as Protestantism has emphasized since its inception, is an experience. Out of that experience there grows an ideal. The expression of that ideal is the essential religious activity. It becomes an attitude — the attitude of faith, which if well maintained constitutes faithfulness to the ideal.

Some kind of belief about the source and consequences of this experience is, inevitably, a part of the activity (thus of the attitude, or faith) that results from this experience. But it is plain that metaphysical explanations concerning its source, and hopes concerning its distant implications for another world, are not the most important part of this faith. The really important part for the present relations of that individual to others, and of others to him, is his understanding of what his religious experience implies regarding those human relations, and his willingness to follow the promptings of the reality discovered within his religious experience — the altruistic or disinterested will. This understanding and willingness constitute the religious ideal and attitude. For the enlightened Christian and for the humanist it is essentially the same. They *have* the one faith. It is only when they pay attention to what each thinks are its more far-reaching cognitive implications and content that differences appear.

Now when people have a common attitude to reality, a common faith — i.e., when they believe *in* the same ideal — it requires only that they communicate that faith or ideal to each other and recognize each other, for them to find themselves spiritually bound together in a psychological group, a communion of faith. When it is a religious faith that is thus communicated and recognized they become a church. If they subsequently discover differences within the intellectual content of their faith these constitute a certain divisive element within the spiritual group, a lesion of the spiritual body. But unless emphasized to the point of refusal of recognition they do not tear the psychological corporate whole asunder. The question, therefore, that the church has to face is whether the discovery of differences of belief on personal immortality and the divine transcendence justifies the destruction of the unity of the whole religious body in the pursuit of its common ideal. The early Christian church thought that loyalty to truth demanded that it do so. Surely two thousand years of history have sufficiently shown the error of that way of supporting truth. It becomes evident then that the church, in support of orthodoxy, should not cut off (refuse recognition to) those who are unorthodox even as to these beliefs, but should invite them to co-operate in loyalty to the common faith.

The word " faith " has been so often used with reference to an exclusively cognitive content, or belief, that perhaps some explanation of the usage here adopted is required. That usage is, I think, essentially in accord with the Christian concept, except when a certain dogmatism or careless emphasis upon the intellectual content distorts the fundamental notion. St. James vigorously rejected such intellectualism. Faith, he asserted, is something that can be demonstrated only by " works." It is no mere belief, for " the devils also believe, and tremble." [3] In the magnificent phrase of the Epistle to the Hebrews, it is " the substance of things hoped for, the evidence of things not seen," [4] which means, in the terminology of modern philosophy, that it is the realization of ideal values. For Jesus, faith was an attitude of trust in God that gives man the power to move mountains. For Paul, the *Chris-*

[3] Jas. 2:17–20.
[4] Heb. 11:1.

tian faith was, in particular, an attitude toward Christ that overcomes the destructive power of sin in the human heart. We shall have more to say, in another chapter, about faith, but these references are sufficient to show how secondary in it is the element of belief. Faith in God, or in Christ, or in the Christian and humanitarian ideal, like faith in a friend or in a bank, is an active attitude of the whole person toward the object in question, as an object of value; and it is based primarily upon a judgment concerning the value of that object.

THE TOLERATION OF ORTHODOXY

The fundamentalist revival that occurred in the first two decades of this century has already faded out. The Barthian movement [5] arose in the postwar pessimism of Germany, crossed the seas with the rising tide of post-Versailles disillusionment, and created an impression upon minds distressed by scenes of economic injustice and disorder. But its effect appears to be no more than to cause a wholesome re-examination of features of religion that the liberal theologians had been neglecting. Thus we may expect the spirit of toleration to continue to grow within the Christian church and, throughout the greater part of Protestantism at least, to find the barriers to free belief within the church continuously set aside.

But it is not enough that the orthodox become tolerant if the unorthodox remain intolerant. It is not likely that the theistic metaphysic and belief in immortality will disappear, for while it must be admitted that many of the arguments *for* these beliefs have been robbed of their cogency by the advance of science, it must also be admitted that the same advance is showing that science has no arguments against them. So if there is to be unity in the religious pursuit of the ideal the unorthodox must be prepared to manifest the same tolerance

[5] For a sympathetic account of this movement see Adolph Keller: *Karl Barth and Christian Unity* (New York: The Macmillan Co., 1933).

they have always asked of the orthodox. And that tolerance must not stop short of active co-operation. It is therefore necessary to examine the position from this angle also.

In his Terry Lectures [6] Professor Dewey maintained that historic Christianity, with its belief in the supernatural, is committed to an aristocratic and exclusive attitude toward those who do not share its beliefs, and also to such a reliance upon the supernatural that it tends to adopt a laissez faire attitude with respect to natural and human intervention in the social process in support of human values. The latter accusation seems to me to betray a strange ignorance or lack of appreciation of what the religious forces of the world have been doing, especially in the last quarter of a century, toward the solution of social problems; but with that aspect of the religious life we were concerned in the previous chapter. The assertion that Christianity must always divide the sheep from the goats according to their metaphysical beliefs we will take pains to refute. But, assuming that these charges against the orthodox are not true or should cease to be true, what then should be the attitude toward the church of those who, like Professor Dewey, " feel the stir of social emotion " and would devote themselves to that " common faith of mankind " which he has so finely stated?

" Were men and women actuated throughout the length and breadth of human relations with the faith and ardor that have at times marked historic religions the consequences would be incalculable. To achieve this faith and *élan* is no easy task." [7] Thus Dewey clearly recognizes the need and the fact that there is something in religion that gives a unique power to personality. But the way to achieve this dynamic and canalize it in the right direction is not to destroy the organization in which it is characteristically known to rise and

---

[6] *A Common Faith,* especially pp. 80–87.
[7] *Ibid.,* p. 81.

flourish. The unorthodox religionist must meet the more orthodox part way. Instead of calling upon the believer to give up cherished and helpful beliefs against which there is no valid scientific objection, he should respond to the believer's expression of welcome and tolerance wherever it is made. He should not demand that the believer in the supernatural give no expression to his beliefs, but should join in an organization where all may express their beliefs and all co-operate in all that they can find in common. Increasingly the Christian churches are letting down the barriers of creeds, making possible a fellowship of spiritual culture and a community of social service where each is free to speak the truth as he sees it and a wholesome respect for the opinions of others is shown by all. The response of unorthodox religious persons has as yet been slow. Yet the extension of this invitation and a willing response to it is the only way to the creation of that dynamic implementation of human ideals that is visualized in the quotation with which this paragraph begins.

It is the only way, first, because mutual respect for honest and intelligent opinion and open-minded seeking of truth is part of the ideal; and second, because no social ideal can be implemented unless it be first incorporated as the activating principle of a group of people who stand for it, publicly declare their adhesion, cultivate their own enthusiasm for it, train the oncoming generation in the knowledge and appreciation of it, and co-operatively seek to put it into effect. If an ideal contains nothing that is not accepted by everybody then it is either already achieved or utterly meaningless. " Woe unto you when all men shall speak well of you." If an ideal contains something that is good and true but not universally accepted then it will meet with opposition. And if it is in the vanguard of human progress it will meet with much opposition. It is not true liberalism to shrink from being a partisan. There is need, as Dewey says, for faith and ardor. But unless they form a party, an active striving group, acutely conscious of its distinctive goal, the faith and ardor are an ineffective flash in the pan. There must be a church, a church militant and, as far as possible, a church united.

If we would learn the psychological (i.e., the spiritual) conditions of the existence of such a church we must learn our lesson from history; and we must not scorn to take our place in the historic movement of religion, the historic church. This does not mean that anyone should bow to an authority that he believes wrong, or be silent on a concept he believes false. The church, if it is to be powerful, militant and united, must give freedom for expression of opinion, for independent forms of organization within it, and for large differences in form of corporate spiritual culture and worship. It can keep clear the unity of its central ideal and give it power by mutual recognition of the multitude of people of different types and points of view who uphold it, and yet develop a rich and varied life of individual and corporate expression. But organization and corporate expression there must be; and this expression must take the forms that have proved their power over the human mind throughout the history of religion. Ceremonial, symbol, witness in words, meditation and public speech we still must have. The modern attempt to develop a religious life without these is as crass as the modern attempt to write poetry without rhythm or rhyme and without metaphor, simile or verbal beauty. The spirit of religion, like the spirit of poetry, requires something more than that we should try to be clever.

THE CONDITIONS OF CORPORATE UNITY

(a) *Leadership.* — The conditions of group activity may be briefly stated as follows: (1) the possession of a common desire, purpose or interest; (2) the communication of this fact to each other and reciprocal recognition of the fact of association; [8] (3) a concrete objective and means to its attainment sufficiently clear to direct co-ordinated activity, or else a recognized leader whose words and example point to such concrete objectives as occasion rises; (4) a recognized organization or pattern for division of labor in the pursuit of the concrete objectives wherein the common interest is attained. On the basis of our previous analysis we may take the disinterested will to the good of others as the common interest that creates the religious association. But we have seen that this will is very vague and ill defined in most people, so that its implementation in pursuit of concrete objectives is extremely difficult. And even supposing that its general nature has been made fairly clear and is accepted in terms such as we have used, the kind of concrete objectives to be sought, the leadership to be followed and the organization needed are questions so difficult that differences as to both means and subsidiary ends are inevitable. But one fact becomes clear. Freedom of individual thought and the moral responsibility of the individual are a part of the goal. So organization for its attainment must be entirely free. Co-ordination must be sought for the sake of efficiency, but not at the cost of destroying that liberty of thought and freedom of conscience which are essential to the realization of the goal. The spontaneity and vigor that come from freedom of organization in the long run produce more power than a uniformity attained through suppression.

The chief practical problems therefore center on the means of communication and recognition and on the selection of concrete objectives and leadership. And here, I would sug-

[8] I use this term in the technical sense defined by R. M. McIver: *Community* (New York: The Macmillan Co., 1928), chap. 2 and p. 155. It is "a body of social beings as organised for the pursuit of some common interest or interests." As such it is distinguished from mere community, "the common life of social beings," and from an institution, which is merely "an established form of relation between social beings."

gest, is the great contribution to the cause of religion that has
been and may still be made by historic Christianity. We shall
return again [9] to an interpretation of the significance of the
work of Christ, but enough may be said here to show the significance of the Christian recognition of his leadership. The
early Christians saw the nature of God revealed in him as in
no other person in history. And whether God be merely immanent or also transcendent this insight must be recognized
as sound. Jesus' place in history is unique. The richest and
noblest succession of religious leaders and teachers in human
history, that of the Hebrew prophets, culminated in his personality. The great religious leaders who have adequately
and unprejudicedly known him, in all the centuries since
his day, from Paul and Marcion to Mahatma Gandhi, have
found in him both inspiration and guidance. The particular
concrete objectives of religious effort must change with time
and place. No set terms can define them. But the broad
principles Jesus enunciated, and the magnificent example of
his life, illuminate our successive problems and, in reflection,
define for us our successive goals, in a way that no other concrete object or person can do. Further, no mode of succession of local and temporary leaders is so likely to be sound as
that of a group that keeps clearly in mind the picture of Christ
as *the* leader and selects its subsidiary leaders by their likeness
to him. In so far as the church has failed to select well its
particular objectives and leadership, its failure is due not to
its recognition of the supreme leadership of Christ, but rather
to its inattention to the meaning of an acknowledgment of his
leadership, or to sheer lack of understanding of the persons
and situations involved.

The validity of the honor thus paid to Jesus in no way
depends upon theological conceptions of the peculiar nature
of his personality, still less upon traditions concerning his

[9] Chap. 11.

birth. These beliefs should be treated in the spirit of scientific investigation and broad tolerance, but they do not affect the question of his leadership. That depends upon his actual place in religious history and the contribution of his life and teaching to religious thought and work. It rests also upon the actual, practical, psychological value found in giving him that place. The religion of intellectual people tends to be too coldly intellectual even for their own best personal development. For the general community, whose value judgments arise out of their concrete feelings rather than out of abstract principles, such intellectualism is hopelessly inadequate. The richness and strength of human feeling can, in most of us and most of the time, be aroused only by concrete objects.[10] In Christ the ideals of love and service, of sacrifice and forgiveness, of kindness and courage, take on flesh and blood. His stature is heroic. His personality has proved itself capable of kindling a like response. And the day has not yet passed, if ever it can, when the cause of humanity calls for sentiments cast in the heroic mold.

(b)   *The Means of Communication.* — Primitive peoples did not attempt to put into words the hopes and ideals that vaguely stirred them. For them, as Professor Marett says, religion was danced out rather than thought out. It is no disparagement of the value of thought to say that the elemental experiences out of which religion arises are "feelings that do lie too deep for words." The primitive expressed them in gesture, and gesture became formalized in ceremonial. If we would retain the broadest possible foundations of religious unity, the simplest and most elementary communication of our religious experience and common ideal must also be in the language of gesture. Words are too specific. They miss

[10] The great difference in strength of concrete and abstract sentiments is well brought out by W. McDougall: *An Introduction to Social Psychology* (rev. ed.; Boston: John W. Luce & Co., 1927) .

the deeper half of the meaning of that which is felt and place all the emphasis upon our interpretations of it, which are always more or less dubious. For this reason the unity of the faith can never be expressed in creeds. Creeds are divisive, and they are inevitably outgrown. They are as wrong as idolatry, and for the same reason. The idol gives too definite a form to the conception of God of those who first devise it. It is an inadequate instrument for the presentation of the idea; and the idea it presents in fixed outline, to rivet upon the future, is always an inadequate idea. Like the creed, it is divisive and perpetuates error. But the language of gesture, if simple, is not definite enough to perpetuate error. Moreover, it can be vivid enough to express the feelings that words cannot utter. If simple, vivid and appropriate it can be handed on from generation to generation; and each successive age reads into it the new meaning it has wrought out of its own religious experience, and reads out of it the continuity of experience of religious reality in every age and every land.

It is not always realized that in the primitive Christian church that communication and recognition which expressed the unity of its faith and bound individuals together in the community of one brotherhood, one religious society, was expressed in the symbolism of gesture rather than that of words. It is not exactly known just how and when its two principal ordinances originated, but before the church had completed the writing of the documents that it later gathered together to form the New Testament these ordinances had become so firmly established that, rightly or wrongly, their institution was attributed directly to Jesus himself. Thus they long antedated the formulation of the first creed. The informal expressions of acceptance of Jesus as Lord and Christ found in the New Testament cannot be regarded as a creed.[11] In the

[11] The request for a brief creedal statement prior to baptism in Acts 8:37 is a late interpolation.

book of Acts it is obvious that it was by the act of baptism itself (a symbolic gesture) that the new convert declared his faith and the church recognized him as one of its own.

What gave the significance to the act was that it was done "in the name" of Jesus. The convert thus took on his name and received the recognition of the church as a kindred spirit, a member of the new religious society. Thereafter he periodically reaffirmed his faith, and joined in mutual recognition of his brethren in the fellowship of Christ, by taking part in a solemn ceremonial meal, symbolic of the "communion" existing between the brethren and between them and their Master. Thus the language of gesture first declared the faith and later continuously reaffirmed it. And the meaning of these solemn gestures was contained, not in any words of explanation, but in the personality of him toward whom they were directed. They were acts of affirmation of the religious *leadership* of Christ, of the adoption of his ideals. Simple and significant in themselves, they were made eloquent by his personality. As expressions of that community of ideal and purpose whereby a number of individuals may be made to feel their religious unity and inspired to work together in the service of a common concrete ideal, they, taken together with the personality of the leader in whose name they were performed, were peculiarly appropriate.

The church at that stage was not yet an organization possessing common metaphysical opinions. It was rather a group of persons bound together by common hopes and ideals which they found expressed in the personality of a great leader. They did not demand unity of opinion among themselves. As Professor McGiffert and other scholars have shown, they did not have it.[12] What they expected of each other was loy-

12 Cf. McGiffert: *The God of the Early Christians* (New York: Charles Scribner's Sons, 1924). It is here shown that there was no clear and consolidated opinion in the early church even on such important doctrines as the unity of God and the divinity of Christ.

alty to their leader in action, and the honoring of his name and expression of their common religious ideal in public ceremonial. The tragedy that underlies the church's disunity is the effort that was later made, not merely to formulate the thought of God and of Christ more fully and exactly, but to insist that the acceptance of these verbal symbols, the creeds, should be a condition of admission to the symbols of gesture whereby loyalty to the common ideals embodied in the personality of the leader was declared. If the church had kept open access to its ordinances, independent of the acceptance of creeds, it would have saved itself much of the tragedy of division and the shame and injury of its heresy hunts.

It is therefore fairly clear that, without a departure from the spirit of historic Christianity — indeed rather through a restoration of its early spirit and practice — the conditions of unity with liberty within the church can be fulfilled. It is plain, of course, that before the ancient ceremonies can function again in this way they must be cleared of the magical beliefs that have been associated with them. This, however, would be only a part of that broadening of understanding which is necessary before a church is ready to remove all creeds from its requirements for membership; and in many churches this attitude to both creeds and ordinances is already attained. With similar tolerance, and a proper recognition of the real values of ancient tradition in ceremonial, it should be possible to secure sufficient agreement on the time and mode of performance of the ordinances to make them real expressions of that unity of the Christian community, amidst wide freedom in belief and action, which offers the brightest hope for the future of the church and the world.

THE CONDITIONS OF CORPORATE VITALITY: PUBLIC EXPRESSION

Here is an inspiring vision of Christendom, united in one great brotherhood around the personality of Jesus, welded into unity of purpose by a common loyalty to the ideal, the way of life, embodied in his person. It would be a brotherhood in which each was free to think and to speak his thoughts on the deepest things of life, and within which groups would be free to organize their religious and social life to meet their differing needs. Such freedom would not interfere with unity, for it would be a part of the common purpose that all should thus be free. Further, all would express, in acknowledged common symbols, their faith in a common leader as source and inspiration of common ideals, and would unite in many ways in common practical programs for the implementation of those ideals. Organization and institutionalization are inevitable if group purposes are to be put into execution, but they can be so designed as not to restrict essential freedom of thought and worship. To create that sense of unity which makes for the reality of brotherhood all that is necessary is that there should be a genuine common purpose, periodic common witness to that purpose in terms that all understand and appreciate, and real co-operation in its practical execution. From such basic unity there may grow a superstructure with great freedom of form.

Today we have freedom of form in the superstructure and, to a larger extent than is generally realized, an underlying unity of spirit. What is needed is to give more concrete form and expression to the underlying unity and more explicit recognition to the rights of freedom.[13] Such unity cannot be achieved by trying to tear ourselves out of our roots in history, though the history of Christendom has for centuries been divisive. It can be achieved only by digging to the depths of the underlying unity of Christendom. In that underlying

[13] As a practical program this must, of course, begin with the liberal religious groups' working out their own problems of unity and adopting a positive and vigorous program. By their active work and example of fraternal recognition of all other religious groups the spirit of unity and freedom would be spread.

unity the Jew shares with the Christian and, with the growing recognition among Jews [14] of the significance of their great contribution to the world in the person of Christ, it is not too much to hope that they too may yet share in that united devotion to the spirit of one great leader which would make one brotherhood of all Christendom and set its face toward the creation of one brotherhood for the world.[15]

But the realization of such a vision, while it needs clear thinking and tolerance, requires something more also. Such brotherhood is not merely an intellectual state of mind, to be achieved by learning and logic; it is a dynamic attitude that must incorporate feeling, habit and will. It is here that so much liberal religious thinking fails. It begins and ends with thinking. It fails to touch the life of feeling and practice. If there is to be real human brotherhood it must consist of personalities that have grown in an atmosphere of brotherhood. If an ideal is to come alive in personalities they must breathe its expression in their daily associations. And if they are to do that they must periodically come together in groups for its expression. For clear thinking one must think alone and unemotionally. But the ideal endorsed by clear thinking can be socially implemented, it can be made to grip and mold the personality even of the thinker, only by being given pub-

[14] For example, see C. G. Montefiore: *Liberal Judaism* (New York: The Macmillan Co., 1903) ; also *Synoptic Gospels* (rev. ed., 2 vols.; Macmillan, 1927) , especially II, 594.

[15] It is not arrogant for Christians to hope that the Christian religious brotherhood may become all-embracing. Brotherhood is a personal relationship and it must find its center of unity in loyalty to a common leader. No metaphysical conception, such as the idea of God, will suffice. No succession of contemporaries could attain the required prestige. And no historic personage could fill the role except Christ. Outside of Asia his place is already acknowledged, and he is gaining increasing recognition in that, his own, continent. The development of a new loyalty to Christ as religious leader of the world would not involve any disloyalty to teachers such as Mohammed, Confucius and Gautama. It would be incompatible only with religions that are narrowly nationalistic or otherwise exclusive.

lic expression. Religious idealism and other forms of idealism can be refined in quiet meditation, but they acquire power by being expressed in company. This is the reason for public worship. Where it is neglected religion wilts and fades. If religion is to be revived as a power to instill into the community a sense of brotherhood, of social solidarity and of Christian idealism, it cannot be done without measures that will call the multitude back into the organized worship of the churches. To wish, as does Professor Dewey,[16] for the manifestation of a typically religious faith and devotion throughout the length and breadth of human relations, while neglecting the typically religious means of spiritual culture, is wishful thinking of a very futile kind.

But if public religious devotion is to perform its function well it must not merely be urged as a duty. It must be carefully planned to meet varying human needs. Here, as in thought, there must be ample room for individuality and for different types of personality to find, among those of like mind, the kind of spiritual exercise most helpful to their own souls. Those of refined sensibilities must not be shocked at the apparent crudity of the religious expressions found helpful by those of coarser or tougher stripe. Nor should they seek to impose upon them forms of worship lacking in the emotional vigor and strong appeal that they need. Religious unity does not require that the whole form of worship be everywhere the same. Even in the performance of those symbolic ceremonies which, as the fundamental language of mutual recognition within the religious society, ought to be universal, there must be wide liberty. It is necessary only that there be sufficient uniformity to secure mutual recognition. But in other phases of worship no such conformity to common patterns is even desirable. What is desirable is only that those means of spiritual culture be adopted which shall

[16] *A Common Faith*, p. 81.

be found most helpful to those concerned. So far as this is concerned, all that I would wish to say further here is to point out some general considerations concerning the place of art in spiritual culture.

RELIGIOUS EXPRESSION AND THE AESTHETIC EXPERIENCE

When we speak of the use of art for some ulterior purpose, even that of spiritual culture, we enter a field of controversy in the theory of art. Between the advocates of " art for art's sake " and those who would regiment the artists as instruments of social propaganda there are fierce battles waging. Into this strife we need not enter, except so far as to claim that art is a part of life, not apart from life, and that, like everything organic, it can contribute to the wholesome functioning of the whole and be the better for it. It is art in isolation that is artificial, not art in functional relation to the rest of life. The distinction between nature and art is not really fundamental. All true art must be natural, and nature is by no means devoid of art. That which is artificial is unnatural only because it is bad art. The artificial is something intended to have the appearance of art, but it is not produced or enjoyed naturally as an expression of life. It is an imitation of art for the sake of money or praise or for some other ulterior motive. The true work of art is a natural outpouring of the soul, and it is an activity that must be an end in itself. The artist may need money and may take money for his work. But if he works merely for money he destroys his artistic soul, just as surely as the minister, if he merely serves for money, destroys his spiritual life. The pursuit of beauty, like the pursuit of holiness, is the pursuit of a *spiritual* value; and it turns to gall and bitterness if it is made subservient to Mammon or to any lesser thing.

Art, then, is both spiritual and natural. It is found in the homes and the cathedrals of men and it is displayed in the song of a bird and the prancing of a horse. Nor is it a paradox to see this manifestation of the spiritual even in the humbler creatures around us, for the life of man is only a finer development of the life below him. But of all creatures it is man who is the supreme artist. Art is not only the flower of the finest civilizations; it is among the lively interests of the humblest races of mankind. No student of primitive man can fail to be impressed by the amount of attention that people who are constantly under pressure for the very means of existence devote to these labors that produce no bread. Weapons, utensils, clothes, houses, canoes are everywhere adorned with pictures and designs; dance and drama are elaborately developed; as much ingenuity is shown in the construction of musical instruments as in that of weapons of war and the chase. And to no phase of life has art been more assiduously applied than to religion. From the primitive to the highest civilizations, it is on his religion that man has lavished the highest products of his artistic genius. Art is thus shown to be a manifestation of characteristics deeply rooted in human nature. When we consider its essentially spiritual character and remember how closely, all through the ages, it has been associated with religion we see that it is a sphere of human activity which no program of spiritual culture can afford to neglect.

But when we inquire more closely as to the place which art should occupy in religious life and work we find ourselves in a realm of thought in which there is still much confusion. The problem of the nature of the beautiful was discussed to some extent by Plato and Aristotle, but was not very seriously investigated until that task was undertaken by Immanuel Kant. Kant's theory definitely connected aesthetic experience with the activity of the imagination and suggested that it was further dependent upon the harmony of the object with the cognitive activity that contemplates it, and of the imagination with the rest of the activity of the mind. This theory, however, is obviously too intellectualistic to account for all the facts, and it was largely ignored in the romantic era, which followed close upon Kant's own age. In more recent times Ruskin has preached the prophetic mission of art. Croce has interpreted it as self-expression. Lipps has attributed it to the development of sympathetic insight and feeling. Among leading recent investigators we find that Professor Prall [17] has claimed that it depends on a distinctive type of highly active and peculiarly heightened awareness, and Professor Collingwood [18] has returned to a theory somewhat akin to Kant's. For my own theory [19] I am indebted to both these writers.

These two thinkers call attention to two different types of aesthetic experience: Prall to the enjoyment of purely sensuous beauty, such as color and melody, and Collingwood to the higher, more intellectual types of beauty, such as are found in poetry and drama. Collingwood points to two requirements for beauty in the object: it must stimulate the imagination, and it must direct a self-harmonious process of imagination. The capacity of the subject to appreciate the beauty of an object therefore depends on three things: first, on his imaginative capacity; second, on his readiness to respond to the suggestions of the beautiful object; third, on his capacity to dismiss from his mind any *practical* concern with the object, any concern with his own particular desires, with truth and reality or even with moral interests, and to allow the aesthetic object to have its own way with his imaginative responses. Thus we enjoy the beauty of an ob-

[17] D. W. Prall: *Aesthetic Judgment* (New York: Thomas Y. Crowell Co., 1929).

[18] R. G. Collingwood: *Outlines of a Philosophy of Art* (New York: Oxford University Press, 1925).

[19] See my *Reality and Value* (New Haven, Conn.: Yale University Press, 1937), chap. 10.

ject to the fullest when we give ourselves up to contemplation of it, losing ourselves in the imaginary world that it
creates for us.

Now imagination, we may point out, is an incomplete
cognitive activity, yet a very important one. The complete
act of constructive thought must begin with the creation of
imagery and the weaving of this into significant patterns of
thought; but it remains incomplete unless it passes on to
test the truth or reality of these patterns by reference to previously known truths or present experienced fact. In aesthetic contemplation, however, we are not concerned with
truth or reality, but only with the self-consistency of the web
of imagination being woven. Yet nature rewards us for this
activity with the joy of aesthetic experience. The reason for
this would seem to be that imaginative activity, so long as
it is self-consistent, is activity of a kind which contributes to
the realization of the fuller values of life in the discovery of
truth. No student of the methods of science can fail to recognize the importance of what we call the scientific imagination in the weaving of hypotheses, and thus in the search for
knowledge.

These higher types of aesthetic experience are then to be
explained as obtained in the exercise of an *incomplete but
important cognitive activity*, the incomplete act of thought
which is imagination. But there is a form of cognitive activity, lower than that of thought, which we call perception.
And here, too, we can distinguish two stages of operation.
The first is the sheer awareness of sensory quality, such as
color or sound. This, as Prall emphasizes, can be a very active and intense process. But perception is not complete until we go on to give meaning to this color or sound as indication of the presence and nature of real things. In true and
complete perception we never merely perceive green or blue;
we perceive green grass or blue sky. However, in aesthetic

appreciation, Prall says, the elementary activity of sheer awareness of color quality or tone quality is greatly heightened, while we become less concerned with the realities or objects which the colors or sounds present to us. Then, providing there is an intrinsic harmony within the sensory data presented, the experience is one of beauty, the harmonies being smoothness of line, balance of form, harmony of musical tones and of colors.

Prall here, I think, calls attention to something that is lacking in Collingwood's account of aesthetic experience; for Collingwood scarcely does justice to our appreciation of sheer sensuous beauty, though his theory is much more nearly adequate than Prall's if we had to take one theory to the exclusion of the other. They can be brought together by the recognition that in both cases aesthetic experience is seen to rise in the harmonious exercise of an incomplete though valuable cognitive activity, i.e., imagination or incomplete thought, and sensory awareness or incomplete perception. Delight is felt in these activities because, when thus exercised incompletely and for their own sake, they can attain a greater degree of intensity and continuity. But this aesthetic delight is felt only so long as this exercise is not only intense but harmonious.

In much of our aesthetic experience, of course, both sensory appreciation and imaginative activity are at work together, the one helping the other. But it should be noted that the higher forms of aesthetic enjoyment are to be attributed, as in Collingwood's theory, to the imagination. The weakness of Prall's theory is shown in his inability to give any satisfactory account of the higher types of beauty, such as that of poetry. Sensory appreciation, we may agree, is an important part of aesthetic experience and can be enjoyed alone and for its own sake, as perhaps it sometimes is in listening to music which has no words and conjures up no pictures. But the most important aspects of the beautiful are those which call into vivid play the activity of imagination.

From this analysis of the nature and conditions of our experience of the beautiful we pass to the question of the place of aesthetic activity in the cultivation of the spiritual life. But it will first be necessary to say something of the general features involved in the growth of character.

AESTHETIC EXPERIENCE AND SPIRITUAL CULTURE

Character consists of an organization of habits and sentiments which overlays the native endowment of impulsive tendencies. But habits are more than mere motor reactions of the conditioned reflex type. Or rather, such motor habits exist but explain only the skill with which an action is performed, not the motive which prompts the action. Habit, in the sense of an acquired motive, is due to the acquirement of *meaning* on the part of the object, especially the attribution of values to the object. The burned child avoids the fire, or at least approaches it more cautiously, because the fire has come to *mean* for it "something that burns." It is because objects acquire meaning for us in this way that we build up our habitual reaction-tendencies in relation to all the familiar things of our world. And it should be noticed that we respond to an object in accord with its acquired meaning without needing explicitly to recall that meaning; e.g., we avoid stepping into water because we know it is wet, although we do not need to think of that fact explicitly in order for its known meaning to affect our reaction. Thus we step aside from the puddle without thinking of the wetness and yet we are perfectly sure that the reason why we stepped aside is because we *know* that water is wet. Similarly a host of objects have for us acquired meanings of which we rarely stop to think, and which we would probably find difficult to recall, but which nevertheless affect our conduct in regard to them. This is so in all our normal behavior as well as in those abnormal cases where certain elements of meaning attributed to an object are repressed.

Character, however, consists not only in habits, but in something of a more far-reaching nature which many psychologists, following A. F. Shand, call " sentiments." These are love, hate, and respect.[20] They are usually regarded as merely very complex types of habit, but seem to me to be better explicable, along lines suggested by William James, as due to the development of the idea of the self. Habits depend on the acquirement of meaning on the part of objects. Sentiments are due to acquirement of meaning on the part of self. It was a very valuable insight of the great Harvard psychologist, much neglected by the stimulus-response theorists, that the idea of the self tends to enlarge to include other persons within it. We grow to identify ourselves with others so that their pleasures are our pleasures, their pains our pains, their triumphs and their shame ours too. For such others we seek good as we do for ourselves; we fear and fight against their evil as we do our own. They are our larger self, and at our best we put our larger self before our narrower self.

This enlargement of the self to gather others into it is the ground of the attitude we commonly call " love." It is distinctly a growth of *meaning* in the idea of the self. Its antithesis is hatred — a development in which a person comes to think of himself as a being whose good is wrought by another's pain or suffering, and one to whom it is an ill that a certain other person should have cause to rejoice. Hatred is too sweeping to be explained, like a habit, as merely the growth of a certain meaning attached to the other person. When a hatred is formed it is the hater's own idea of himself that has changed. Yet another feature of our typical attitudes is that of respect. This too is sentiment rather than habit,

20 For a fuller discussion cf. my *The Mind in Action*, chap. 6.

in that it depends on the development of the idea of the self. We learn to attach to ourselves certain ideas of rank and worth in various scales of value, and we attach similar ideas to others. Respect is the valuation of a self (our own or another) as having the rank or scale of worth it ought to have, or the valuation of some other self as having great worth in comparison to our own. That evaluation of one's own worth which we call self-respect is of very great importance for character.

Now this growth of meaning, on the part of both external objects and the self, depends upon experience. But "experience" is a broad term. For our purposes here we may recognize three types: (a) experience in actual relation with persons and things; (b) the experience of hearing things talked about (and hearing ourselves talked about) in a way which suggests to our minds that those things possess certain qualities or that we ourselves possess certain qualities; (c) imaginative experience. Experience in the first sense, which we may distinguish as experience proper, is, of course, the greatest of all teachers and tends most strongly and vividly to affect the meanings which we give to things and the development of the idea of the self. Yet the range of this type of experience is very limited compared to that of the other two, to which we must, therefore, pay more particular attention.

The second type of experience we may call hearsay or, better, suggestion. It is really extraordinary how habitual attitudes are instilled into people by the mere fact that certain ideas are constantly suggested to them. The power of sheer constant repetition of an idea is well recognized by advertisers, who make great use of it as a means of cultivating the habits of their customers. When the suggestions come from persons and institutions of high prestige, such as school and teacher, church and minister, they are very powerful. Yet attitudes (whether habit or sentiment) which have been cultivated by suggestion can be unmade by suggestion. Everyone knows how readily the moral and religious attitudes of a young person, instilled by careful and constant suggestion in the home and the home church, can be broken down by countersuggestion when the young person goes away from the home environment to college or to a job in another town or city. The trouble with the attitudes formed in this way is that the values which the person has been taught to attribute to the objects concerned have not been personally felt; they have formed no part of actual lived experience. Further, suggestion, while it can cultivate habits and form sentiments of respect, can do little to formulate the great sentiments of love and loyalty which are the most powerful and far-reaching elements in formed character. Love and loyalty grow only with the *activity* of the self, especially in actually living through the experiences in which it performs the deeds of love and loyalty. Likewise, any real strength of habit, against the influences of countersuggestion, comes only when the original formative suggestions are in some way frequently acted out. The problem of cultivating the higher loves and loyalties and finer habits of life in any strength is therefore that of finding spheres of action in which they can be displayed and their values actually felt.

It is here that the third type of experience comes to our aid. That which we cannot live through and experience in actuality we often can go through in imagination; and if the imagination be sufficiently strongly cultivated the values concerned can be very deeply felt and a strong impression made. The power of suggestion is therefore greatly intensified if it can stir the imagination. It is here that the fine arts come to our aid in the building of character. The effect of a work of art is to stimulate the imagination. It lures us to give ourselves up to the influence of its suggestions, to fly with it into a world of imagination and *live*, with its own peculiar type of reality, in a new world, thinking the thoughts of the artist, entering into the experience of other minds, discovering and feeling for ourselves the values involved in experiences and activities that have never been ours in actual life. It stimulates us into an intensity of activity in living these strange experiences through, though it is only the activity of imagination. And it rewards us for this activity with the experience of the beautiful. But if the imaginary world into which we have thus entered be one of high and holy thoughts, of lofty deeds and fine resolves nobly executed, then it rewards us with something else as well. Because we have been made to feel for ourselves the glory of a high devotion, even though it has been only in imagination, those ideals take a stronger grip upon us. Art has enabled us to see their reality.

This is the function of art in religion. And to produce this effect in the community is one of the prime purposes of the public services of the church. It is not the only purpose. Combined with it are those of instruction and devotion, public pledge and witness, mutual support and fellowship. Nor is art the only medium. There is power in the silence of a Quaker meeting. There is virtue in the logic of sound discourse. It is in the combination of all these things in ways empirically found most helpful by different groups of people that the common religious life can best be cultivated. Nor must private meditation and devotion be neglected. There are few, however, who have the energy to maintain a private religious culture without the public. Above all, the nurture of the religious life of youth can be maintained only in the religious community, for religious growth is a process of *social* orientation. Thus it is true not only that the great society needs the religious devotion of the individual, but also that the religious life of the individual needs that of the religious community.

PART III

INTERPRETATION OF THEORY

The Nature of Man

THE HEBREW BELIEF IN IMMORTALITY

THUS FAR we have been able to elucidate our problems without raising metaphysical questions. It has been sufficient to draw light from history and from the critical analysis of various forms of religious experience. Some of the psychological and historical data are vague, but in so far as our analysis and history have been correct we have thus far appealed only to fact. And it is certainly of very great importance that so much of religious life and thought should (if our facts are correct) be open to validation in this purely empirical manner.

If this much of our argument is accepted it establishes a wide basis of agreement for a vivid and valuable co-operative religious life without the attaining of agreement on further philosophical questions concerning the divine transcendence and the destiny of the soul. Yet these questions of religious belief call for an answer, partly because differences of opinion upon them hinder perfect co-operation of religious people, partly for their intrinsic interest, but chiefly because there are certain values enshrined in a rational, positive faith in these doctrines which are lost if we feel logically forced to surrender them. So we turn our attention now to an inquiry into these further questions of the interpretation of our religious experience. We shall deal first with that of immortality, although the positive grounds of belief in it rest on a prior belief in the divine transcendence. The reason for this apparently reversed procedure is that, in considering the *possibility* of im-

mortality, we shall be chiefly concerned with an analysis of
the nature of personality; and this must necessarily be undertaken before we pass on to any further consideration of that
element within personality which we have seen to be the
foundation of the idea of God.

The primitive belief in the soul and its survival of the
body was, as we have seen, a piece of primitive psychology
usually unconnected with belief in moral and religious rewards. The soul itself was simply a refined form of matter,
such as breath or shade, and its life in and around the grave or
in some special abode of the dead was generally pictured as
poor and dull. The early Hebrews shared these typical primitive beliefs, as witnessed by many Old Testament passages. A
typical description is contained in the following prophetic
address to the king of Babylon:

Sheol from beneath is moved for thee to meet thee at thy coming: it stirreth up the dead for thee, even all the chief ones of the
earth; it hath raised up from their thrones all the kings of the
nations. All they shall speak and say unto thee, Art thou also
become weak as we? art thou become like unto us? [1]

Neither is the lot of the righteous any better, as is indicated
by the following lines from a hymn of praise attributed to
the good king Hezekiah: " For the grave cannot praise thee,
death cannot celebrate thee: they that go down into the pit
cannot hope for thy truth. The living, the living, he shall
praise thee as I do this day." [2]

That no religious significance attached to the afterlife is
strongly indicated in the latter passage and in many others.
Indeed, as the tone of Hebrew religion rises the belief in the
future life fades. Many passages echo the pessimism of Job:
" So man lieth down and riseth not: till the heavens be no
more they shall not awake, nor be raised out of their sleep." [3]

[1] Isa. 14:9–10.   [2] Isa. 38:18–19.   [3] Job 14:12.

The whole significance of religion is attached to the life on earth. Man reaps his full reward here for his good and evil deeds. The problem of evil, as we saw in an earlier chapter,[4] was largely met by the survival of the primitive notion of collective responsibility. When this false ethic was condemned by later prophets and the notion of individual responsibility gained ascendancy it could still be assumed, as by Job's comforters, that if an apparently righteous man suffered it indicated that he was really a secret sinner. However, as confidence in the power and goodness of Jehovah grows there begin to appear passages asserting a faith, or at least a hope, that God had something better than the silence of the grave in store for his faithful servants. "The fool and the brutish together perish, . . . They are appointed as a flock for Sheol; . . . But God will redeem my soul from the power of Sheol: for he shall receive me."[5]

Yet, even when we have made the most of such passages as this, we still are forced to recognize that the religion of the Old Testament at its best was a religion without a faith in immortality. And the religion of the Old Testament prophets, it must be acknowledged, was one of the most significant and fruitful of all human history. However, lest too much be inferred from this, it must be remembered how inadequate was their conception of the problem of evil. In spite of the abandonment of the notion of collective responsibility, they were so much concerned with what they believed to be God's dealings with the nation as a whole that they were often blind to the injustices suffered by individuals. He was surely not a very good observer who wrote: "I have been young, and now am old; yet have I not seen the righteous forsaken, nor his seed begging bread."[6] The Hebrews' trust in Jehovah was for this life and it was for his provision of material goods that they chiefly praised him.

---

[4] Chap. 4.   [5] Ps. 49:10, 14, 15 (R. V.).   [6] Ps. 37:25.

But as the tragedy of the nation deepened in captivity upon captivity, and as the sense of Jehovah's care became less material and more a matter of inner spiritual strength, the conviction grew not only that God had some better lot in preparation for his people as a whole, but that all his deserving children should live to share it. Thus, in the wisdom literature and in the apocalyptic literature of the time between the Old and New Testaments, there is a steady growth of the faith in immortality. This was not conceived as a mere spiritual survival. The Hebrews nowhere developed a belief in the necessary immortality of the soul. It was rather to a resurrection of the body that they looked, and to a new and glorified earthly life. The belief was not universal. It was rejected by the Sadducees at the time of Jesus, but accepted by the Pharisees. What is important, however, is that it is not a philosophical conception nor one based on theoretical grounds, but a distinctly religious conception growing out of a sublime faith in the goodness and power of God.

It is this faith, somewhat modified by Greek philosophy, that was later incorporated into Christianity. Though opposed to the Pharisees for their rigidity and exclusiveness, Jesus defended their teaching in this respect. And he rested his own conviction squarely on his conception of the nature of God. " He is not the God of the dead, but of the living." [7]

THE GREEK THEORY OF THE SOUL

The early Greeks, like the Hebrews, shared the primitive conception of the survival of the soul, and for them too it was a dismal state of being. " I would sooner be the hireling servant of the most penurious man alive," says Achilles, " than the ruler over all the kingdoms of the dead." [8] But in the classical period this primitive belief gives way, on the one hand to skepticism, particularly among the followers of De-

[7] Mark 12:27.   [8] *Odyssey*, Bk. XI, ll. 484 ff.

mocritus and Epicurus, and on the other hand to a high belief
in the immortality of the soul. Among the philosophers this
latter doctrine owed its adoption to Socrates and Plato, but
they in turn had been influenced by the mystery religions
which were spreading the belief among the common people.

The earliest influence of this kind in Greece was the Eleu-
sinian mysteries, but the chief, undoubtedly, was the cult of
Dionysus,[9] especially as developed by the Orphic sects. In
its Phrygian home this was a wild and horrid orgy by which
the worshiper achieved an ecstatic condition in which he believed he obtained union with the god and thus a share in
his immortal life. This suggestion was taken up, purified,
reinterpreted and ennobled by the Orphic brotherhoods,
among the early leaders of which, if not the founder, was the
philosopher Pythagoras. The experience of ecstasy suggested the soul's independence of the body, and the idea of its
union with the god suggested its divine origin. Its present
state was then interpreted by the Orphic religion as due to a
prenatal sinful defilement, and its salvation was to be achieved
by the ceremonial purifications of the cult.

The essential difference between the Greek and the Hebrew-Christian conceptions of immortality is that the former
arose chiefly out of reflection on a mystical ecstasy and the
latter out of reflection on the deeper problems of the moral
life and a lofty conception of the divine goodness and power.[10]
The result is that the Greek conception does not connect
salvation directly with any inner change of the moral life.
The sin from which it delivers is a generalized sense of sin
attributed to the prenatal stage, and its mode of cleansing is

[9] " The worship of Dionysus must have sown the first seed of belief in an
immortal life of the soul." — Erwin Rohde: *Psyche,* translated by W. B. Hillis
(New York: Harcourt, Brace & Co., 1925) , p. 255.

[10] For an excellent exposition of the Greek mystery religions and their relation to Christian beliefs cf. S. Angus: *The Mystery Religions and Christianity*
(New York: Charles Scribner's Sons, 1928) .

chiefly ceremonial. This is so in spite of the fact that the Orphics did prescribe an ethical rule of life and, especially in later times, required that their initiates be men of good character. The most important result of this difference in the origin of the belief, however, was that in defense of the doctrine the Greek philosophers appealed, not to their moral experience and their sense of loving communion with God and trust in his goodness, but to psychological grounds. These emphasized the distinction between soul and body, and suggested a necessary and universal immortality instead of a new life made possible by spiritual development attained in this life. It was the prestige of these Greek philosophical concepts that shaped the later development of the Christian doctrine and the general lines of the apologetic by which it has been defended.

For the Hebrew, the early Greek and the primitive alike the soul was but a fine form of matter. It was the great contribution of Socrates to have recognized that the distinction between the mental and the physical involves more than this. We cannot now endorse the form in which he stated the distinction, nor all the arguments with which he and his great disciple, Plato, supported it, nor all the implications they drew from it. But the fact that experience here presents us with an irreducible difference, which demands the drawing of some clear distinction in our thought, is one that no sound philosophy can ignore. The discovery was joyfully applied by Socrates to the elucidation of the new concept of the soul which the mysteries were popularizing and which his own mystical nature (indicated by his well known belief in his own guidance by a familiar spirit) inclined him to accept. In the *Phaedo* he jocularly replies to Crito's question, " How shall we bury you? " with confident good humor: " As you please, only you must catch me first." But then he reveals that this distinction between body and mind lies at the root of his belief when he adds: " My friends, I cannot convince Crito that I am the Socrates who has been conversing with you and arranging his arguments in order. He thinks that I am the body which he will presently see a corpse, and he asks how he is to bury me."

This discovery of Socrates was made in the realm of logic. It turns upon the fact that, while all physical events are transitory and particular, the mind grasps truths that are timeless and ideas that are general. All the more important arguments for immortality that Plato puts into the mouth of Socrates turn on this point. The arguments are vitiated by two false assumptions: first, that the capacity of the soul, or mind, to discover universal ideas and necessary truths while observing a world that apparently consists only of particular, temporal facts, can be explained only as a process of recollection of perfections experienced in a previous existence; second, that the distinction between the mental and the physical thus indicated must be one of " essence " or " substance," and not merely a difference of process, activity or function. Aristotle, Plato's great successor, gave up the former assumption, and also the latter so far as it concerned those parts of the soul which man shares in common with plants and animals — merely vital and sensitive processes. But he retained the distinction of substance as holding between the rational part of man's soul and his body.[11] From this Aquinas drew the Scholastic doctrine of the immaterial, and therefore indivisible and indestructible, soul. And under the same influence Descartes put forward his theory of two substances — matter, which has extension but no thought or experience, and mind, which has thought or experience but is unextended.

[11] De Anima, III, 5.

BODY AND MIND

This dualism of substances, spiritual and material, which has its roots in Plato and came to full florescence in Descartes, was a plant that produced bitter fruit. It set the problem of the relation of body and mind in an insoluble form. How can an immaterial, unextended soul control the movements of a solid, material body? Or, in more modern terms, how can an idea, as a mere nonphysical content of consciousness, effect a physical change in even a single molecule of the brain? And, on the other hand, how can such a mind receive any impressions from a physical world, with which it has nothing in common, so as to be aware of its existence? The former of these two questions led to mechanistic materialism, in which matter or force was regarded as the only substantial and permanent reality, mind being a mere " epiphenomenon," a strange by-product of the complicated chemistry of the brain, having no effect upon its changes.[12] The latter question led to idealism, on the ground that, since the physical world certainly is known by our minds, it must in its essential nature be really akin to them. But this simply obscured the real difference between the mental and the physical and destroyed the significance of individuality. It made the individual human mind appear merely an evanescent phase of a vast " ideal " world order. Thus idealists have divided on the question of the survival of human personality, Bradley and Bosanquet, for example, taking the negative, and Royce and Pringle-Pattison the affirmative.

Since the Cartesian two-substance theory has proved unworkable, and since the criticisms of Berkeley and Hume showed how shadowy the notion of substance, as distinct from its qualities, really is, there has been a strong tendency to

[12] Typical nineteenth century representatives of this view are Büchner, Spencer, Haeckel and Huxley.

drop the term from philosophical discussion. We speak today of distinctions of quality, relation, process and function without attributing these to differences of substance. In regard to the nature of the soul this has led to a return to a theory of life and mind, in all their phases, akin to the Aristotelian theory of the vegetative and sensitive parts of the soul. Life, says Aristotle,[13] is self-originated nutrition, increase and decay; i.e., it is the "actuality" or function of the bodily organism. If the eye were a living being then seeing would be its soul; and similarly, the function of cutting is, as it were, the soul of the ax. So the soul of a man is defined by his capacities — of nutrition, sensitivity, reason and movement. This, put in modern terms, is to say that life, mind and soul together constitute the system of functions distinctive of the human organism, the term "function" here including the latent potentiality or capacity for these distinctive activities, as well as their actual operation. Thus mind, or soul, is defined in terms of *process,* not of substance. And this is certainly the predominant modern view. It is involved in the theory, adopted in this book, of personality as a system of volitional tendencies; and in different forms it is held by idealists, instrumentalists, and the various schools of realists, English, German and American.[14]

For Aristotle, the only one of the functions constituting the soul that is separable from the body is reason.[15] This he recognized as, in some very vague sense, immortal. But the psychological reasons he gives for distinguishing the generalizing capacity of reason from perception, memory, feeling and will no longer convince us. Even so strong an upholder of the spiritual nature of man as James Ward deplores this dis-

---

13 *Loc. cit.*

14 C. W. Morris: *Six Theories of Mind* (Chicago: University of Chicago Press, 1932).

15 *Loc. cit.*

continuity.[16]   There is abundant evidence of the gradual evolution of the mental capacities of man. From the simplest
feeling-responses of humble organisms to human abstract
thought there is no break that is not explicable as a further
differentiation of function among capacities present at a
lower level. These developments of mental capacity are correlated with elaborations of brain structure. And this correlation occurs in such a way as to indicate that neural processes play essentially the same part in the higher mental
activities as they do in the lower. These and many other physiological facts, such as the effects of brain injuries, of glandular
secretions, of drugs, disease and blood supply, have sufficed to
convince most students of the subject that the higher mental
processes are just as much dependent on the physical organism as the lower.

This, however, is not to say that the *only* factor involved in
the occurrence of mental activity is the physiological. That
the living and active brain is essential to knowledge of the
sensory world and to the type of mental activity in which human beings are engaged in their physical impact on the world,
seems to be true. That we have no knowledge of any purely
mental activity to which the brain does not seem to be necessary may also be granted. But it does not follow that the physico-chemical organs we call body and brain are the sole factors
involved at any stage of mental activity, even the lowest. And
if there is another factor it may also be the case that it is
capable of finding or developing some other medium of expression when permanently deprived of its customary medium, the living brain. It may be that a living organism
involves, besides the system of physico-chemical processes we
call its body, another and distinct system of processes which
constitutes its life and mind. The living organism would then
be a co-ordinated system of the two kinds of process, and the

---

[16] *Psychological Principles,* p. 5.

dissolution of the one would not necessarily imply the entire dissolution of the other.

Whether this is a reasonable and probable view we shall have to inquire. It is certainly the case that the opinion of a very large number of scientists and philosophers is at present against it; and the conclusion is drawn that human personality does not survive death. So our first task is to inquire into the reason for this state of affairs.

THE MECHANISTIC THEORY

Materialism and mechanism in the old sense have ceased to trouble us. The new physics has destroyed them. Matter is no longer conceived as something permanent, occupying space, and real events are no longer something that happens to matter. Matter is itself simply a system of "events," and these events, as Bertrand Russell says, "just happen, and do not happen 'to' matter or 'to' anything else." [17] The modern physicist is too wary even to say that they happen to the "ether." These events have an orderly way of happening, which science formulates as natural laws, but the apparent rigidity of these laws in physics and chemistry is only a statistical uniformity. A single atom is a manifold system of events and there are many millions of atoms in a pin's head. The laws of mechanics hold only among these aggregates — among macroscopic events. Among the microscopic events that physics must postulate in explanation of the macroscopic there is irregularity and perhaps spontaneity.

Thus a physico-chemical theory of life and mind which gives full recognition to these modern physical theories, if it is still called "materialism" is a materialism with a difference. It allows for genuine chance variations in the order of nature. This opens the way for still greater departures from mechanism. It makes it entirely possible that new phenomena

[17] *Philosophy* (New York: W. W. Norton & Co., 1927) , p. 278.

thus developed may be subject to natural laws not deducible from those holding good of antecedent events. It thus makes it theoretically possible that vital and mental phenomena may manifest modes of behavior not even theoretically deducible from physics and chemistry, because of effects of new emergent factors upon microscopic events. It even makes it possible that microscopic events may be affected by some independent nonphysical factor and organic behavior be thus subjected to a higher type of control. The former view, since its rejection of mechanism still does not allow of any independent nonphysical factor, may be called physicalism.[18] The latter view, though unacceptable in many of its forms, finds reasonable empirical expression in a theory we shall call activism.[19] As representative of a modern type of mechanism we may take Professor Cohen, who, while recognizing that such views are theoretically possible, thinks that there are good empirical grounds for rejecting them.

He bases the case for mechanism on three arguments: [20] (1) That the principle of continuity implies that, since life as we know it has been possible on earth only in recent geological times, it must have developed out of inorganic matter at a time when conditions were more favorable to such a development than they are now. The idea that any nonphysical factor could be involved he dismisses (quite unjustifiably, as will be shown later) as a theory of " supernatural creation." But he admits that this argument alone does not disprove the theory we have called " physicalism," which accepts " spontaneous generation " but insists that organismic behavior is not entirely subject to physico-chemical laws.

[18] Different but typical examples of this view are to be found in the realism of R. B. Perry (cf. his *Present Philosophical Tendencies* [New York: Longmans, Green & Co., 1912]) and in the instrumentalism of John Dewey.

[19] Theories of this kind seem to be historically derived from the " act psychology " of Brentano.

[20] Morris Cohen: *Reason and Nature* (New York: Harcourt, Brace & Co., 1931), pp. 243–48.

(2) The rejection of this possibility, however, is urged by the argument " that the actual progress of biologic science along physico-chemical lines demonstrates the validity of that type of explanation." It is admitted that mechanical explanation is far from complete and that many biologists are convinced that increasing knowledge indicates more and more clearly that there are limits to the physico-chemical explanation of biological phenomena, but it is claimed that the faith of the mechanist is abundantly justified by the past progress of his method.

(3) The third argument shares the weakness of the second. It is urged that if biology is to be a natural science it must assume its phenomena to be subject to causal laws subject to empirical, physical verification. This is precisely the argument the behaviorists have used for their procedure in psychology. But, of course, the question is begged in both cases. The real question is whether the phenomena of life and mind *are* such that they *can* ever be dealt with completely by the methods of natural science. The contention of all nonmechanists is that there are limits to natural science. The vitalist and the activist think that these are prescribed by the operation of an independent nonphysical agency. The physicalist thinks that it is sufficient to postulate that a certain indeterminacy in the physico-chemical system permits of the " emergence " of new forms, not strictly deducible from the laws found sufficient to describe the antecedent conditions. Such new forms, he points out, may have qualities and functions which can be described only in a new set of laws superimposed upon the others; and these new laws *are* subject to empirical verification. Yet science as a whole cannot be made complete, partly because of the complexity and variability of the new phenomena, and partly because the new laws cannot be deduced from those of the earlier stage.

It is obvious from these arguments that the case for mechanism is anything but conclusive. It is perhaps justified as a methodological postulate in physiology, biochemistry and kindred sciences — though many workers in these fields regard it as a positive hindrance.[21]   But as a metaphysic it is only a desperate flight from one absurdity [22] to another, or else the expression of a will to believe.   In defense of this rather emphatic statement it is not necessary to quote the mass of evidence concerning the teleological character of biological phenomena and to point to the radical differences between the behavior of living organisms and that of inanimate things. Nor would it be sufficient to do so, for it is impossible to prove the negative proposition that in these cases no mechanistic explanation is possible.   Science has often discovered physicochemical explanations where it seemed that there could be none.   The real reason why the faith in mechanism is contrary to common sense is that it denies that feeling has any function in life and that knowledge makes any difference to conduct.   It means that the experience of pain and pleasure has nothing to do with our behavior, that nature has elaborated sensation in the course of evolution all to no effect, that these things are mere accompaniments of the neural processes of living organisms and play no part in the causal order of the physical world; and yet the causal order of the physical world causes them!   Such a theory ought, surely, to be the last resort of thought.   Instead, we find not a single argument for it that a cautious advocate can claim as conclusive, and no facts suggesting it that are not balanced by equally suggestive facts on the other side.

THE THEORY OF PHYSICALISM

The type of theory we have called physicalism avoids the difficulties of mechanism.   It recognizes that as we pass from

[21] E.g., J. S. Haldane: *The Sciences and Philosophy* (New York: Doubleday, Doran & Co., 1929).

[22] This term is not meant to be invidious, but to indicate the kind of theory that even the philosopher must abandon in his ordinary practical affairs.

the less complex to the more complex type of entity — e.g., from the molecule to the plant cell and to the higher animal — new qualities and characteristics emerge which are not predictable from a knowledge of the earlier forms, and that these involve principles of interaction not reducible to the simpler law. It maintains the principle of continuity but so interprets this that, to quote a leading proponent, " its meaning . . . precludes reduction of the ' higher ' to the ' lower ' just as it precludes complete breaks and gaps." [23] Yet it also maintains that the new and " higher " vital and mental processes are completely dependent for their occurrence on the forms previously attained by the older, or " lower," physical processes. The vital and mental are not features of nature co-ordinate with the physical but are dependent upon it. The difference between the animate and the inanimate " is not that the former has something in addition to physico-chemical energy, but simply in the *way* in which physico-chemical energies are interconnected and operate, hence different consequences mark animate and inanimate activity respectively." [24]

Now if it were merely the more complicated mechanical structure of a living organism that determined all the differences in its behavior this theory would still be mechanistic. It would still leave no room for the efficacy of purpose and intelligence and would involve the same absurdity we have pointed out above. But this is not Dewey's view. It is the fact that the more complicated mechanical structure in some mysterious way acquires new " emergent " properties nowhere present before, such as sensory experience, pleasure and pain, that makes possible intelligent and purposive be-

[23] Dewey: *Logic: The Theory of Inquiry* (New York: Henry Holt & Co., 1938) , p. 23.

[24] Dewey: *Experience and Nature* (Chicago: Open Court Publishing Co., 1925) , p. 253. This statement is made specifically of plant cells, but both plant and animal life are described in the same chapter as " psycho-physical."

havior. Dewey is emphatic that these also belong to nature and, specifically, to the organism, and that the organism as a whole reacts to its environment. And, apparently because it is this new kind of whole,[25] its reactions are different in the striking way that characterizes animate organisms. The sensitivity of the plant cell and the simple reactions of lowly animals he is willing to call " psycho-physical." Somewhere at this level feeling emerges. But he is emphatic that " psychophysical does not denote an abrogation of the physico-chemical; nor a peculiar mixture of something physical and something psychical." [26]

Is this a tenable position? To clarify the issue we may take the specific example of the qualitative character (the conscious experience, not the neural process) known as pain. Does it play any effective part in behavior? If it does not, then we are left with the absurdity of mechanism. If it does, then either it directly affects physico-chemical process or it affects some nonphysico-chemical process which, in turn, affects physico-chemical process. The latter alternative is the one adopted by activism. The former is the one that appears to be involved in Dewey's [27] position and, generally, in the type of theory we have called physicalism. But it certainly involves a radical departure from the ordinary conception of the physico-chemical. Whether the activist theory involves a similar difficulty we shall inquire later. But the notion that

25 *Ibid.*, p. 256: " This pervasive operative presence of the whole in the part and of the part in the whole constitutes susceptibility — the capacity of feeling — whether or no this potentiality be actualized in plant life."

26 *Ibid.*, p. 255.

27 *Ibid.*, p. 268: " Qualities actually become specifically effective however, in psycho-physical situations. Where animal susceptibility exists, a red or an odor or sound may instigate a determinate mode of action; *it has selective power in maintenance of a certain pattern of energy-organization.* So striking is this fact that we might even define the difference between an inanimate body and a vital and psycho-physical one, by saying that *the latter responds to qualities* and *the former does not.*" (Italics mine.)

a qualitative character, such as a pain or a color, can directly affect the course of a dynamic process, such as molecular change in a nerve cell, is precisely the unintelligibility that has caused so many scientific minds (since they have not seen a reasonable alternative) to relapse into the acceptance of mechanism.

On the ordinary conception of physical objects as dynamic agents completely describable in physico-chemical terms, physicalism is absurd. But Dewey's position is saved from this absurdity by a radical reinterpretation of the physical world.[28] Matter, or the physical, is not itself an event or existence. Natural existence is a world of events. These events, at the lowest level we know them, are characterized by the external interactions we call physical. But natural existence involves much more than this and reveals its basic traits more fully in its later developed effects — i.e., in life and mind — than in the mere physical order. So a physical event is always a natural existence involving potentialities that are more than physical. And it is for this reason that a " red " or a " dry " quality may be able to exercise a selective power over patterns of energy organization.

Thus " natural existence " is regarded as containing the " potentialities " of feeling, willing and thinking, only waiting for the appropriate structure of physical events to " release " them. This is a metaphysical theory very closely akin to that which will later be presented as necessary also to activism. But Dewey insists upon the *dependence* of life, feeling and thought upon physical events in a way that is not necessitated by such a metaphysic. The recognition that there is something in natural events besides their physical character is covered by the vague word " potentialities," and no inquiry is made as to whether any further light can be cast on these. The claim is made that somehow " natural events

[28] See especially *Experience and Nature,* pp. 262, 271, 272.

having matter as a character, ' cause ' life and mind." [29]   Yet it is admitted that this is so marvelous as to be miraculous.

That things should be able to pass from the plane of external pushing and pulling to that of revealing themselves to man, and thereby to themselves, and that the fruit of communication should be participation, sharing, is a wonder by the side of which transubstantiation pales.[30]

This marvel, however, would cease to be miraculous if we could discover in mental process an observable factor that is neither a physical process nor a physical quality, nor any mere relation between these.   For then, without committing the metaphysical crime of inventing an entity to fill a gap in our theory, we would have something to point to as the factor that mediates between the quality (such as pain) and the physico-chemical process of the nervous system.   We should have to admit that such a factor could be actually observed only by each person within himself, and that its presence could only be securely inferred in other persons and to a lesser degree in the higher animals.   But there would be no reason to believe that it first came into being at the point in nature where we first find evidence of it, and that it must have been miraculously produced by natural events containing nothing akin to it.   Since the " basic traits of natural existence " — to use Dewey's term — must necessarily be recognized to include more than merely its physical characteristics, there would be every reason to believe that the nonphysical factor discovered in experience is one of them.

THE ACTIVIST THEORY

The question before us then is whether we can find, within experience, a nonphysical factor that is responsive to differ-

[29] *Ibid.,* p. 262.
[30] *Ibid.,* p. 166.

ences of quality (such as red and pain) and that might be
regarded as having an effect, in turn, upon physical processes.
The best approaches to the solution of this problem, it seems
to me, are those made by that school of realists who recognize
a distinctive mental " act of awareness " as involved in all
experience. Professor C. W. Morris describes this as " the
theory of mind as intentional act " [31] and includes in this
school Whitehead, Samuel Alexander, G. E. Moore, Broad,
Laird, Stout, Brentano, Meinong and Husserl. Very similar
views are held by some American critical realists, such as Lovejoy and Pratt. The essential feature of the activist position
is therefore seen to be endorsed by a very eminent group of
philosophers who, in other respects, hold diverse metaphysical
theories. We can therefore with some confidence make it
the basis of a theory of the connection between the qualitative
and the dynamic characters of reality, i.e., between the data
of actual experience (such as pain and color) and the physico-
chemical structures and processes whereby science explains
them.

The existence of the mental act of awareness, however, is
not merely a hypothesis to be adopted on authority. Nor do
those who believe in it regard it merely as a hypothetical entity
invented to explain mental phenomena. They claim rather
that it is a datum of experience. They point to the fact that
when we see, feel, want and will we are distinctly aware, not
only of the objects seen, wanted and so forth, but also of the
fact that we are seeing, wanting, etc. There is no sharp distinction between such acts as seeing and wanting (i.e., between cognition and conation, or knowing and willing) , for
every process of experiencing involves a process of striving and
vice versa. Cognition and conation are not two distinct
mental processes but two aspects of the one mental process.
And it is this total mental process, involving experiencing and

[31] *Six Theories of Mind,* chap. 4.

willing, that we are more or less clearly aware of in all our mental life. These facts are matters of fairly general agreement. But those who deny the existence of the mental act, as distinct from the other contents of consciousness, claim that what they are aware of as their own seeing and willing (for example) is not a distinctive mental act but simply the general attitude of the organism as a whole toward its data. This general attitude, they claim, turns out upon closer examination to be known simply as the changing system of relations among the various sensory and affective data.[32]

Now there are two very good reasons why introspection often fails to convince people of the existence of the distinctive mental act. The first is that we are very apt to have the wrong sort of thing in mind when we look for it. It is not an object, such as a physical movement or a sensation of muscular strain or warmth; and when we engage in introspection it is these objects that catch our attention; and so we are apt to say nothing else is present. It is not something of which we can form an isolated mental image so as to have a correct idea of what to look for; and it is notoriously difficult to find anything of which we cannot first form a correct mental image. The second difficulty is connected with the nature of attention. If we attend to an object it becomes impossible at the same time to attend to our awareness of that object. Thus the person who seeks the act of awareness or will by introspective attention to the contents of his consciousness will inevitably attend less and less to the fact of his own awareness or will. Consequently introspection tends to confirm him in the theory that there is no such distinctive fact.

It is therefore the nonintrospective consciousness that is

[32] The two classical statements of this position are in Hume's *Treatise*, 1:3:4 (" Of Personal Identity ") and William James's essay, " Does Consciousness Exist? " in his *Essays in Radical Empiricism* (New York: Longmans, Green & Co., 1912). Cf. also Perry: *Present Philosophical Tendencies*, chap. 12, and Morris: *Six Theories of Mind*, chap. 4.

most clearly aware of its own distinctive activity. That is why common sense never doubts the fact of mental activity until it tries to become scientifically introspective. The man who says he wants his dinner has no doubt that he knows the *want* as a given fact. And it is not the vague, uncomfortable feelings inside him that constitute the want, nor is it the smell coming from the kitchen, nor mental imagery of eating, nor feelings of incipient movements of the kind involved in seeking food. Neither is it any passive relation among all these data, or any particular movement or change of any of them, that constitutes the want. The want is an entirely unique fact that he feels as his own *active tendency*. It is, of course, inseparable from some of the other data. It is that which gathers them all into a whole and gives them their significance. In so far as it is a relation it is the kind of relation we call an act; and it is a unique kind of act, entirely distinct from the spatio-temporal change we call physico-chemical action, or from any kind of merely qualitative change such as a change of sense data.

Just as clearly present to the normal consciousness is the act of seeing or of thinking. I see a white patch and I think it is a wall. And I have no more doubt of the existence of the seeing and thinking than I have of the white patch and the wall. If I try to introspect the seeing and thinking I find various data such as sensations of eyestrain and a dull feeling in the head, etc. But now I am aware of *feeling* these and I am certain that they do not themselves constitute the previous, or still present, seeing and thinking. Nor is the seeing or thinking any relation between these or any other data that enter into experience, unless it should be that unique relation in which they are brought together in a distinctive mental act.

Briefly to show that the mental act is more than a qualitative change and is different from a physico-chemical activity, it should be enough to summarize the things it does: (1) It analytically discriminates one sensory or affective quality from another.   (2) It apprehends the discriminated qualities together with the relation of difference and other nonspatio-temporal relations between them.   (3) It distinguishes past and present and anticipates a future.   (4) It responds to distinctions of value with an act of preference or choice; i.e., it *wants* this rather than that.   (5) It responds to some given data, not simply as to what they are as given, but as symbolizing, indicating or meaning something that is not given.   If all these reactions to qualitative data, such as colors and pains, are to be called " physico-chemical " then that term has lost its distinctive meaning.   If not, then the organism does contain a factor that is nonphysico-chemical.[33]   Our next problem, therefore, becomes that of the relation of the three features found together in organic life — the qualitative, the physico-chemical, and the nonphysico-chemical activity which we shall call mental.

THE STRUCTURE OF AN ORGANISM

Now this distinction of three features instead of just two — body and mind — leaves the qualitative feature neutral. What, for short, we shall call " the physical " is molecular structure and change and interchange of energy.   The mental is the process and order of our striv*ing*, experienc*ing* and think*ing*.   The qualitative is the changing panorama of that which is experienc*ed* — e.g., color, sound and the felt " pushiness " [34] or hardness-softness of matter; also joy, pain, beauty and the pricks of conscience.   Of these qualitative data the former group seems more closely associated with the physical and the latter with the mental activities.   But it is impossible

[33] For a fuller discussion of these points see my article, " Functionalism and the Intentional Act," *Philosophical Review*, July 1940.
[34] This delightful term was coined by Whitehead.

to be sure, for example, that a purely physical entity would have color, or that a purely mental entity could feel the pricks of conscience; and it is also impossible to say whether there really are any purely mental or purely physical entities. But if we divide the qualities into two classes, the sensory-motor (color, sound, etc.) and the valuational (joy, pain, etc.), then it seems that changes in the former depend upon physical changes, while changes in the latter depend upon mental changes. What is commonly called "physical" pain and unpleasantness is only an apparent exception to this rule for, while such sensations are always unpleasant or painful to the normal person, those with certain forms of insanity and abnormal mental attitudes known as masochism sometimes actually enjoy them.

Now, so far as our evidence goes, the correlation between physical change on the one hand, and change in sensory-motor quality (e.g., color and felt hardness) on the other, seems to be one-sided. One physical change seems to be fully accounted for in terms of other physical changes; and the changes of color, sound and so forth seem to be simply correlated with the physical without effect upon them. Between mental changes and changes in value experience, however, there seems to be a reciprocal relation. It is certainly the case that attention and will respond to changes in the value qualities of a situation; e.g., we tend to dwell upon and seek to maintain the pleasant and to avoid the painful. But it is also evident that changes of mental attitude affect the nature of the values experienced in any situation; whether we enjoy a certain play or approve of a certain moral judgment depends to a considerable extent upon the frame of mind with which we approach it; and yet value qualities are far from being entirely dependent upon our will, or we would always make everything pleasant and good. We may sum up the situation by saying that, although the value qualities experienced depend in part upon our frame of mind, yet in a given frame of mind they force themselves upon us as relentlessly as the sense qualities. Thus the total system of physical and mental activities acquires and presents to us an assortment of sensory-motor and value qualities, and the further course of our mental activity is forced to take account of them in selective responses.

These relationships involve an effective influence of the physical upon the mental activity, for the sensory-motor qualities to which the mental activity must selectively respond (attention, perception, etc.) depend upon the course of physical activity. Changes in value experience, however, depend chiefly upon the course of attentive effort; and these induce new choices and different efforts. We cannot say that the course of physical change *determines* the course of mental activity, because there seems to be a certain spontaneity about attentive effort and also because the nature of the values felt (to which response is made) depends upon those mental factors we have called the person's " frame of mind " as well as upon the sensory-motor content. However, it certainly seems obvious that the physical activity, through its correlated qualities, exercises a large measure of *indirect* control over the mental and largely defines for it the problems to be faced and the limits of its capacity.

Finally, we come to the vexed question of the influence of the mental activity on the physical. Can this be made any more intelligible than the idea of the direct effect of qualities like color upon physical processes? I think it can if we consider the nature of time and space. Time is not merely an abstract measurement; it is concrete activity. An inactive world would be a timeless world, and a timeless world an inactive world. Neither is space a mere abstract set of relations. Physical activity, says the physicist, is " space-time." But, if so, it is not a marriage of two abstractions that produces the concrete being of the physical world; it is the concrete being of temporal-activity, operating in the concrete being of the spatial continuum, that constitutes the units or fields of physical energy. These science discovers through their effect in displaying the varied sensory-motor qualities latent in the world plenum. Those activities that form physical energy are not themselves directly responsive to the qualities they display. They have spatio-temporal quantitative characters, and the laws of their occurrence can be formulated in these purely quantitative terms. But in certain parts of space at least there occur activities that have no measurable spatial quantity, though they do have temporal extensity. Mental activity is a change that occurs *at* a place (e.g., in a human brain) but is not, like physical energy, a change *of* place.[35] But it *is* responsive to the qualities displayed by the physical energy of that place.

Now it is a matter of observed fact that, where there is evidence of the existence of these active responses to sensory and other qualities, the course of physical activity occurs in a peculiar way. The transition of physical energy from its kinetic to potential form, and vice versa, is affected. Careful experiment seems to show that there is, in the metabolism of the living body, neither addition to nor subtraction from the total quantity of physical energy; but this energy is stored and released in organic process in a way not duplicated in the inorganic. The natural explanation is that this modification of the one kind of activity is due to the presence of the other. But this implies some common nature of the two. Here the most likely explanation, it seems to me, is a form of the neutral substance theory. This suggests that the two concrete activities are activities of the one concrete entity, the activities of which constitute the physical and men-

[35] The same may be said of many of its objects; e.g., a change of color occurs *at* a place, but is not a change *of* place.

tal world. We could then understand their interaction — how the " pushiness " of physical energy impresses itself upon the striving-experiencing processes of mental activity to create the awareness of a physical world; and how the positive and negative volitional responses to positive and negative value qualities affect positively and negatively the metabolism of a living cell, so that it absorbs or emits physical energy.

This presupposes, of course, that these striving-experiencing processes go on in *every* living cell; and although we cannot prove it this is entirely probable. Single-celled organisms such as the amoeba show essentially the same evidence of feeling as do larger animals, though of course their feeling must be much simpler. And although the immobility of plant cells makes it well-nigh impossible to obtain evidence of feeling in them their metabolism is essentially so similar that there is no reason to believe them absolutely devoid of feeling. As for our own bodies, there is no reason to believe that feeling is confined to the cortical cells. Consciousness varies from the limelight of attention (involving probably the activity of a small proportion of cortical cells) to a vague background in which a mass of feeling is fused. This peculiar fact of attention can even make us apparently unconscious of experiences of which special psychological methods (such as hypnosis) may afterwards show we were not really unconscious. This negative effect of attention seems to be the explanation of all forms of psychic blindness. Sleep is probably a generalized and normally recurrent form of psychic blindness. There is thus no reason to regard feeling as the miraculous and peculiar prerogative of the cells of the higher animal cortex. It may much more reasonably be supposed to be operative through the whole range of life.

AN ACTIVIST METAPHYSIC

The metaphysic to which activism thus points might possibly be described as a neutral monism of substance [36] with a duality of process, rather than, as in Spinoza, a duality of attributes. One omnipresent concrete entity, which may well be space itself, exerts itself in two forms of activity, these operations constituting time. One of these two series of events (the physical) has a spatially quantitative character. It is a spatial change, a movement dispersing itself through space and producing a multiplicity of changing forms. The other is a feeling-response to the shock, or pushiness, of the spatially quantitative activities. It feels both these and a selective display of other qualities (e.g., color) latent in the spatial plenum, attention to some of these rather than others being apparently facilitated by the changing course of physical events. The content of perception is thus made to include both quantitative and qualitative characters selected and organized by the physical system and habits of attention of the organism.

The first of these two forms of activity has been going on for many millenniums; perhaps it has always been going on, but science cannot tell for certain. Concerning the second we know less, for it does not leave behind it mathematically calculable effects, except certain of its effects in modifying physical structures. These indicate that this second type of activity began a unique course of constructive modification of physical forms on this planet in the Pre-Cambrian period. Probably opportunity for the commencement on earth of this type of constructive activity, which we know as vital and men-

---

[36] The term "substance," as used here, does not carry with it any of the traditional definitions. It is simply an entity postulated as ground of that relational order manifested by physical and mental processes which are empirically discontinuous.

tal, was afforded by the purely physical synthesis, in the peculiar conditions of the period, of some highly unstable carbon compounds, presenting distinctive qualities. If the new active response to these qualities elaborated a more complex structure, presenting further new qualities that called forth further response, we can understand how the constructive effort of life went on from that point.

The new control of physical process became an instrument for further control. Positive value experience presents itself when activity tends to be progressively and harmoniously constructive, and negative when it is the reverse. Mental activity responds to changes in value experience. Thus the activity that tends to be constructive is maintained, and is changed only when constructive achievement is no longer being obtained in that way. Then a new course is tried, and so the experimental activity of life, guided by its sense of value, goes on. The organism grows, and growth leads to multiplication. Multiplication leads to differentiation and new forms of development, culminating in the life of the present day.

In the multicellular life of the higher animals, and especially in man, there is elaborated a highly complex structure, not only physical but mental. The mental processes of man, quite obviously, do not consist simply of those of the individual cells of his body.[37] The facts of selective attention, with its degrees of consciousness, indicate that. This peculiar unity of the human consciousness, its capacity to fuse into a single uniform experience the activities involved in a multitude of cells,[38] and its ability to select some experiences for vivid attention and to be blind to others, indicate the play of a system of mental activity *between,* as well as *within,* the cells. It

[37] For a fuller discussion of this question see my *Reality and Value,* pp. 34 ff.

[38] As in the case of seeing white light when a complex light ray stimulates a large array of nerve endings, most of which are susceptible to one wave length only and, operating alone, would produce an experience of color.

is this superimposed system of experience, it would appear, that constitutes our normal consciousness and obscures from us the vague and simple feeling-tone of the great mass of bodily cells.[39] And this system has its structure, its interlacing of active tendencies that affect each other. Its integrated order is the finest achievement of intelligence. Mental acts are not transitory. They establish a mental " set " which may constitute an abiding purposive tendency. This structure cannot be regarded as depending merely on the physical structure, though it is vitally affected by this latter. The mental structure is a system of acts, and each act is a new contribution to the total. Its effectiveness remains even after attention passes on and it is no longer explicitly conscious, as abnormal psychological phenomena have strikingly demonstrated. Personality is a system of will, and will is not merely a momentary willing, but the purposive set or tendency given to personality by the momentary act of willing. Personality thus possesses a nonphysical structure, built up during the course of life, and actively responsive to the kinds of value that it has experienced in life.

If this account be true it does not necessarily follow that personality survives the destruction of the physical organism in a way in which it could live a new life. But it certainly makes such survival a practical possibility, and even a proba-

[39] If, as Dewey suggests, the difference between an animate and an inanimate body is that the former responds to qualities while the latter does not, then it would seem to be necessary to assume that the unconscious physiological processes of the higher animal organism involve a great deal of feeling, however dim and vague, of which there is no explicit awareness. This is quite probable. The human (and other higher animal) consciousness is highly attentive; and attention excludes masses of feeling while concentrating on a few details. Cases of psychic blindness and similar abnormalities show that even strong feelings normally attended to can be shut out of the central stream of consciousness. Probably even sleep is only a generalized and normal case of periodic psychic blindness, resting the higher brain cells while simple feeling-responses still go on. There is thus good reason to believe that wherever there is life (vital process) there is some degree of feeling.

bility. It means that when the physical organism ceases to function there still survives a mental organization, consisting of set tendencies to respond in certain fairly specific ways to the values that present themselves in certain typical situations. But these typical situations are, to a considerable extent, such as present themselves only through the related activity of the physical organism. This is true of the whole range of habits or tendencies that constitute what we have called the ego. To these tendencies the specific values that stimulate their responses can no longer appear. Thus the ego, the whole early structure of human personality and the whole system of non-physical tendencies concerned simply with the physical organism, must remain inactive. But for the disinterested will the situation is different. This is a will to constructive activity of any kind possible, and responsive positively to values as felt and anticipated. The question is whether there is any kind of constructive activity open to this general active tendency and the more specific active tendencies that have developed out of it. These latter include the interests in the general development of personality both in ourselves and in all others with whom we are in communication, the interest in the imaginative creations of art, and the disinterested pursuit of knowledge.

The question whether the formal structure of personality that survives the body must remain inactive, or can find stimulus and opportunity for a new life, therefore depends on the question whether it can discover any medium of creative activity and communication with other persons. The resources of the universe must indeed be poor if it cannot. Even the resources of the physical universe would seem to offer some scope. For mental activity, as we have seen, tends to modify to some extent the physical activity that occurs in the same place. So if it is able to modify to any extent the radiant energy that flows through it, and if other minds can become sensitive to these modifications, then communication would be established. Social life, knowledge and art would then be possible. The community thus established would be a genuinely co-operative community, for the power of the divisive and hampering ego would have gone. The new community would be composed of personalities whose initial richness and power would depend on the degree of development that had taken place in this life, on the basis of the disinterested will, and whose great interest would be in the co-operative development of that fuller life for all which had begun here.

This theory of personality, of course, cannot be regarded as proved. If our analysis is correct it is a reasonable probability, and no more. But at least we can say that those alternative views — mechanism and physicalism — which, if true, would make personal survival possible only by a miracle, cannot be regarded as substantiated. It cannot be maintained that modern scientific knowledge, in physics, biology or psychology, has rendered the doctrine of personal immortality incredible or even improbable. In our analysis we have taken the facts and well established theories of all the sciences at their face value. Our inquiry has proceeded on purely empirical lines. We have sought to explain the interconnection of mental and physical phenomena with a minimum of hypothesis. And our conclusion has been drawn, by these empirical methods, from the facts, as their most likely result and explanation. Nevertheless, it must be recognized that it is not on this sort of empirical argument from science that the religious faith in immortality really rests, but on an inner moral conviction that that faith is implied in the goodness and power of God. Without such a faith any belief in immortality must be exceedingly weak. Our long excursion into the field of empirical scientific inquiry was made not so much to establish the validity of a faith in immortality as to disprove the frequently repeated contention that science has discredited it.   So we return now to a new examination of the real grounds out of which, in the great ethical religions, the belief has grown.

THE GROUND OF FAITH IN IMMORTALITY

As shown in our discussion, at the beginning of this chapter, of the development of the belief in immortality, it grows out of faith in the goodness and power of God.   This is its first premise — that God is good and is able to give good gifts to his children.   The second premise is that life is good and the *sine qua non* of all good gifts.   No ethical religion doubts the first premise, except in so far as it doubts the very existence and power of God.   And these doubts of his existence and power arise chiefly from observation of evils which seem incompatible with his goodness.   This question we take up in our next chapter, but here we may point out that, from the standpoint adopted in our present analysis and interpretation of religion, the question of the power of God is secondary to his goodness.   We are seeking, not the God of some metaphysic, but the God of religious experience.   And this God, the object and ground of that experience, we have found in the disinterested will to the good, which is felt as active within us and is the ultimate ground of all our religious experience and thought.   So the primary fact, with which our knowledge of God begins, is that of his disinterested goodness.   But as yet we have not inquired whether, in range and power, God is anything more than this particular element of human personality.[40]   If he is not, then he is certainly not able to confer

---

[40] If this be the whole nature and extent of the divine then it is obvious that there are, in one sense, as many gods as there are moral personalities. Yet in another sense — i.e., in quality, intent and meaning — God is one and the same in all of us. A comparable case is that of a book. The Gospel of Matthew, for example, is one book; yet it is, in another sense, many, for it is manifest and operative in millions of copies, each of which is a book.

immortality as a gift upon others and it is an open question whether the divine element in any of us is able even to maintain itself. But if this divine element in us is but the immanent operation of a divinity that far transcends us, then there can be little doubt of his power to continue in some form the distinctive constructive activity in which each finite personality consists, so far as that activity is good.

The question that still remains resides in the last phrase. How far is the activity or life of human personalities good? It is obvious that if the human life really is an active process initiated by a Will that far transcends it, then, in the course of its particular development, it has passed beyond the control of the originating Will and has developed tendencies contrary to it. It has thus produced evil as well as good. This sense of the evil of finite human life has found expression in some religious minds (particularly in India) in the conviction that it must eventually be brought to an end, that the human spirit must lose its individuality by returning to the unity of the eternal and absolute Spirit, attaining immortality by re-absorption into God, so that evil is blotted out and there remains only the eternal perfection that ever was.[41] This theory, however, is contrary to the nature of the good, as discovered in our earlier analysis, and must be rejected if that analysis is to stand. The good is not an eternal perfection, but is something progressively realized in constructive activity, and above all in that activity wherein personality is developed. We know God primarily as a will disinterestedly concerned with constructive achievement, wherein the development of the fullest life of finite personalities is found the most supremely good. Thus God, as we know him, is a being who seeks the completest life for all; and if it be in his power that these lives should go on to realize a still more abundant life

[41] For an Occidental exposition of this type of view, cf. Bernard Bosanquet: *Value and Destiny of the Individual* (London: The Macmillan Co., 1913).

after their release from preoccupation with the affairs of this body, then it must certainly be his will that they should do so.

However, certain doubts of the possibility of continuation of any features of the life developed here, coupled with a sense of the obvious elements of evil in all personalities, have suggested to many minds that we should content our thought with the good to be realized in this world. Virtue, it is pointed out, is its own reward, and the good man seeks not so much his own continued enjoyment of life as the continuity of his influence for good in human society. This latter is assured so long as human society lasts, for, while evil is self-destructive in the long run, the good that men do tends to live after them in its influence upon the lives of others. This, it is argued, is all that the good man should desire for himself.[42] To this it may be replied that even if it were granted that this is all that the good man should desire for himself, it certainly is not all that he should seek for others. The essence of the good life is to seek the completest life for all. This is the very nature of the divine as found within us. And, in so far as that divine nature transcends the human in existence and power, it must seek to give life and give it more abundantly, here and hereafter. Else would the transcendent God be false to his own nature as it is revealed in us and would fail himself to perform the duty he imposes upon man.

This failure to recognize that individual personal immortality must be an object of the divine good will, so far as it is possible, is at bottom due to the interpretation of the good in terms of desire and to the fact that many good people have ceased to desire immortality. The common tendency to fall a little below our ideals makes us weary of the struggle. Dis-

---

[42] For a criticism of this type of theory cf. John Baillie: *And the Life Everlasting* (New York: Charles Scribner's Sons, 1933), pp. 194–214. For a favorable exposition of it cf. R. W. Sellars: *Religion Coming of Age* (New York: The Macmillan Co., 1928), chap. 11.

appointments make us feel that we have overrated the joy of life; and we become ready, when our natural span is finished, to lay it down. We become more interested in the social process and the ideals we wish to see realized in it than in the thought of prolonging our own enjoyment of life. So the idea that our own task may at length be laid down, that our errors will in the long run meet their negation and the good we have done remain, has a satisfying appeal. In a somewhat world-weary mood it seems all that we really desire; and then, if we interpret the good in terms of desire, we may be inclined to say it is enough.

But the good is not to be measured by what we desire *most;* it is rather what we desire when we are at our *best.* At other times we desire the lesser good — as, often, we well know. The good is rather to be measured in terms of the more abundant life; and if we rightly understand it we shall see that it is good. It is not the ego that we should expect to survive, but the higher personality realized and developed through the conscious expression of the disinterested will. If this is so then the inner discord due to the conflicting tendencies of the higher and lower self will be over, for there will be nothing to which the egoistic habits can respond. The ego and its body are a stage in personal development that can be left behind. What would survive of the whole personality is that which is in true harmony with the divine; and it would go on to develop and share in the life of a new stage of the divine society. This is the hope that has come out of our empirical analysis of human personality. And it is the faith which has grown out of man's deepest religious experience. Whether this faith is justifiable, however, depends upon the truth of its major premise — the superhuman reality of God.

The Nature of God

IMMANENCE AND TRANSCENDENCE

IF THE ANALYSIS of our earlier chapters is sound then religion arises from the experience of a disinterested will, within the individual, seeking the good of some other person or persons in circumstances which conflict with natural egoistic tendencies. This altruistic will is thus an immanent personal agency, seeking the conformity of the whole individual to the general good; it is the source of that sense of inner peace and joy that comes when such harmony is attained, of the sense of obligation that impends when it is threatened, and of the sense of sin or guilt that imposes itself when it is broken. There are other sources of the feelings of peace, obligation and sin, but they are secondary, being largely the result of inadequate and unjustified interpretation of the primary experience. At its origin, and in its most clearsighted and intelligent expression, harmony with the disinterested will is what men have called harmony with God. We are therefore justified in saying that the disinterested will *is* God as immediately and normally present in human experience. As such God is a personal agent (for personality is essentially a system of will) and is immanent in every human being.

But man has rarely been content to regard his God as merely a part of himself, even though the most fundamental and noblest part. Nor is there any special reason, immediately evident, why he should do so. His physical organism is part of a larger physical order, out of which it has developed its own distinctive existence, and within which it still remains an organic part. There is no *a priori* reason why this should not also be the case with the spiritual, or mental, part of his total organism. Unsophisticated common sense, however, has found this extension of the spiritual order not altogether simple. It conceives the physical as too substantial and the mental too much in terms of the conscious contents of individual minds. It thinks of personality, therefore, as an isolated consciousness inhabiting a distinct substantial body. So, in these terms, if God is to be thought of as more than a part of human personality he has to be conceived either as impersonal or else as anthropomorphic, i.e., as an isolated consciousness inhabiting some sort of body.

This results in an inadequate conception of God. If he is regarded as personal his relation to man becomes merely social, the closest analogy being that of the family, with God as father. This conception however, though rich in poetic value, does not do justice to the reality of the divine immanence; for how can one isolated center of consciousness (such as personality is ordinarily conceived to be) be an immanent part of another? Neither does it fit any better the concept of the divine transcendence; for how can a localized center of consciousness be as omnipresent as religion requires God to be? With such a conception of personality man's early belief in divine transcendence readily became polytheistic; and when the inadequacies of polytheism became manifest the new monotheism had to help out its concept of the divine activity by surrounding the deity with a host of angels and other semidivine beings. Christian theology, from its inception, has wrestled with the problems of immanence and transcendence without finding a solution that can be harmonized with the common-sense notion of the isolated personal consciousness and its associated, traditional, physical substantialism.

When personality is interpreted as a systematic organization of will, however, these difficulties disappear. As pointed out in the previous chapter, the human organism consists of a multitude of subsidiary organisms (cells) each of which is itself a systematic organization of "mental" (in the broadest sense) or vital as well as physical processes and tendencies. And what we call our consciousness achieves its unity and apparent isolation only by the process of exclusion which, at the level of deliberate control, we call attention. The striving processes thus excluded from our consciousness are not, therefore, to be regarded as entirely devoid of feeling; abnormal psychology very clearly indicates this. Consequently, our own personalities, we are now forced to recognize, involve highly complex systems of "mental" process, containing subsidiary centers of more or less experiential activity in a hierarchy of many grades. None of these organized centers of experience is entirely self-contained. They are organic to each other. Each to some extent lives its own life, yet all share in a common life. All, together, constitute a person. Yet each has, in a sense which is not entirely metaphorical, a personality of its own.

If the personality of God includes anything more and greater than that element of human personality we have called the disinterested will, then our relation to this transcendent divine person must be of an organic character, for, as we have seen, the disinterested will is the root of human personality and also the determining factor in its complete and well integrated growth. And, on the analogy of the animal organism, it is quite intelligible that our personalities should be organic parts of a larger organic whole. The analogy is, of course, not exact. We should not jump to the conclusion that God is a very large animal, of which we are living parts and the inanimate world a sort of skeleton. But the analogy is more suitable to the modern understanding of personality, and better fits the facts of religious experience, than that of the family. This latter — the fatherhood of God and the brotherhood of man — is aesthetically and emotionally more appealing, but that of the organism (which also may be given aesthetically beautiful expression, as in the parable of the True Vine and in Paul's metaphor of the church as the body of Christ) is probably intellectually more accurate. But both are metaphors. There is a very loose organic relation between the members of a family, and a very close one between the parts of a living body. If the personality of God transcends its presence in man then our relation to him would appear to be organic rather more in the latter sense than in the former.

A fairly good analogy, but still inadequate in many respects, is the relation of the white corpuscles in the bloodstream to the organism as a whole. These corpuscles live a very independent life, moving freely about in the performance of their functions and responding to various stimuli which direct them in their activity. Yet they are a part of a larger, living whole, drawing from it their comparatively independent existence, contributing to its good and finding their proper function in doing so. If each of these cells had as much intelligence as is possessed by the whole human organism in which they live, they would probably find themselves in much the same puzzling position as to the meaning of their lives as we do. They could explore the whole body without finding any organisms with capacities for free and intelligent behavior greater than (or equal to) their own. They would find their world to consist (like ours) of an inanimate structure, a structure of fixed living organisms, and a more limited number of freely moving living organisms. But they would find no supraindividual consciousness above that of organisms like themselves. Their only inkling that they belonged to any such larger life would be in the teleological structure and relations of function within the whole, and in the experience that they found their own profoundest impulse to be, not merely a securing of their own needs, but a devotion of themselves to a

kind of activity which they might discover to be to the good
of the whole.

It must be recognized that there are no very obvious facts
that indicate the reality of a divine transcendence. Yet it
has been a generally accepted belief in almost all religious
circles; indeed, of the two features of divinity, it is that of
immanence that has been more often rejected or overlooked.
We must therefore ask the reason for the origin and persistence of the belief in spite of the difficulties involved in it and
the lack of clear evidence for it. This is not the same as to ask
what arguments religious thinkers have brought forward in
proof of it, for arguments are often ingeniously discovered
to support beliefs that rest on mere tradition and vague intui-
tions; and this is certainly the case with the belief in a transcendent God. What we must do is to go back to that experience of the altruistic will in which religious belief originates
and inquire what there is in this experience that suggests that
its datum presents an indication of the existence of something
much more than that which is immediately given in experience. We can then take up these features or associations of
the immediate datum to see whether, in reflective and enlightened examination, they justify the belief to which they have
led. Finally we can pass beyond the range of religious experience to test our conclusions by seeing whether they fit what is
known of reality from other sources and whether there is anything in these further ranges of experience that suggests the
same conclusions.

This is the same procedure as has to be adopted in testing
the validity of our beliefs in a physical world and in other
minds. We begin with the relevant experience from which
those beliefs arise, particularly our sensory-dynamic experience, and we inquire what features of that experience sug-

gest the existence of a larger reality than that immediately given and indicate its nature. We then submit these suggestions and indications to reflective and enlightened examination and, so far as they seem justified, test the conclusions by comparison with knowledge from other ranges of experience, such as logic and ethics. In regard to both the physical and the mental (or spiritual), I think, the evidence is such as to justify the conclusion that the little order of processes immediately experienced is but a part of a larger order of processes of both kinds. If so, our knowledge of God and of the physical world rests on essentially the same kind of evidence. With this introduction, we shall turn first to an inquiry as to what are those features of religious experience which lead to a belief in divine transcendence, and then to the specific re-examination of those features to see whether they justify the belief founded on them.

The first feature of the disinterested will that suggests that it is more than merely a part of the individual human personality is its conflict with the ego. A man's egoistic tendencies are obviously his own, directed toward what he conceives as his own good. But the disinterested desire for another's good sometimes issues in serious conflict with the ego, and it is the cases of conflict that suggest that its power is derived from some agency beyond the self. In our analysis of the religious experience and practice of the primitive we saw this internal conflict at work, and also in the cases of modern conversion crises. Where the internal conflict is strongest the conviction of the divine transcendence tends to be most vivid. To a very large extent, however, human personality becomes so integrated that the conflict is slight. Also, such conflict as there is concerns chiefly the will to the good of members of our own family and other close personal groups, and these tend to be so closely identified with the self that we hardly distinguish between their good and our own unless some unusual personal sacrifice is involved. In these normal conditions the altruistic will does not strike us as other than our own. Also, so far as it merely points to ideals which are so much a part of the social tradition that it would seem unnatural to do anything different, the " otherness " of the disinterested will does not strongly impress us.

It is out of the cases of *strong* conflict that the conviction arises in a man that he is faced with something within himself which is greater than himself. The prophet whose unique experience and thought have left him in the grip of a great new ideal feels it. The follower, whom the prophet inspires to strive to realize that ideal in spite of the lethargy and opposition of the community, also often feels it. The sinner, who awakens to despise the mean and sordid ego he has developed and from which he can scarcely escape, recognizes it. Any one of us, faced by unusual circumstances which constitute a moral crisis, may tend to experience it. In brief, it is the fact that the disinterested will can set itself in opposition to the whole familiar body of tendencies we are accustomed to recognize as constituting the self (even to the point of demanding the sacrifice of life itself) that gives man the impression that it proceeds from beyond himself. Probably all of us have felt its " otherness " to some extent, and to some the experience has had an overwhelming intensity. It has been something too great, too high, too difficult and too much opposed to the desires of the familiar self to be felt as their own will. They may or may not have fought against it. But, when they have consented to it, it has been a surrender of the familiar self to something higher. It has conveyed the feeling expressed in the saying, " Not my will but Thine be done."

Closely attached to this tendency to conflict with the ego is the second of those features of religious experience which suggest that the disinterested will is rooted in something beyond the individual self. This is the positive feeling-tone and the access of personal power that come with the surrender of the ego and the identification of the self with the larger purposes of the disinterested will. The experiences of St. Paul, Tolstoi and the Sadhu Sundar Singh, referred to in an earlier chapter, furnish typical examples. But religious biography is full of records of this experience. It is as natural as the emotional exaltation of falling in love. Like this latter, it varies enormously in intensity in different cases but always brings an access of personal vigor and a sense of deep and real values attained. And in both cases the conviction is inescapable that something of the deeper meaning of life is revealed in such experience, that a man enters here into touch with a reality greater than himself, that it is fitting and proper and in accord with the true nature of things that he should so act and so feel. If the nature of things is such as to provide such a reward for an inner spiritual adjustment, it is very natural to interpret that adjustment as an adjustment to something spiritual in the nature of things. As the values experienced in love impress us, not merely with the co-operation of another body, but also with the kinship of another soul, so the values experienced in religion suggest that the world in which we live and strive contains something more akin to our striving than the obvious, dead matter of it appears to be.

The third feature of religious experience that suggests a spiritual presence transcending our own is also closely connected with the inner conflict. It is the sense of obligation. We may follow Sir David Ross [1] in taking the notions of " right," " ought to be " and " moral obligation " as practically synonymous; but these terms are extremely difficult to

[1] *The Right and the Good* (New York: Oxford University Press, 1930), chap. 1.

define.[2] We are inclined to define *what* " right " means by presenting a theory as to *why* certain actions are right; e.g., that they " will produce the greatest possible amount of good in the Universe." [3] But the very fact that egoists, nationalists and others deny any such obligation shows that this is not simply the *meaning* of the term. To argue " that only that action which produces the greatest good possible in the circumstances is right " is not a mere tautology. It is to say of a certain kind of action that it " ought to be done." And this " ought " has reference to an ideal of behavior. As Professor M. C. Otto remarks, " In every day speech ' right ' has a specific connotation by reference to an ideal order set over against nature." [4] Bentham regarded the word, used in this sense, as really meaningless.[5] And Otto suggests that there is probably no justification for any such moral philosophy. But he adds: " Yet it is beyond question that this much at least is what right means in the popular and even in the cultivated mind." Few will question this statement; and most moralists today will also agree that G. E. Moore's statement describes the kind of actions that really conform to the requirements of the ideally right as formulated in their own minds.

We have referred particularly to Moore and Otto because both refuse very definitely to connect their ethics with any theistic metaphysics. Yet they have defined for us exactly what the enlightened religious consciousness also declares — the duty to seek the good, not of ourselves alone, but also of our fellow men. The disinterested will, which puts the

[2] In a strict sense of " definition " they cannot be defined, but can only be indicated, as when we " define " a color by its place in the spectrum. I would certainly agree with those who say that ethical terms cannot be defined in nonethical terms. But it seems to me possible that " right " and " good " may yet be successfully defined in terms of each other.

[3] George Edward Moore: *Principia Ethica* (New York: The Macmillan Co., 1903), p. 147.

[4] *Things and Ideals*, p. 94.

[5] *Principles of Morals and Legislation*, chap. 1, section 10.

greater good of others before the lesser good of the self, asserts itself within our consciousness with a peculiar authority. It furnishes the clearest and strongest examples of the experience we call the "sense of obligation." The order of behavior to which it points determines, for all save the egoist, the dominant features (if not, directly and indirectly, the whole) of that ideal order we call "right." Even if, like the tribal moralist, we limit the circle of those to whom we will recognize obligations, it is still the concept of the good of the recognized group that tends to dominate the system of moral ideas. Even the egoist, to justify his theory, usually feels it necessary to argue that by *wisely* pursuing his own good each person will contribute much (or most) to the general good.[6]

With greater or lesser extent and tenacity this sense of obligation imposes itself on the individual. He may disobey its mandates and sometimes he may ignore it. But he cannot *think* about his relations with his fellows without feeling it; and when he disobeys or ignores it, it often comes back to inflict upon him a sense of remorse. He cannot change it at will; and the more he reflects upon it the wider and stronger its claims tend to grow. Yet he can trace it to no origin that can explain it away. It is not merely the voice of his own deeper interests, for it often impels him to go against what he believes to be his own interests. It is not merely the pressure of society, for it often impels him to resist social pressure. It is a still, small voice in his own heart, making demands that are contrary to those of the will he recognizes as his own. He may resist it passionately, and yet feel that it "ought" to be obeyed. He does not feel it as a *strong* desire. Perhaps he hardly recognizes that he desires its goal at all. It is a demand that voices itself within him and claims authority over him. Yet often it does not appear to be any human demand, and it

[6] Epicurus, for example, placed great importance on friendship and asserted that justice is necessary to a life of true pleasure.

exerts itself within him as no human demand can do. Is it surprising that men who have struggled thus with conscience have become convinced that it is the voice of God? Whence, otherwise, could this weak desire gain so much authority?

THE ARGUMENT FROM THE FACT OF CONFLICT

(a)   *Kropotkin and McDougall.* — These three features of religious experience seem to me to be chiefly responsible for the tendency to interpret its object, the disinterested will, as having its roots in a spiritual reality transcending that of the individual mind having the experience. Our next task is to examine each of them in the light of all our scientific knowledge, to see whether this natural and common interpretation is justified.

The first feature to be examined is the fact of internal conflict. There are many conflicts that arise within a personality which certainly do not imply that any of the discordant elements is related to a spiritual source outside the organism. Is there anything unique about the conflict of the ego with the disinterested will that it should do so? In reply, it must first be recognized that egoistic desires are readily intelligible as direct or indirect expressions of the needs of the organism. They spring from appetites and other natural tendencies serving biological needs, and have been developed into their various forms in the mature personality through interaction with the material and social environment. But the desire for the good of some other person is not so readily intelligible. Until very recent decades moralists were inclined either to seek to explain it away as ultimately derived from egoism or to attribute it to some peculiar divine grace in the human heart. Setting aside these explanations as too often shown to be unsatisfactory, we must attend to more modern theories.

The modern explanation attributes altruistic desires either to instinctive impulse or to processes of social conditioning.

The former view has been championed by Kropotkin and Mc-Dougall. Kropotkin [7] pointed to the fact that many species, including man, owe much of their success in the struggle for existence to the development of tendencies to mutual aid. Thus spontaneously appearing impulses of the family and the herd have been strengthened by natural selection until they attain great force. McDougall [8] developed this theme by showing how natural instinctive tendencies, by force of association of ideas, become extended to a wide range of objects beyond those to which they originally respond, and argued that in this way the parental instinct to care for the weak and needy has become the source of all altruism. Most psychologists today doubt the reality of such fixed instinctive patterns as this would imply.

But even if they be admitted, the explanation seems very far-fetched when applied to the wider range of altruism. Disinterested social service is by no means merely a sympathetic response to the weak and needy. It is often a desire for lofty ideal goods to enrich the life of the general community. It is also too reflective, too analytical and intelligent, to be the mere result of an illogical extension of emotional impulses to regions to which they are not naturally appropriate. Nor can altruism be any more plausibly explained as arising from a mere fellow feeling of the herd. Rich and powerful though these feelings are, they are very narrow in scope, attaching themselves to a group that is *differentiated* from other groups, and are therefore by their very nature incapable of universalization.[9] And altruism so overrides these divisions, through a logical thinking that denies their significance, that it can hardly be due to an impulsive extension of emotions based

[7] P. A. Kropotkin: *Mutual Aid a Factor of Evolution* (London, 1900).

[8] *An Introduction to Social Psychology.*

[9] Henri Bergson: *Morality and Religion,* translated by Andra and Brereton (New York: Henry Holt & Co., 1935).

upon them.   Much of our merely impulsive altruism may certainly be traced to these instinctive tendencies.   But the deliberate verdict of duty obtained when we sit down in a cool hour, and the rational extension of our desire for human good wherever men are found, are so far beyond mere animal impulse, and yet manifest such power to set aside the animal impulses of the ego, that their roots must go far deeper into the nature of personality than these biological theories would allow.

(b)   *Westermarck and Dewey*. — The predominant current tendency in social psychology treats fixed instincts as of comparatively little importance in human motivation compared to the effect of social influences upon the growing personality, and attributes all our higher altruism to this latter source.   Among the most influential proponents of this view are Westermarck,[10] C. H. Cooley,[11] and Dewey.[12]   Westermarck regards altruism as due to " retributive kindly emotion," which he describes as a friendly feeling toward those who are found to be a cause of pleasure.   But if all our motives were egoistic, except so far as we tend to reciprocate with a desire to give pleasure to those who give pleasure to us, this would fall far short of explaining the range and strength of the human desire to advance general human welfare.   Further, is it not the case that the more closely we examine this desire in ourselves the more obvious it becomes that it is *not* merely because others have given us pleasure, or that we expect that they may do so, that we want them to be happy?   Rather, we want other human beings to enjoy welfare and security simply because we *like* them to be in that condition.   To desire the good of others is just as natural to man as to

[10] *Origin and Development of the Moral Ideas* and *Ethical Relativity* (New York: Harcourt, Brace & Co., 1932) .

[11] *Social Organization* (New York: Charles Scribner's Sons, 1909) and *Human Nature and the Social Order* (Scribner's, 1902) .

[12] Especially *Human Nature and Conduct*.

desire his own good, and is just as incapable of further explanation, though the egoistic desires are usually the stronger.

Dewey would seem to agree with this. But, following out
and developing the sociological theory of human nature propounded by Cooley, he regards all our distinctively human behavior as rooted in habits arising from interaction with the
social environment. Habit, he says, means " will "; it is " an
acquired predisposition to ways or modes of response," a
standing predilection or aversion rather than a specific act;
and because every man is born into a family and a social group
these, from the beginning, shape his habits. " Conduct is always shared; this is the difference between it and a physiological process. It is not an ethical ' ought ' that conduct *should*
be social. It *is* social, whether good or bad." [13] Now, obviously, the word " social " is here used in two senses. When
people say that conduct *ought* to be social they mean that it
ought to be consistent with social welfare. When Dewey says
that all conduct is social, whether good or bad, he means
merely that it is conditioned by society and affects society.
But he also assumes that, since conduct is social in this second
sense, it will, if only it is sufficiently intelligent, be social in
the first sense also.

Dewey is well aware that intellect can be misdirected,
turned to a mere seeking of " the instrumentalities of success " or to an " apology for things as they are." [14] But these
activities are not sufficiently intelligent to be truly good.
" Good consists in the meaning that is experienced to belong
to an activity when conflict and entanglement of various incompatible impulses and habits terminate in a unified orderly
release in action." A " superficial compromise " or " a victory of a temporarily intense impulse over its rivals " is only
a " seeming unification " which will end in further complica-

13 *Ibid.*, pp. 42, 17.
14 *Ibid.*, p. 258.

tion, inhibition and dissatisfaction.[15]   There are no separate instincts.   Life is essentially active.   Desire is simply " activity surging forward to break through what dams it up." Its goal is the object which " would secure re-unification of activity and the restoration of its ongoing unity." [16]   Intelligence seeks this solution of every problem; and Dewey is so convinced that the only really adequate solutions to be found by the individual must always tend in the long run to be " social " in both the senses we have distinguished that he is prepared to sum up our social obligation in the present day as that of fostering and developing the spirit of scientific inquiry.[17]

We are here concerned not to decide whether this optimism is sound, but with the question whether all altruistic desires can be explained in Dewey's way — as due to situations wherein the " life-activity " of an intelligent organism, socially conditioned in its development, finds that the reunification and ongoing of its activity require that certain goods should be obtained by others.   Now if it were supposed that the life-activity is originally directed only to satisfaction of its own organic needs or its own pleasure, this would merely be another of the oft-refuted attempts to derive all altruism from egoism.   But Dewey's life-activity is in itself neither egoistic nor altruistic, but devoid of desire.   " When the push and drive of life meets no obstacle, there is nothing which we call desire.   There is just life-activity." [18]   Nevertheless it *is*, initially, only the push and drive of a single organism.   Its concern for the unification and ongoing (the good) of other organisms is not, so far as Dewey indicates, a disinterested will to obtain this good for all, such as we have posited.   Its altruistic tendencies are simply habits due to its reaction to social pressure and example.

[15] *Ibid.*, pp. 210–11.

[16] *Ibid.*, pp. 249–50.

[17] *Ibid.*, p. 329.

[18] *Ibid.*, p. 249.

When we consider the nature of this social pressure and example we cannot but feel that this view is not really tenable. It posits an aggregation of organisms each striving to maintain a unified and expanding life-activity. In doing so each often finds it necessary and helpful to adjust its behavior in ways which allow others to do the same. Thus they develop habits of mutual response and adjustment involving co-operation and occasional sacrifice of their own self-expression to that of others. They even grow to *desire* the self-expression, or good, of others in situations they have found to contribute to their own, and these desires become habitual. But can we imagine habits thus formed becoming extended to the point where one finds a genuine satisfaction in changes that promote the welfare of utter strangers, foreigners, and even of people whom one dislikes? Still further, can we explain in this way the abiding satisfaction a man may have in such measures even when they are known to be contrary to very important interests of his own? And when we consider that the social conditioning to which most people have been submitted directs their attention only to the good of narrow groups, and even cultivates animosities toward others, can we believe that a mere intelligent seeking of the best way to maintain the unity and ongoing *of an activity thus conditioned* can sufficiently explain the way in which many such people have, at great cost to themselves, set aside the narrow traditions in which they have been trained and devoted themselves to the good of the alien race or class? Again, consider the history of the individual, and how egoistic his early set of habits necessarily is before he becomes aware of the possibilities of similar satisfactions and dissatisfactions on the part of others. Can the rapid response he makes to the needs of others when he becomes aware of them, the flaming idealism that youth so readily manifests, be due simply to an intelligent perception that his own good is bound up with that of these others, or to

habits formed by a mere uncritical acceptance of the suggestions of impractical idealists?   When the implications of
Dewey's theory are thus pointed out its inadequacies become
obvious.

We may conclude, therefore, that if the life-activity were
social only in the sense of being socially conditioned, it could
never have developed altruism as we know it. It must be
social also in the deeper sense of being directed toward social
welfare, or it could never have developed more than spas-
modic tendencies, in the majority of individuals, to pursue
the good of others except so far as this seemed conducive to
their own.   If it is true, as Dewey claims, that between " un-
scrupulous pursuit of self-interest " and " beaming benevol-
ence . . . the difference lies in the quality and degree of the
perception of ties and interdependencies," [19] then the " life-
activity " of each organism cannot be ultimately concerned
only with its own expanding life.   The clearest perception
must link the present interest with the ultimate interest of the
life-activity, setting aside all habits that do not minister to it.
And if, as is true, our clearest and most penetrating percep-
tions of our own deepest interest, when divested of passion
and prejudice, reach out disinterestedly to concern themselves
with the good of all men, then the simple " life-activity,"
which is the core of our whole organic life, can be no mere
expression of the struggle of a single organism to maintain
and expand itself amidst its fellows.   It must be a constructive
activity with a deeper source and a wider reach, creatively expressing itself in the initial development of organic life, becoming absorbed in the limited experience of each organism
developed, and reaching out to a wider " social " constructive-
ness through the individual as individuals become aware of
each other's presence and needs.   Thus our critical examination of the altruistic will in its conflict with the ego leads us

[19] *Ibid.*, p. 317.

to a conclusion that substantially endorses that of unsophisticated common sense: that the roots of altruism lie in a spiritual agency — i.e., an agency responsive to values — beyond the individual organism, an agency that is concerned with the good of all.

THE ARGUMENT FROM THE SENSE OF VALUE

(a) *The Place of Values in the World.* — The second of the features of religious experience from which belief in a transcendent deity is derived is, as indicated above, a value experience. Now it is fashionable in some quarters today to describe values as merely constituents of emotion. This is too loose a use of the term " emotion " for exact psychological purposes, but we need not press that objection here. What needs emphasis is the utter futility of any suggestion that by characterizing values as emotions we can thereby dismiss them from scientific consideration. This attitude is reminiscent of the Cartesian-Newtonian world view which cast everything subjective — everything with which the physical sciences cannot deal — out into another world. But this bifurcation of the world is bad science and worse philosophy. The psychological subject and all its contents are as much a part of the world as the body and the earth it stands on. Emotional changes are as fully integral to the world order as summer and winter. There are no degrees of reality among concrete facts; and the value qualities of our inner experience are as much a fact as any other. Indeed they are the most important of all facts, for it is only in relation to them that other facts have importance. An argument as to the nature of the world drawn from value experience is therefore an argument based upon the only intrinsically important facts in the world, and is the most important of all considerations for understanding the world.

Sensations of sight and touch have a fairly distinct spatial character which permits of measurement, and thereby of the discovery of an order of events of a nonsensory character which has a considerable permanence. But this order is no more real than the sensory qualities of sight and touch that reveal it. And the sensory qualities of sight and touch are no more real than the qualities of smell, taste, beauty, ugliness, pleasure, pain, joy and sorrow, which have no spatial character. All are equally transitory. They appear within the range of consciousness, disappear and reappear in a most mysterious manner. Something of the order of their going and coming we do learn. But where they go and whence they come, who knows? Whither do our joys and sorrows fly when we fall asleep, and where do all the pretty colors go when the light blinks out? These questions of a child are the profoundest problems of philosophy. All we can say for certain, and perhaps all we need to say, is that they are latent characters of our world which the world thrusts within our actual experience according to the way we behave in relation to the other active agencies of the world. We, as active systems of experiencing will and physico-chemical motion, are an organic part of the world; and the content of our experience is a part of it. To some of our activities the rest of the world responds by presenting a vision of color and beauty, to others with an excruciating pain, to others again with a sense of inner peace and joyful confidence. To interpret these responses of the rest of the world as entirely deliberate is a stupid anthropomorphism; to interpret them as entirely devoid of purpose is an equally unwarranted " physiomorphism."

Man is a psycho-physical organization, organic to a larger world. It would be strange if all the rest of the world were akin to only one phase of the human series of activities. Such a hypothesis becomes still stranger when we consider that every new phase of the development of life is met by a response from its world manifesting new qualities — qualities which, on the whole, tend to help and encourage further development and to discourage and destroy developments that stand in the way of the general onward movement. Thus each new specialization of the sensory nerve endings has discovered some new quality hitherto (so far as the life we know is concerned) latent in its world, yet usable for the refinement of distinctions in experience. Even pain has played a useful part in the direction of the onward movement of life. At the human level each refinement of the organization of personality has discovered new distinctions of value manifesting themselves to the moral consciousness, leading us on from the few rough virtues of the primitive savage to the finer graces of cultured personality and saintly living.

There are involved in this progress not merely new combinations of mental activity and physical motion, but new qualities that are felt. One *feels* different if one can manage to be brave, from the way one feels in giving way to fear. One feels the difference between overcoming anger in forgiving an injury, and planning a spiteful revenge. And these qualities of feeling that enter into *us* are bits of the world stuff. Out of the manifold resources of that stuff we are made. This complex gyroscope of electrons and protons and mental acts that we call our " body-and-mind " performs its evolutions in a few cubic feet of space and gathers out of the world order all the qualitative richness of experience — color and sound, the beauty of holiness and the misery of pain and guilt. Do we create these qualities *ex nihilo* at every moment of conscious existence, and drop them into nothingness again? And if not — if they are somehow part of the permanent resources of the world — is the world-whole, which is full of such marvelous potentialities, devoid of all power to realize and respond to them, save that which runs its brief course on the surface of this planet? To say " Yes " is to make a tremendous assumption based on nothing but our ignorance. To say we have no facts on which to base an answer is to ignore not only certain metaphysical considerations, but the evidence of that religious and moral experience which is the actual root of faith. We are dealing with the second of three features of this experience. An analogy will help to make its significance clear.

(b)   *Value as Revealing the Range of Mind.* — We cannot directly observe the activities of other minds. We infer them primarily [20] from the fact that the other minds communicate with us, guide us and reveal their will to us in the changes of experience they succeed in imposing upon us. Can any reflective person say that the changing course of his inner experience of values, which the world thrusts upon him, suggests or reveals to him no wider will in the world than the human? It is not quite like a human will, for it is not vacillating and inconsistent. The hierarchy of our values is somewhat vague and it does change — as when we learn that mercy is better than vengeance. But when the vagueness clears and the changes come, the new value scene is not seen as a change in the relative quality of the values themselves. It seems rather that we see better the values as they really are, and that the former view was due to our blindness — that mercy always was better than vengeance, and only the hardness of our hearts prevented us from seeing it before. When we pay attention to the fact of the changes in the value scheme it suggests that it cannot reveal the will of God, simply because it changes. When we pay attention to its fixity it suggests that it manifests, not a will at all, but a part of the eternal world order.[21] But when we reflect that every change in our value scheme comes to us as a clearer insight into an order of values that we had not seen clearly enough before, we realize

[20] Secondarily, we infer their existence from the teleological control over their bodies manifested by them. We shall refer to this again below.

[21] The point of view of Hartmann's *Ethics.*

that our value experience is best interpreted as our partial understanding of an order of values that is stable and objective. And we see that that stable and objective order of values is just what we should expect if it reveals the will of God.

But why should we connect values with will? The answer is that experience connects them with will. All the empirical philosophies of value, from Aristotle to Spinoza and to Ralph Barton Perry,[22] have emphasized the connection of value with want and desire. The difficulties that have arisen in their interpretations have been due to the fact that the hierarchy of our wants is so complex, and that they have not realized that its ultimate roots lie, not in the ego,[23] but in a will that transcends the ego to seek its creative expression in and through the good of all. Every positive value quality felt is experienced in the attainment of, or movement toward, some goal of the living organism.[24] And every goal is but the end of a stage, and a new beginning in the ongoing of life. This non-finality and instrumental character of all our particular values is the truth so well emphasized by Professor Dewey, and it has done much to enhance the influence of his teaching. Yet, as Aristotle saw, values cannot all be instrumental. There must be some ultimate end. So we can bring together the insights of Aristotle and Dewey in the recognition that life itself is the ultimate end — "that they may have life, and have it more abundantly." And life is creative activity.

But if we assume that all our wants and desires, in the pursuit of which our particular value experiences are felt, are ultimate goals, or if we assume that they are ultimately instrumental only to the good (the onward-going life) of the particular organism we each call "myself," then sooner or

22 *The General Theory of Value* (New York: Longmans, Green & Co., 1926).

23 This term is used in the sense defined in chap. 2.

24 Cf. my *Reality and Value,* chaps. 6–9, especially pp. 221–27.

later our world thrusts upon us a negative value experience
that tells us of our mistake. It is not only that positive wrong-
doing tends to bring pain and punishment, but in so far as
we live for self the game is not worth the candle. The experience of the young Tolstoi is peculiar here only in his
thoroughness and his sensitivity to the barrenness of the result. It is as we take an interest in other individuals and the
larger life of the social order that we discover those subtler
and more satisfying qualities of value entering into life.
These are not the intenser pleasures. It is as interests more
worth while that they are felt. Our world is rewarding us
for reaching out to pursue a good that is not our own. It
encourages us with a new sense of the worthwhileness of life
as we devote ourselves less to our own ends and more to the
common good. There are those who have grown up in a
community whose vision of the common good was narrow
and exclusive, bound in by barriers of race, caste, creed, or
personal resentments; and yet they have somehow broken
those barriers and given themselves to the cause of justice
and reconciliation. In return, their own community often
has made them suffer; and perhaps those they served have
been ungrateful. But *the world that is wider than the men
and women in it* has responded in another way; the world
reality that is immediately felt — as color and sound, beauty
and guilt are felt — has pressed upon their souls a new experience: not just a pleasure, though sweet enough to com-
pensate for the pain, but a sense of the abiding value of the
thing that they have done. Then, sometimes, they have had
the gifts and the courage to become prophets of a new way
in the relationships of men. And then, most wonderful of
all, when others, following, have tried the new way, the felt
reality of its value has pressed itself upon them too.

Throughout most of the range of our value experience we
are clearly aware of the wants or desires in the service of which

our experience of value is found. Where there is a will to attain an end there is a sense of value (more or less permanent) to be found in the attainment of it. Where there is a sense of value in the attaining of a result there is somewhere, however hidden, a will to its attainment. But the sense of value is not permanent unless the result, and the will that achieves it, are in harmony with the more ultimate purposive tendencies of the organisms that are affected. Our values form a hierarchy defining goals in which one is instrumental to another, and that to yet another, and all at last to the creative forward movement of life. And the only values that are permanent are those whose goals fit into the purposive scheme of the whole. Here we have the key to the ultimate organization of life. For when we make the goal the mere expression of our own psycho-physical organism alone, its values rapidly perish. When we take for our goal the common good to which all selfish ends must be subordinated, the sense of value in life as a whole deepens, strengthens and grows richer.

Thus from our value experience the organization of our human personality grows clear. Its ultimate root lies, not in the will to self-expression of the individual organism, but *in a principle of creativity common to all organisms,* which, as through one organism it becomes conscious of another, concerns itself with the creative expansion of the life of all. This principle of creativity is so organic to the world as to be responsive to the scale of values with which the world presents it. Thus here·again, through the analysis of our highest value experience, we find our own being to be rooted in that disinterested will to the good to which we have given the name of God. And we see how the unfolding value experience of man reveals to him the nature and aim of the divine will.

But something of still deeper significance emerges from

our analysis of the place of value qualities in the world order. We have seen that, though their felt qualities may be called a part of the content of an emotion, that does not make them any less essential features of the world. We have seen the organic relation of these qualitative potentialities of the world to our own life-activity and, above all, to the disinterested will present in us all. We have seen that disinterested will revealed as not dependent upon our organisms, but as that on which our organisms depend and from which they rise to pursue their independent way. We have found a principle of creativity that must be antecedent to the kind of organic life we know, and we have been able to trace its identity with the higher will within ourselves. And we have seen that we never lose touch with this higher will, nor can we, with all our independence, pass beyond its influence; for it is the ultimate determining factor in all our value experience, guiding and encouraging us in those developments consistent with the whole onward movement of individual and social life. In *our* lives is the experimentation, the failure, and the triumph. Beyond and within us is the abiding Will to universal good. It never controls us, but reveals itself to us in its ultimate determining influence upon what, in the long run, we shall find most truly good.

The Nature of God
(Continued)

THE ARGUMENT FROM THE SENSE OF OBLIGATION

THE SENSE of obligation is the third of those features of our moral and religious experience that have suggested the idea of its source in some superhuman spiritual reality. The peculiarities of this experience may again be noted. What we feel we " ought " to do there seems always to be *some* desire to do, but commonly it is not what we desire most to do; and, whether or not the opposing desires win out in action, we feel that it does not affect the question of what we ought to do. The " ought " thus represents a desire but is independent of the strength of desire. It is commonly altruistic in its directional tendency but not necessarily so. Yet reflection upon it has brought about a very widespread endorsement of the principle of doing the greatest possible good for all concerned, with equal consideration for all. In the details of its operation it reflects strongly the current moral tradition and the personal prejudices and interests of the individual, though its own verdict is that these are really extraneous influences by which the moral judgment " ought " not to be affected. It thus points to a unique order of activities, actual or ideal, which it marks as the way things ought to be or ought to be done. It allows for differences of obligation relative to differences within the individual and in the external circumstances of each case, but assumes a universality in the nature of the ought in that it asserts that in so far as the relevant features of the total situation are the same for each person concerned it contains the same obligations for each of them.

(a)   *Obligation as Reasonable Self-Interest.* — This then being the general character of the notion of obligation, an empirical philosophy must look for its source in experience. From the beginnings of empiricism we find a strong tendency to look for the roots of obligation in reasonable self-interest. Among recent writers this point of view is ably represented by F. C. Sharp and W. T. Stace.

In defining the moral ideal Professor Sharp emphasizes the requirements of impartiality. The " authority " of this ideal, he says, consists in its " reasonableness." From a wide variety of examples of " unreasonable " conduct he concludes that such conduct consists essentially in a person's acting " in defiance of the demands of an objective valuation of his own interests." If we accept this definition we should conclude that the contradictory term " reasonable conduct " would describe conduct that is in accord with an objective valuation of one's own interests. But Sharp draws a different, and quite unwarranted, conclusion: " This analysis of the unreasonable reveals the nature of the reasonable . . . those actions are reasonable which would flow from a complete knowledge and perfect realization of the sum total of their consequences," so that such knowledge, applied consistently throughout, " would result in the willing subordination of self to the claims of that majestic whole of which we each form a part." [1] This argument shows that, when only the individual's own interests are at stake, reasonableness consists in the selection of what, on the whole and in the long run, constitutes the greatest good. It then assumes that the same principle will hold when the interests of many people are involved. But such an assumption obviously begs the whole question.

This fallacy, however, would never have deceived anyone

[1] F. C. Sharp: *Ethics* (New York: Century Co., 1928) , pp. 481–84.

were it not that, to all morally sensitive people, it does seem perfectly reasonable that we should consider the welfare of others equally with our own.   Sharp is on sounder ground when, in an earlier chapter, he states that "egoism . . . is no more primitive in the child's mind than is altruism." [2] But this is close to saying that what is really primitive is the disinterested will.   And, as we have constantly urged, this is the reason why, to the reflective moral consciousness, it seems increasingly reasonable and right to pursue without favor the good of all.   But to say that will is *primitively* disinterested means that it is not primarily a response to the needs of the organism, that it is not merely an organic adjustment in its origin and a habit in its developed form.   It is to recognize, therefore, the only alternative, that will is responsive to the objective value qualities that its *world* presents to it.   Thus its early apparent egoism, in the child and in the animal, is due merely to the fact that its early feeling of values is limited to those associated with the organism immediately concerned, and its later egoism is due merely to the survival and extension of early habits thus formed.

Without the recognition of this priority of the disinterested will to the reactions and needs of the organism every attempt to explain the sense of obligation breaks down.   Professor Stace's more confident exposition from the standpoint of egoism is, for example, no more successful than the rather hesitant egoism of Professor Sharp.   Stace's view is not that *all* our motives are egoistic.   He finds in "disinterested altruism" one of the most important sources of morality.[3]   It is the notion of obligation, he feels, that has to be put upon an egoistic basis.   He can find no meaning in the notion of a categorical obligation, except in the sense that these notions have

[2] *Ibid.,* p. 88. Allowance must, of course, be made for the fact that altruism can be *manifested* only as the child becomes aware of other selves.

[3] W. T. Stace: *The Concept of Morals* (New York: The Macmillan Co., 1937), p. 281.

a powerful effect upon people's minds and behavior.[4] Why they should do so is left a mystery. But Stace cannot find any fact that such statements of obligation describe. Hypothetical moral judgments however, he points out, may describe a factual connection and may therefore be true or false; i.e., they are meaningful. In such judgments, " This ought to be done " means simply, " If certain needs or desires are to be fulfilled then this ought to be done." Thus morality is regarded as relative to the needs of human nature, and a universal or objective morality has to be shown to be " relative to the universal needs of human nature." [5]

From an empirical examination of recognized human duties and of concepts of the ends of moral action, Stace concludes that the goal of moral action is happiness and that human duties may be summed up in the command, " You ought to be unselfish." The only empirical basis he can find for this conclusion is in the contention that this is the only way for a person to attain his own happiness.[6] In support of this contention he points first to the social nature of man, which makes him dependent in so many ways upon the presence and cooperation of his fellows; and, second, to man's " capacity for being made happy in some degree by the bare fact of the happiness of other persons." [7] These two sources of satisfaction, it is claimed, yield values so high in the scale " that between them they are capable of yielding more happiness than all the rest of our satisfactions put together," and " supreme happiness " is attainable only " by reaching up to, and practically carrying out, the highest imaginable moral ideals." Thus the conclusion is reached: " You ought to be moral because without morality you cannot attain . . . that high happiness, which you yourself desire." [8]

4 *Ibid.*, pp. 22 ff.   7 *Ibid.*, p. 262.
5 *Ibid.*, p. 67.   8 *Ibid.*, pp. 277–79.
6 *Ibid.*, pp. 252–54.

Now, as a general rule, it seems to me profoundly true that a really rational unselfishness, even involving considerable self-sacrifice, makes for the happiness of the unselfish person. In certain extreme cases however, where the right and unselfish thing has been done at great cost and has met only misunderstanding and ingratitude, the conclusion hardly seems justified. But whether or not it is the case that to be just and unselfish will always make us happier, it seems to me quite obvious that this is not the reason why we feel that we ought to be just and unselfish. Is it not the essence of the moral situation that we feel that there are certain ways we ought to behave toward our fellows, *whether we want to or not, and whether or not it will make us any happier?* If a man could prove with certainty that to pay his debts would make him unhappy, that would not prove that he ought not to pay them. The essence of morality is in the recognition that there are certain obligations we owe to our fellows, not in a canny calculation as to how to get the most out of life for ourselves. We may cherish a high faith that virtue is its own reward, but it is not the fact of its great rewards that makes a certain line of conduct a virtue.

Thus, plainly, the root of our sense of obligation does not lie in the promise of happiness attached to the doing of our duty. But does this rejection of the effort to base morality on the desire for our own happiness leave the moral imperative hanging in empty air — an ought-to-do without a reason to be found for it? If the "ought" had no relation to any fact it would be strange that the notion should have the deep influence upon people's minds that Stace rightly admits it possesses. When we turn to our previous analysis, however, we find the reason for the "ought," and the reason why it so strongly influences people even when they cannot clearly explain what they mean by it. It expresses a more or less clear sense of the *proper* order of our purposive activity that is rooted in the *actual* order of the teleological structure of our own personalities.[9]

In the actual order of the purposive structure of the organism, for example, the will to eat is instrumental to the will to live. If we pursue the will to eat in circumstances which are detrimental to the more fundamental will to live, then, upon reflection, we see that this relation is wrong; even without reflection we may vaguely feel that there is something wrong without being able clearly to isolate the functional disorder and say what it is. Similarly, when we set the pursuit of our own lesser good before the greater good of the community, we see, more or less clearly, that there is something wrong about this choice. The disinterested will to the realization of the greatest possible good may be almost swamped by the subsidiary desires to realize certain particular goods in our own persons. But the more we reflect upon and analyze our own desires, the more the conviction grows that the (at the time weaker) disinterested desire for the general good was the one to which the other desires " ought " to have been subservient. The values attached to this desire seem " higher," its satisfaction " deeper "; there is an obligation attaching to it; it is not so strong but it ought to be allowed the primacy.

---

[9] This is the reason for the success in interpretation of ethical problems achieved by the important British school of moral philosophers known as deontologists. They make the term " right " more fundamental for ethics than " good," and, for decision as to what is right, appeal to our sense of what is fitting or proper in the circumstances. If our analysis is correct, however, this method succeeds only because our sense of what is fitting is a sense of what is fitting to the structure of personality as an order of will, and because the feature of that structure that ultimately determines what is fitting is the disinterested will to the greatest possible good. Thus, in spite of the success of the deontological approach in clarifying ethical problems, it remains true that it is the nature of the good that ultimately determines what is right. For an exposition of deontology see Ross: *The Right and the Good* and *Foundations of Ethics* (New York: Oxford University Press, 1939) . For a critical reinterpretation of this theory see my article, " Deontology and Self-realization," *Ethics,* July 1941.

This inescapable feeling that the disinterested will ought to be recognized as having primary claim is, if our analysis is correct, simply due to the fact that it really is the primary feature of that system of purposive tendencies which constitutes the personality. The "ought" describes a fact, a fact which is also a norm, the normal functional order of the system of conative tendencies, or forms of will, that constitute our human nature. And it is for this reason that, when we reflect calmly and deeply upon what we ought to do, we feel that the way of our highest obligation is also, in general if not always, the way of our truest welfare and deepest happiness.

Thus the very reasons advanced in support of an egoistic interpretation of obligation turn out, upon examination, to point to the primacy of the disinterested will and the merely instrumental position of the system of purposive tendencies that constitutes the individual organism. The good of the individual finds its place as a real part, but only a part, of a larger good in course of realization. And the individual will finds itself as a necessary organic part, but only a part, of a larger system of will directed toward the larger goal.

(b) *Obligation as Social Pressure.* — The theory that conscience is due simply to the acceptance, under various forms of social pressure, of the traditional moral ideas of the community or of some group within it has always found many supporters. The fact that individuals do tend thus to derive their moral ideas is, of course, quite obvious; we similarly derive most of our ideas on every other subject, and comparatively few people give much critical overhauling to the traditional beliefs in morals, politics, science or any other field. But this fact, and the resulting differences of opinion among different groups, do not prove that all these bodies of belief are *nothing but* beliefs accepted under social pressure, that they are not all more or less accurately grounded in experience and capable of being tested by experience. Empiricists

in ethics are usually quite emphatic in insisting that there are
objective empirical criteria whereby we can decide what is
good.   Yet many of them assert that the notion of an *obligation* upon the individual to conform his conduct to the pursuit of the good has no other basis than the natural and social
sanctions.   We shall briefly examine this interpretation as
developed by Dewey, Moritz Schlick (representing the recent
and active school of logical positivism) , and Westermarck.

Dewey. — " The stuff of belief," says Professor Dewey,
" comes to us from others, by education, tradition and the
suggestion of the environment."   This is so with science and
with conscience.   " When a child acts those about him react,"
showing approval and disapproval.

> We foreknow how others will act, and the foreknowledge is the
> beginning of judgment passed on action, . . . there is conscience.
> An assembly is formed within our breast which discusses and
> appraises proposed and performed acts.   The community without
> becomes a forum within. . . . Moral judgment and moral re-
> sponsibility are the work wrought in us by the social environ-
> ment.[10]
>
> Right is only an abstract name for the multitude of concrete
> demands in action which others impress upon us, and of which
> we are obliged, if we would live, to take some account.   Its au-
> thority is the exigency of their demands, the efficacy of their in-
> sistencies. . . . Accordingly failure to recognize the authority of
> right means defect in effective apprehension of the realities of
> human association . . . indicates a defect in education.[11]

This, if it were true, would reduce the whole notion of right
and wrong, of moral obligation, to the mere blind force of custom.   Yet, sandwiched in the midst of the argument, there is
a grudging half-admission that gives the whole case away:

> There may be good ground for the contention that in theory the
> idea of the right is subordinate to that of the good, being a state-

[10] *Human Nature and Conduct,* pp. 314–16 *passim.*
[11] *Ibid.,* pp. 326–28 *passim.*

ment of the course proper to attain good. But in fact it signifies the totality of the social pressures exercised upon us to induce us to think and desire in certain ways.[12]

It is surely a very superficial impression from the facts which ignores the inner meaning given to the idea by every thoughtful person who admits an obligation. A little questioning of any intelligent person, be he savage or scientist, as to why he recognizes a certain traditional custom, institution, law or principle as right and obligatory will bring forth the defense that it is good for the individual or for society. That which society approves is accepted as an obligation simply because it is assumed that society has approved it as good because it *is* good. When a moral critic attacks any accepted law or principle he does so by proceeding to argue that it is not good. Both sides agree that the only way to show that anything is obligatory is to show that it is good — for society if not for the individual. Even Kant felt this necessity. And when appeal is made to authority it is to an authority recognized as knowing what is good.

Thus at every level of consideration the notion of obligation is connected with that of the good and derived from it.[13] Dewey himself cannot escape the connection. With a delightful inconsistency he follows up his dismissal of the notions of right and obligation as mere names for social pressures by telling us what our obligations are and grounding his contention, not on facts of social pressure, but on his own insight into what is good. All morals, he has claimed, are social. And then he adds:

But there are enormous differences of better and worse in the quality of what is social. Ideal morals begin with the perception of these differences. . . . We have at last reached a point where

[12] *Ibid.*, pp. 326–27.
[13] For a reference to the objections of the deontologists to this point of view cf. footnote 9, this chapter.

social conditions create a mind capable of scientific outlook and inquiry. To foster and develop this spirit is the social obligation of the present because it is its urgent need.[14]

Thus Dewey himself feels an obligation and wants us to feel it. It does not arise from social pressures, but from the " perception " of qualitative differences of good and evil in the social order and in the character of different minds, and from the further recognition that the individual *ought* to do those things which meet the social need. Dewey's own moral sense is obviously rooted in the disinterested will to the general good; but he does not do justice to the man in the street and the man in the jungle when he suggests that *their* sense of obligation is not also rooted in some " perception " of " differences of better and worse in the quality of what is social " — a perception which, in their case as in ours, rests ultimately on the primacy of the disinterested will.

Moritz Schlick. — In the work of Moritz Schlick we have a much more careful statement of essentially the same point of view, though linked with a hedonism which Dewey rejects. " Those dispositions are called good," Schlick finds, " which human society *believes* are most advantageous to its general welfare." [15] Or again: " The word ' good ' has a moral sense when (1) it refers to human *decisions,* and (2) expresses an approbation by human society." And approval means " *desired* by a large majority of those persons with whom the individual comes into contact through word or deed." [16]

The conscience is formed by external suggestion, whose whisperings resound in the mind as through a powerful trumpet.[17]
The moral demands are established by society *only because* the fulfillment of these demands appears to be useful to it. . . . The

---

14 *Human Nature and Conduct,* p. 329.
15 *Problems of Ethics* (New York: Prentice-Hall, Inc., 1939) , p. 195.
16 *Ibid.,* pp. 82–83.
17 *Ibid.,* p. 91.

material meaning of the word " moral " *exhausts* itself in denoting what, according to the prevailing opinion in society, is advantageous (its *formal* meaning consists in being demanded by society) .[18] . . . The philosopher could, for his purposes, *define* as moral that behaviour by means of which an individual furthered his capacity for happiness, and could designate the precepts of society as " truly " moral if this criterion fitted them.[19]

" I ought to do something " never means anything but " Someone wants me to do it." And in fact the desire of another, directed upon me, is described as an ought only when that person is able to add pressure to his desire and thus to reward fulfillment and to punish neglect, or at least to point out the natural consequences of observance or neglect. . . . When the command of another person confronts me under [these] conditions . . . , then definite conscious processes take place in me, which represent just that experience which in everyday life we call " ought." It is complex, yet not so difficult to analyze. The decisive thing is the consciousness of " compulsion," which consists of the fact that a persistent idea is established by the one who commands, and is equipped by means of his sanctions with feeling tones so strong that they affect adversely the pleasure components of all other ideas, and (in the case of obedience) suppress them.[20]

The utter inadequacy of this exposition of the empirical roots of our sense of obligation, and of the notion of a *moral* good, may perhaps be sufficiently shown by its application to the problem of international morality. The notion of moral obligation of nation to nation has been of slow growth, but it certainly is growing and its expansion is the greatest moral need of today. Its growth is due to the logical extension to the international sphere of moral principles already recognized between individuals. If it is wrong for me to rob my neighbor and right for me to protect him from a robber, then

18 *Ibid.*, pp. 96–97.
19 *Ibid.*, p. 197.
20 *Ibid.*, pp. 110–11, 114 *passim.*

it is wrong for my nation to rob a neighbor nation and right to offer protection.

But if we accept Schlick's interpretation of what constitutes morality and obligation then this argument is based on a false premise. It assumes that essentially the same relevant moral relations hold between the populations of one country and another as between individuals within the one country. But, for Schlick, the act that would have the best result on the whole is not thereby to be accounted morally good or obligatory. Morality and obligation enter in only when it is approved by society as useful and society is able to exert such compulsion as to make it unpleasant to go against its will. This means that, in pre-world war days, when international society expressed no disapproval of the exploitation of Asia and Africa and the annexation of small countries by their larger neighbors, there was nothing really wrong about such actions. And even today, when world opinion disapproves such things, there is no moral obligation upon any country not to do them, for world society has not yet developed the means for making it really unpleasant for the aggressive and exploiting nation so long as it attacks only weaker peoples.

Now what proves that Schlick's exposition of the roots of our sense of moral obligation is empirically incorrect is the fact that the intelligent, calm and reflective moral consciousness endorses the analogy between interindividual and international morality as basically valid, allowing for such differences of circumstance as those due to the difficulties of collective action and relative remoteness of relations. The fundamental reason why the capitalists of America and England ought not to exploit the peons of South America or the Negroes of Africa with the aid of bombs and bullets is precisely the same as the fundamental reason why they ought not similarly to exploit their own workers at home. It rests in the common nature of humanity and in what is *due* from man to man by reason of that common nature. The reflective moral consciousness has always supported the view that human beings have certain rights which *ought* to be socially approved, whether they are or not. And this conviction, as we have seen, rests in the fundamental constitution of human nature as rooted in the disinterested will to the good.

Westermarck. — Both Dewey and Schlick acknowledge their debt to Westermarck for much of the evidence to which they point in support of their view that the sense of moral obligation is due to social pressure. But they ignore one feature of Westermarck's exposition of this same theory which is of very great significance. This is the role assigned to the character of " disinterestedness " [21] attaching to the moral judgment. According to Westermarck's finding from his enormous researches into the moral ideas of both primitive and civilized peoples, it is only that social approval and disapproval which bear the appearance of being disinterested that are regarded as moral; and these apparently disinterested judgments of the community are reflected in the mind of the individual as a sense of obligation.

In explanation of the reason why judgments must appear disinterested to be recognized as moral, Westermarck thinks it sufficient to point to the fact " that society is the birth-place of the moral consciousness; that the first moral judgments expressed, not the private emotions of isolated individuals, but emotions felt by the society at large." [22] But this hardly seems adequate. Are group approval and disapproval usually so impartial that impartiality should come to be singled out as so much their characteristic feature that, when the individual holds before his mind two or more alternative judgments or decisions, the one which is impartial should appear to be the kind of decision that the group would make, and so carry

21 Cf. *Ethical Relativity,* especially pp. 92 ff.
22 *Ibid.,* p. 109.

with it the peculiar sense of authority that belongs to the group? Is it not rather the case that, for some other reason, both individual and group judgments are felt to be moral and obligatory only when they seem impartial — i.e., when they appear to be expressions of a disinterested will to the good? [23] Certainly, as Westermarck himself declares,[24] when individuals arise to criticize prevalent moral ideas on the basis of their own feelings, they should be recognized as speaking in the name of morality so long as those feelings manifest an impartial or disinterested concern for the welfare of others or the correction of evils.

Thus, here again, the facts adduced point to the root of the sense of obligation as lying in that experience of the individual which is due to the operation within him of a fundamental tendency to seek disinterestedly the greatest good, rather than merely to respond to private needs and desires or to submit to social pressure.

(c)   *Obligation as Rooted in the Structure of Personality.* — In general, naturalistic ethics tends to oscillate between the two explanations of the sense of obligation that we have discussed, sometimes attributing it to social pressure and sometimes to farsighted self-interest. There is, however, a third alternative, a suggestion of which empiricists might have found in Immanuel Kant: that conscience is due to the felt need of consistency; not, however, merely of thought (as with Kant), but of will; i.e., that conscience is rooted in the felt need of *integration of personality.* Probably the reason why this interpretation has not been more frequently adopted is that, unless we recognize the fundamental character of the disinterested will, it suggests such a hopelessly subjectivistic and ego-

[23] Allowance must be made here for the fact that tradition and prejudice distort the view of what *seems* impartial, and narrow the range of good which the individual is willing to consider.

[24] *Ethical Relativity,* p. 112.

istic type of ethics.   This, nevertheless, is the position adopted
by Professor T. V. Smith.[25]

In characteristically vigorous style Smith submits other
typical explanations of conscience, empirical and nonempiri-
cal, to an acutely critical examination and rejects them.   With
them he rejects all claims of conscience to any kind or degree
of authority.   It is merely a state of feeling depending on our
active inner personal integration, and its only value is to be
aesthetically enjoyed.   But then arises the question why conscience, in general, supports the principle of equity.   Having
dismissed the usual empirical explanations, which all grant
some remnant of moral importance to conscience, Smith calls
in the psychoanalysts to destroy the last of the claims of conscience to respect and to explain away its last claim to dignity:
" the drive of conscience toward equalitarianism is its self-
punitive bid for absolution from its ancient power curse." [26]
It is a defense mechanism unconsciously erected by conscience
in the effort to secure " allies in the great task of self-mastery."
The distressing need which we feel as an uneasy conscience is
the need of an inner integration of personality, involving control over the ego and its unruly desires.   So conscience, by
an unconscious reaction, calls society in to help in its own inner problem of self-control.   It asserts that all persons must
behave in the way it feels it necessary to behave for its own
inner peace, and that society must insist that all persons, including itself, recognize the equal rights of all.

The demand of conscience for the recognition of equal
rights for all is thus explained as a sort of fortunate compulsion neurosis, developed by civilization and making its continuation possible.   Like so many of the psychoanalytical the-

---

[25] *Beyond Conscience* (New York: McGraw-Hill Book Co., 1934).   For an
able critique of this point of view cf. A. E. Murphy: " Conscience, Tolerance
and Moral Discrimination," *Ethics*, April 1939.

[26] *Op. cit.,* p. 341.

ories of human behavior, it sounds a bit far-fetched. And, since it requires us to postulate subconscious reactions the existence of which can never be verified, it must always remain a hypothesis to be accepted only if the situation is susceptible of no explanation better supported by facts. Psychologically considered, it is a most unlikely hypothesis, since it explains a feature of conscience which emerges most strongly with the calmest possible reflection (the principle of equity) as being a mental reaction due to the severity of the inner conflict. On the other hand, when we attribute this principle to a natural disinterested tendency to seek the good wherever found, we see precisely why it should emerge most strongly in times of calm reflection, when the coarser habitual desires of the ego are in abeyance.

However, the central feature of Smith's explanation of conscience may, I think, be accepted. It does arise out of the felt need of inner personal integration. But the reason why it, upon reflection, leads to the endorsement of the principle of equity is that complete integration is to be achieved only through the organization of all egoistic tendencies in due subordination to the deepest tendency of personality — the tendency which tends to make itself felt the more our self-understanding grows; the will that responds disinterestedly to what it feels as good. It is not sufficient to recognize, as does Professor DeWitt Parker, that the obligatory and objective character of the moral consciousness is due to the need of integration of personality, and to postulate that this need culminates merely in an " interest of the self as a whole." [27] We are glad to be able to cite Parker as another supporter of the view that the sense of obligation derives from the need for personal integration; but what requires emphasis is that this need would not take the form it does if the dominating interest were

[27] DeWitt H. Parker: *Human Values* (New York: Harper & Brothers, 1931) , chap. 5.

any mere interest of the particular self in its own particular self-expression.

The fact that has to be faced is that genuine integration of volitional tendencies requires that those which have been developed (whether in the history of the individual or of the race) as mere means to more fundamental purposive drives have to be subordinated to the ends they serve. We therefore can learn which purposive tendencies are the more original by finding which have to be subordinated to which in order to achieve integration — and the deepest integration is marked by the deepest satisfaction, by inner peace and harmony. The whole ethical history of mankind then bears witness to the fact that this is achieved when the particular appetites and habits are subordinated to the fundamental will to self-preservation and self-expression, and when this in turn is subordinated to the will to pursue the greatest good, irrespective of whether that good accrues to the experience of the self or of other selves. This means that the primary form of will, to serve which all the others (even the will to self-maintenance) have been developed, is the disinterested will to the good. It means that every appetite and tendency to organic adjustment, the whole purposive organic life, is a secondary development subservient to it.[28]

It is for this reason that the reflective moral consciousness, acquiring by calm reflection a deeper insight into the functioning of its own desires, discovers that its egoistic desires (though often, by reason of habit, the strongest, and, by reason of the immediacy of the values concerned, the readiest to respond) are not the most fundamental. Its really fundamental aim is the increasing realization of values in every center (i.e., in every consciousness) where values are being and can be realized. To this fundamental will (the will to constructive activity in which the greatest possible values are

[28] For fuller exposition see my *Reality and Value,* chaps. 6–12.

realized) all particular organic desires are thus more or less clearly seen to be instrumental. This more or less adequate insight into the actual order of our own will thus determines what we see as the *reasonable* order of our desires. It also determines which of our desires we feel *ought* to be subservient or instrumental, and which *ought* to be fulfilled. When we thus recognize the fundamental position of the disinterested will in the development of organic life, all the mystery disappears from the sense of obligation. It is seen to consist in a more or less adequate insight into the purposive order of one's own life, into the teleological structure of one's own personality. And the reason for its objectivity, and for the tendency of moralists to reach unanimity on fundamentals through progressive reflection, is the fact that the fundamental aim of each individual is the same (the disinterested pursuit of values) and that each is active in a common world of value potentialities.

If now we sum up the results of this analysis of moral experience we find that we have three very significant facts concerning the disinterested will. First, it is a direct response to objective situations according to their value-tone which seeks creatively to develop those situations in ways that maintain or increase their value; it is not merely an impulse developed by the specific needs of the individual organism or the race. Second, it is organic to a world order of values, distinguished as greater and less, higher and lower; and this world order progressively unfolds new values to call forth ever fresh creative activity. Third, it is the root of the sense of obligation, thus asserting its unique importance above that of all other impulses and desires; in the structure of personality it is fundamental and there is something wrong in the teleological order unless all specific interests are made to harmonize with it. In brief, the disinterested will appears as a part of the world order, responsive to the world order of values; and it is not dependent on the individual psycho-physical organism, but the individual psycho-physical organism functions in rationally recognized subservience to it.

But will, as we have seen in an earlier chapter, must be regarded as a process within an omnipresent neutral substance. The set tendency of the disinterested will therefore is seen to be a feature of neutral substance present in each organism as the fundamental feature of its nonphysical structure, and existing independently of both the physical and the rest of the nonphysical structure. It is a feature of the world order to which the individual psycho-physical organism is instrumental and upon which it is dependent. It is both immanent in and transcendent to the individual organism. It is the basic structural feature common to every organism. Individual organisms are so many particular developments of its original creative initiative. They work out that initiative as opportunity develops and according to the values discovered in their own peculiar perspectives of the world. They are each independent developments because each new act of will is a spontaneous response to values as they are discerned. But the values that enter their experience depend upon the harmony of each new act of will with its ground in the earlier structure. Thus their deepest and most abiding values are ultimately determined by harmony with the disinterested will. So the individual remains in living contact with that disinterested will which underlies and transcends the specific organization of will that he recognizes as peculiarly his own. And in the long run he finds the deepest values of his own life realized by bringing the will that is peculiarly his own into conformity with the will that is his and yet more than merely his own.

THE GOD OF RELIGIOUS EXPERIENCE

In our analysis of religious experience we found that it is this other and higher will within himself that man has felt and

called God. Now we have learned that God is not only immanent in man but transcendent beyond him. God exists as a
form of will, as an effective structural feature of the world
order, a set tendency of the neutral substance which underlies
at least all its other nonphysical structures and processes
known to us. And, since personality is neither more nor less
than an organization of will, God is personal. His personality is the source of ours and in his personality ours finds its
basis and completion. His personality includes ours and
transcends it. Each of us finds his good·in the development
of his own personality, but only in such development as is in
harmony with God's, and therefore in harmony with that of
all other personalities. For the one divine will seeks in and
through each the good of all.

Empirical knowledge is rooted in the analytical distinction
of data in their given relations to each other. But it goes
beyond this bare acquaintance to formulate an interpretation
of (i.e., to give meaning to) what is discriminated as given.
Thus from a discrimination of sensory data it passes to thought
about the physical world, and from a discrimination of mental activities and values to thought about the mental or spiritual world. In both cases the validity of the thought (meaning or interpretation) is tested by its interconsistency with
further experience and the thought arising from it. When
thoroughly tested we call it knowledge.

It may therefore be said that we have knowledge of God.
He is not merely a hypothetical entity invented, more or less
legitimately, to explain peculiar facts in our experience or to
fill the gaps in our scientific explanations. Our knowledge
of him begins with the discrimination of a datum, an act of
will, within the active process of our own personality. It goes
on to discover the relation of that datum to other data — to
other acts of will, to the value qualities, to that peculiar combination of value qualities and volitional relations we call the

sense of obligation, and so to the world of persons and things in which we find ourselves. On ordinary occasions the central datum, the disinterested will, is interpreted as a part of the ordinary self; but on certain special occasions its conflict with the rest of the self, its relation to certain higher value qualities, and its place in the experience of obligation, make this explanation seem inadequate. It may then be interpreted as primarily the expression of a greater self on which our own private selves depend.

Traditional philosophical theory, by reason of the notion that a self consists essentially of a unitary center of private consciousness, has regarded these two interpretations as contradictory. But the careful analysis of moral and religious experience upon which we have been engaged tends to validate both interpretations. And the modern understanding of the self allows of the truth of both interpretations; for it depicts the self as a system of volitional tendencies, the feeling aspect of which tends to culminate in a unified attentive consciousness, but is not limited to this and may possess subsidiary centers. It thus becomes possible to regard the private human consciousness as a subsidiary center of attentive consciousness within, and organic to, a larger mental life, characterized by that disinterested will to the good in which our own mental life is ultimately rooted. Freudian psychology has shown us how such divisions of personality within personality may occur even in human life, though a division of personality within a single organism is pathological. But the development of distinct personalities together with distinct organisms is natural.

What our religious experience discloses is that the distinct personality, thus developing, never loses contact with the wider personal order out of which it is developed, any more than the physical organism loses touch with the physical order out of which it is developed. The psycho-physical organism of man is organic to the psycho-physical order of the world. He discerns value potentialities in the world order that are not primarily values of his own organism. The deepest element of his own personality responds in creative effort to effect their realization. In that effort new and unexpected values are realized by reason of the integration of the subsidiary forms of his personality with this disinterested form of will which is its foundation and source. But this personal Will that pursues values beyond the individual, and with which the individual may integrate himself, is, as we have seen, neither derived from nor confined to the will of the individual organism. The individual finds himself integrated with it, but it is not *merely* an integral part of him.

Thus we may justifiably speak of our knowledge of God as knowledge of both his immanence and his transcendence. That knowledge, of course, is very limited — much more so even than our knowledge of the physical world. What we know is that our world manifests in us constructive acts of will, responsive to the values the world presents to experience and directed toward the realization of values beyond our experience. And we have strong reason to believe that this will is not the product of our organisms, but has produced them; that they are organic to it; that it pursues its ends in and through them, influencing though not controlling them. We know that our good is found in the service of this larger will and that in and through us it seeks the good of all. Of the content of its experience we know only so far as its experience, of joy and disappointment in its more or less successful efforts, is also ours. Of its origin we do not know, save that it was in the world before us, since our organisms are organic to it. For the same reason it must be prior to all the kinds of particular organic life we know. It is personal, for personality is neither more nor less than a system of will. In this person our personalities have their foundation and in our personalities this person finds his fulfillment. He is thus not merely *a* person, but, so far as we know, the only complete Person. This is God, as known in religious experience. It is God, " whose we are and whom we serve," in whom " we live and move and have our being." There is no question of his goodness, for we know him first and best as the higher will that seeks in and through us the good of others.

It is plain, then, that we may love God and should serve him. But to what extent can we trust him? He has good will toward men. But what *power* has he to do them good? Regarding the most important question here we can answer with some confidence. Does our knowledge of God support the hope that our lives may be sustained in him and find new spheres of expression, and scope and means for continued growth, after the dissolution of the body? Concerning this there can be little doubt if the conclusions already arrived at are accepted. We have seen that the physical organism is merely instrumental to the constructive activity of will in response to its experience of value. And personality is a system of will. Our personalities are rooted, therefore, not in the physical structure of the world, but in its volitional structure. Our experience of value depends upon the interrelationship of the activities of this volitional structure. The activities of the volitional structure affect, in some way, the course of our physical activity, and are responsive to the qualities presented through physical activity. That concentration of attention upon control of the organism and experiences connected with it would, we may expect, end with the dissolution of the organism. With this release of attention a new range of experience, connected with the relation of the personality to the wider processes of the world in its vast diffusion of activity, should become available. Further development of personality would be found in the organization of this experience in ways found to be of value. And a multitude of persons, organic to a universal Person and organizing their experience in a common world, should not be devoid of influence upon each other through that common world, and should thus find available those means of communication and mutual aid essential to a common life.

Again, concerning the power of God to guide our lives toward the realization of the fullest good for ourselves and others, the answer is clear. His will is the ultimate determinant of the system of our values. Because of this we find our good in activity that contributes to the good of all. When, blinded by passion or ignorance, men do not pursue this good, then they, or society after them, discover the disvalues involved, and experimental search is made for better ways. Thus, tentatively and erringly, man pursues the good and is guided by it toward the realization of a fuller life for all. We are not offered an assurance that all will be well in the long run whatever men may do. But we can go forward with confidence that our progressive insight into the good is an increasing insight into the teleological order of reality, and thus that the way to its realization is open — that the things we value most are not ultimately at the mercy of the things we value least, and that the way to the increasing attainment of the best is to be true to the good as our keenest reflective intelligence sees it.

But when we ask whether God is able to order the behavior of men and the course of the physical world according to his will, then the answer of religious experience must be in the negative. Indeed, as we saw in an earlier chapter, it is chiefly the influence of philosophical speculation that has led to the adoption of such beliefs. Our religious experience reveals God as influencing our behavior through our value experience, but the fact of conflict shows that he does not control it. Nor is there any evidence in religious experience to show that the will of God controls the course of the physical world. In

the fact of the operation of will in the constructive development and behavior of living organisms there is evidence that
the course of physical events is not entirely beyond all influence from the volitional order of the world. But it would
seem to fall far short of complete control. Over the behavior
and development of animate nature there is the same indication, as in our own experience, of influence but not control.
Philosophy and tradition have created much trouble for theology by theories which extend the divine power to the purposive and fixed creation of each particular form of life, un-
affected by the will and striving of the creature concerned, and
by attributing to God a direct control of physical nature and
even of the human will. Much of this is very primitive philosophy and has long been incorporated in religion. But its
roots are, nevertheless, in philosophical speculation rather
than in religious experience.

The extent of the divine power over the physical world and
human behavior seems to be sufficient for our faith in immortality and the validity of our values. Beyond that the interest
of religion in it concerns such questions as the scope of prayer,
providence, and special revelation. The general formula
at which we have arrived is that God is able to influence but
not control the course of human behavior and that our mental
activity (and therefore, surely, the divine also) has *some* effect
upon physical process. But this leaves many questions open.
No answer can be made on general principles that this, that
or the other is possible or impossible. It is a question for
empirical evidence in each case.

An examination of any particular case would be beyond the
scope of this work, but a few general considerations may be
indicated. In the first place, the fact that an event is extraordinary and not even theoretically explicable in terms of known
physical laws does not prove that it is supernatural; neither
does it prove that it could not really have happened; our

knowledge of the borderline phenomena of mind and matter is altogether too vague for any such confident assertions. Second, human testimony is very unreliable even when perfectly honest; rumor grows with extraordinary rapidity and does not require a deliberate intention to deceive in order to originate or propagate it. Third, abnormal psychological experiences prove nothing; yet they are quite consistent with the intelligence and integrity of a witness or teacher; they are a common result of intense inner conflict; and since new moral insights can rarely be achieved without inner conflict, and the sense of conflict contributes to the deepening of religious conviction, they should be expected to be a common feature of the experience of prominent religious innovators.

THE GOD OF PHILOSOPHICAL THOUGHT

It is not to be supposed that the human mind will rest content with that knowledge of God which is directly given and implied in religious experience. Nor is it desirable that it should. To render life and thought consistent we must bring together the results obtained from the analysis and interpretation of every phase of experience — sensory-motor, aesthetic, ethical and religious. This thinking of our results together is a check on the validity of the results arrived at in each sphere. This is synoptic philosophy, or metaphysics. So far as possible we have avoided it in the present work, confining ourselves as much as possible to the analysis and interpretation of religious experience. But we cannot refuse to face the fact that our conclusions from this sphere have implications for synoptic philosophy. They suggest, as we have already pointed out, a monistic theory of the ultimate being, a recognition of determinate, eternal, qualitative potentialities within that being, and a distinction of two kinds of activity — physical and mental — manifested by it which between them realize or display a selection of the qualities.

For theology this raises the question whether the ultimate and all-inclusive being should be called God. We began by recognizing that what is immediately known as God is the disinterested will within us. We next saw that this should be regarded as the immanent presence of a will that transcends the organisms and to which all organisms are organic. Here, then, was a wider concept of God. But philosophical reflection leads to the thought that God, in this latter sense, must be organic to the world as a whole, including the as yet unrealized determinate potentialities and the physical world as well. So thought passes to the concept of God as the universal reality. In each of these phases God may rightly be called personal, and they represent fairly well the three phases of the divine being distinguished in the doctrine of the trinity — except so far as the Logos, or second person, is identified with the personality of Jesus. With the historical elements of the creed we do not here concern ourselves, and its metaphysical terminology is certainly inadequate, but we nevertheless can see that it interprets, with deep insight, the God of both religious experience and scientific thought.

We saw that religious experience of itself leads us to think that there are limits to the power of God to control human behavior and the physical world. The ground of those limitations that should be recognized in the God of philosophic thought is therefore a question at least of considerable academic interest. Theology has usually asserted that God is self-limited in the gift of free will to man. But we have seen that the divine will, as immediately known in us, has only a very limited control over matter also. Whether that will, as transcendent, has any control over inanimate nature is a question for empirical inquiry. The history of the traditional metaphysical arguments for the being of God seems to show that there is no certain evidence for any such control, and that there are reasonable indications of only a limited control.

Combined with the evidence from moral and religious experience this limited control becomes a very well supported metaphysical theory.   But we have still to ask what is the nature of the control and its limitations.

Plato believed that beside God there exists matter as also eternal, and that God's creative activity exerted upon matter found it not entirely conformable to his will.   Thus evil and imperfection in the world are to be attributed to the resistance of matter to the divine activity.   This ultimate dualism has always seemed rather unsatisfactory to both philosophy and religion.   So, too, have pluralisms, such as William James's theory of the universe as a society of spirits of which God is *primus inter pares*.[29]   Yet, until recent decades, monism has seemed to tend logically either to an absolutism in which God is equally responsible for good and evil, or to one in which there is no God at all.   This century, however, has seen a strong tendency toward an organismic conception of the universe which is neither strict monism nor pluralism, but recognizes the universe as a unity in which several distinguishable principles function together.   By far the most original and most thoroughly worked out philosophy of this kind is that of Professor Whitehead,[30] for whom God is the most important, but not the only, controlling principle in the course of the universe, others being certain determinate potentialities, such as those of sense and value, and the spontaneous creative activity manifested in the actual ongoing of the world. Another organismic philosophy recognizing a limited divine control of the universe — and one which has aroused much interest, especially in America — is that of Professor Brightman.   This suggests that God is limited by a factor within his own being which is called " the Given." [31]   It is a passive ele-

[29] *A Pluralistic Universe.* (New York: Longmans, Green & Co., 1909) .

[30] *Process and Reality* (New York: The Macmillan Co., 1929) .

[31] E. S. Brightman: *The Problem of God* (New York: Abingdon Press, 1930) .

ment within his nature, additional to his reason and will, which enters into every one of his conscious states and constitutes a problem for him.

Brightman's statement of the nature of the limitations that must be recognized is made from the standpoint of an idealist, Whitehead's rather more from that of a realist. Brightman includes the limiting factors within God. Whitehead describes God as a factor constituting one whole with them. Whether such a whole should itself be called God is, plainly, little more than a matter of terminology. But of these two accounts of the factors limiting the divine influence and activity, Brightman's, due to the idealist approach, emphasizes its passive nature, while Whitehead's view would explain the element of disorder and evil in the world chiefly by reference to the spontaneous activity of the actual entities that make up the particular things and organisms of the world. In brief, Whitehead explains evil by carrying the principle of freedom down from human nature to all nature, animate and inanimate. And this is entirely in accord with modern science, both in biology and in physics.

If we then recognize that there is a perfectly legitimate sense in which the absolute, the universe as a whole, may be called God, then, though God in this sense is not finite, yet much is beyond the control of his will. But that which limits his will is, as Brightman says, not outside his being but within it. It is, on our view, the fact that the creative activity, which is the expression of his being and which we discover in the two forms of physical and mental activity, is in both forms a creative development of free agents spontaneously active. If we ask why God does not control human history and the physical world and shape them more in accord with human needs, the answer is that he cannot. And he cannot because we and all other entities are free agents. If we ask why God did not create for us a world of unfree agencies, yet malleable to our will, the answer is, again, that he could not. And the reason, so far as we can see, is that he cannot create entities so foreign to his own nature. If we ask why, when we err, our experience should be attended by so much pain, the answer is that all the qualities of our experience are realized by our own activity out of the determinate potentialities of God's own being, which are not subject to his will; that his will works with ours to realize good rather than evil; and that whatever of good or evil we experience is his experience as well as ours, for we are in him.[32]

[32] For fuller exposition cf. my *Reality and Value,* especially chaps. 5, 12.

EPILOGUE

The Christian Faith

FAITH, BELIEF AND KNOWLEDGE

A PROMINENT PART has been played in Christian thought by the notion of " faith," and in Indian religious thought by the kindred notion of *bhakti*. Both are words for a deep and positive and essentially moral element in religious experience. Yet in Christianity so much emphasis has been laid upon questions of doctrine that in the popular mind " the faith " is but another name for a creed, and we joke about the schoolboy who defined faith as " believing what you know ain't true." Even this, however, indicates that faith is no ordinary belief. People cannot, by faith, believe things they *know* are not true; but they can and do, by faith, believe things they would not ordinarily regard as true. This applies both to the supernatural and to natural and social phenomena, as when one has faith in the integrity of a friend in spite of strong circumstantial evidence to the contrary. In such cases there is an element of emotion, or the will to believe, determining the conviction, and it is this feature that suggests that faith is a kind of belief that does not rest on good evidence. It does not follow, however, that all cases of faith are cases of insecure belief. We speak of faith in the skill of a great surgeon or in the security of United States government bonds. Obviously it is not the element of uncertainty that distinguishes faith from other forms of belief.

Further, as was pointed out in an earlier chapter, faith involves much more than belief. To have much faith or true faith is to be faithful; and faithfulness is an attitude in which a person holds fast to pledges and implicit understandings in the letter and the spirit; he trusts and proves worthy of trust. The element of belief in the total attitude of faith may be relatively small, as in the faithfulness of a sentry in a post of danger, which is principally a matter of will. The essential thing in faith would appear to be a value judgment — a judgment that something is good — and faithfulness consists in holding fast to that value judgment and its implications. Where those implications chiefly concern conduct, as in the cases of the sentry and the lover, the element of will comes into prominence and the total mental attitude is usually called " faithfulness." Where the implications under consideration are chiefly cognitive the element of belief comes into prominence and the resultant attitude is usually called " faith," or even simply " belief."

Belief itself is merely the attitude of mental rest in the acceptance of a judgment. Its antithesis is doubt, which is the tentative holding of a proposition in mind without accepting it as a part of that body of meanings whereby we feel we grasp or understand our world. Accepted or believed propositions become bases for deliberate action. Doubted propositions do not, except tentatively, with hesitation. Judgments wherein we simply formulate in significant terms the result of our own experience are always accepted without hesitation unless they are thought to conflict with some long accepted or equally well grounded judgment. Then we may doubt the reality of what has appeared in experience or the accuracy of our judgment concerning it. Judgments derived by inference, and propositions obtained by suggestion and other forms of communication or formulated tentatively in imagination, tend to be accepted or doubted according to their observed agreement with what is already believed.

Thus the general body of beliefs is built up and continuously sifted by checking it with new judgments. Among these beliefs are some that seem to be so well grounded as analytical formulations of experience or as inferences from such judgments that we call them knowledge. Others are held as more or less well substantiated beliefs, shading off into mere tentative opinions. The line between knowledge and the beliefs we feel we can scarcely claim as knowledge is not hard and fast, for the simple reason that, except in regard to abstractions and the immediate particular experiences of the moment, knowledge never amounts to certainty.

The distinction between faith and other forms of belief arises out of a distinction among the data of our experience. Our objective data may be classified as either sensory-motor or valuational. Judgments concerning merely the former are never described as acts of faith, however certain or uncertain, immediate or derived. Yet, even where mere inanimate things are concerned, if the acceptance or rejection of a judgment turns upon a value judgment it is recognized as an act of faith. Any judgment that puts faith in our fellow men is based on judgments concerning the values involved, as values to which they may be relied upon to respond. Even such a marginal case as a boy's act of foolhardy faith in skating on thin ice is a judgment concerning the probable stability of the ice, affected by wishful thinking determined by his high evaluation of the pleasure of skating. In such an act there is faith, but no genuine inference from the value judgment. In a careful man's faith in a good bank there is sound inference, based first on his knowledge of the values involved in a bank's stability, and second on his knowledge of how people in general and the bank's officers in particular respond to those values. He says he *knows* that bank is sound. And he may be quite justified in his claim, for values are sufficiently objective, and human responses to them sufficiently regular, to enable us to include many of our acts of faith not only in the realm of belief, but in that of knowledge — recognizing the limitation of certainty attached to all knowledge, as stated above.

MORAL GROUNDS OF FAITH AND DOUBT

Now, if the analysis of the foregoing chapters is sound, our belief in God [1] is the kind of belief that is rightly called faith; but that does not mean that it is not knowledge. If the argument of the last two chapters should stand the test of critical examination we should be entitled to call it knowledge, even though, like so many other well grounded convictions, it could never amount to certainty. But however well established the belief may become it will still be something known by faith, for it rests ultimately upon judgments of value. The initially given datum — the disinterested will to the good — may be known with certainty as a fact of observation. But like all such facts it is only a momentary particular. The rest is interpretation. We judge it to be an element in a personality greater than our own, one to which our own is organic, by reason of the three characteristics we have seen stamping it as suprahuman and supraindividual — its conflict of evaluations with the ego, the objective values it discloses, and the authoritative sense of obligation attaching to it. The recognition of each and all of these three features involves value judgments; and upon these rests faith in God, a faith which we may call knowledge, belief or opinion according to the degree of certainty we feel to be attached to it.

It is, of course, true that there are other reasons for the belief than these; and some of those other reasons, such as the cosmological argument, do not involve value judgments. If any person's belief in God rested entirely on such nonvaluational grounds it would be a mere intellectual belief, not faith, and would contain no moral element. It may be

[1] What is referred to here, and in the rest of this section, is the theistic belief that God is personal, immanent and transcendent.

doubted whether that is the case with any person's belief in God; but it is certain that the value judgments involved are often slight, unimportant and irrelevant; e.g., a belief accepted merely on the authority or prestige of officials or elders, which is primarily a faith in the intelligence and integrity of these persons rather than in God. The belief that arises or is confirmed chiefly through the individual's own religious experience is, however, a genuine faith; and the moral judgments involved are, I think, always chiefly those brought out in the above analysis. Such judgments involve the exercise of serious moral reflection, discrimination, effort and choice. Thus the faith so developed is essentially a moral attainment.

The recognition of this fact must not, of course, be allowed to suggest that a moral stigma attaches to those who do not arrive at a similar faith. Many who have very earnestly sought to arrive at such a faith have found themselves faced with intellectual difficulties compelling them reluctantly to reject it. Others, in the light of a different experience, have felt that such a faith issues in disvalues which constitute a refutation of the value judgments on which it appears to rest, and so must be rejected in order that those very values may be saved. In cases of both types an entirely different set of conclusions may be based on essentially the same judgments of value. Such conclusions are also acts of faith, often of very high moral quality. Such considerations reveal the truth of Tennyson's trenchant lines:

> There lives more faith in honest doubt,
> Believe me, than in half the creeds.

Only a closer and more careful analysis of the whole range of experience involved can decide the issue here; and only harm is done by one side's casting aspersions on the intelligence or moral integrity of the other. Both belief and doubt concerning God can be acts of faith based on high, sound and earnest moral judgments. The differences and extravagances of opinion are due sometimes to failures of moral judgment, but also to purely extraneous and nonmoral circumstances.

In order properly to appreciate the significance given to faith in religious thought it is necessary to recognize clearly that, whether logical or not, to the thoughtful adherent of an ethical religion his faith appears as an expression of his moral life — and really is so. When asked for the reasons for his belief he will probably try to find arguments of a more objective character than these " reasons of the heart." Yet the lines of Tennyson express a typical religious experience:

> If e'er when faith had fallen asleep,
> I heard a voice, ' believe no more,'
> And heard an ever-breaking shore
> That tumbled in the Godless deep,
>
> A warmth within the breast would melt
> The freezing reason's colder part,
> And like a man in wrath the heart
> Stood up and answer'd, ' I have felt.'

What our analysis has revealed is that this answer of the heart is not mere " wishful thinking " and not a mere expression of emotion of no objective significance, but an expression and interpretation of a deeply rooted and sound moral experience — and thus of the kind of experience of most significance for an understanding of the place of personality in the world order.

RELIGIOUS FAITH AND RELIGIOUS BELIEF

Whatever the theory of the grounds of this belief in God may have been, the actual felt connection (however vague) between the moral consciousness and theistic belief has led to the general conviction that the holding of such beliefs is an important part of the moral life. This is a transference, to the resultant belief, of the moral quality of the moral judgments which underlie the total attitude of which the belief is a part. That total attitude is faith, and many features of it, including the belief, may change without the loss of its essential moral quality. It is thus a mistake to pin the moral quality to the belief. It belongs to the active attitude of faith as a whole. In general this has been fully recognized by Christianity. In addition to the emphatic protests of St. James against the notion of a faith that consists of mere beliefs without works [2] there is the famous essay in the Epistle to the Hebrews in which faith is described as the ground ("substance" and "evidence") of hope, belief, understanding of God's work, and moral and mystical power.[3] Paul rejects intellectualism with the assertion that "with the heart man believeth unto righteousness."[4] And Christian theologians have been careful to distinguish between mere historical and temporary beliefs, on the one hand, and "saving faith," on the other, emphasizing the moral content of the latter even though often denying its moral foundations.

It is the felt connection between their personal moral integrity and their religious faith that accounts for the feeling of Christians that the doctrine of justification by faith is a moral doctrine. Unfortunately, Thomas Aquinas [5] taught that faith is primarily a matter of the speculative intellect and only secondarily of the practical, and he was followed in this by many Protestants. But on such an interpretation, as critics of this theology have so often pointed out, the doctrine of justification by faith is most immoral. It would mean that God's forgiveness is conditioned upon the acceptance of certain his-

---

2 Jas. 2:14-26.
3 Heb. 10:38; 12:2.
4 Rom. 10:10.
5 *Summa Theologica*, 2 II., questions i-iv.

torical and metaphysical propositions which are quite independent of our moral attitudes. On the other hand, if we
recognize that faith is an attitude of the personality, involving
a lively moral experience and an earnest effort to work out
its implications in thought and practice (whatever the resultant beliefs), then justification by faith is the only truly moral
doctrine. It puts both belief and works in their place as the
outcome of faith, differing according to other circumstances.
And it points to moral attention and aspiration as the only
truly praiseworthy moral characteristics, for these are the essential features of faith.

The common human judgment of a person's moral worth is
assessed upon his overt acts; he is judged to *be* as good or bad
as that which he *does*. And he is treated accordingly in our
legal and social sanctions. Yet it does not require much reflection to show the injustice of this treatment of each man
according to his works, for all men do not have the same opportunities. Circumstances of heredity and environment
make it easy for some of us to be highly respectable citizens,
and very difficult for others. So no judgment of any person's
moral worth based purely on externals can possibly be fair, and
legalism must necessarily involve inequity. This fact has
impressed itself upon sensitive souls in the great ethical religions. In India it issued in the doctrine of *bhakti* and in
Christianity in that of justification by faith. Even long before
Christ the Hebrews had realized the problem, as is manifested,
for example, in the statement of the psalmist, " A humble
and a contrite heart, O God, thou wilt not despise." [6]

Judaism, however, never shook off legalism. The only way
to keep the favor of God was by the " works of the law." That
this view was inadequate was the deepest insight of the apostle
Paul. If a person's moral ideals are not very lofty, and if the
circumstances of his life are morally propitious, he can go

[6] Ps. 51:17.

through life feeling that God should be very well satisfied with him; at most, he may persuade himself, a few special offerings, prayers and penances should be all that is necessary to make up for his slight deficiencies and secure full divine approval. But if a person's ideal has been raised by measuring himself beside the moral stature of Jesus of Nazareth, or if unpropitious circumstances have involved him in serious moral lapses, he cannot, if he is in earnest, so easily persuade himself that his deeds must win the commendation of God. In these cases legalism can only suggest strong condemnation. Paul found himself subject to both conditions — convicted of his error in persecuting the Christians, and doubly convicted by comparison with the lofty ideal of Christ. The result was a deep conviction of sin. But yet his conversion experience convinced him he was not rejected by God. So legalism must be wrong. He had been accepted by God, " justified," without the works of the law. Apparently it was some echo from the teaching of Jesus that supplied the answer. It was his faith that had made him spiritually whole. He was " justified by faith without the deeds of the law." [7] Yet Paul could not altogether escape from the legalism of his early training. Before he could be entirely satisfied with the truth of his new insight he had to harmonize it with his former religious beliefs, which he did through a legally phrased theory of atonement. Further, he, and his successors still more, laid too much stress on the intellectual content of faith and not enough on its basic elements — the attentive consciousness of moral values, and aspiration and active endeavor toward their realization.

TEACHING OF JESUS ON FAITH AND ON SIN

In this, Paul and the other disciples of Jesus seem to have missed the profounder insight of their master. We have the

[7] Rom. 3:28.

teaching of Jesus only at second hand, and it is difficult to say how much of what is attributed to him was really his.   But, unlike Socrates, Jesus had no Plato to improve upon his teaching in the recording of it.   The writers of the Gospels were much lesser men than he, so we can confidently credit him with all the more profound and original elements in the sayings they attribute to him.   Other parts may lack authenticity, but not these, even though they may not be quite in the form he gave them.   There is not much doubt but that the general tenor of his teaching is fairly well preserved.

Now any thoughtful reader of the Gospels is sure to be impressed with the emphasis Jesus laid on faith, but full significance of that emphasis is apt to escape us unless we remember the essentially moral character he gave to faith (which generally escapes his biographers) and connect it more closely than they do with his teaching on sin.   The first significant fact about his teaching on sin is that praise and blame are laid, not on the overt act, but on the inner motive or choice of values.   It is not only murder that is wrong, but the harboring of a grudge; it is not only adultery, but the lustful look.[8]   The second point of great significance is the value attached to aspiration.   In the parable of the Pharisee and the publican [9] the Pharisee can boast an impeccable record of overt acts, but he is totally lacking in any aspiration, any consciousness that he might make his life count for any greater good.   The publican is a sinner and knows it, but he repentantly aspires to be something better.   Life has led him into difficulties too great for him and he feels he can do nothing but ask God's mercy. Yet he, says Jesus, is justified rather than the other.   Again in the parables of the lost coin, the lost sheep and the lost son [10] we see the same idea.   Ninety-and-nine " just persons

8 Matt. 5:21–28.
9 Luke 18:9–14.
10 Luke 15.

who need no repentance " arouse no heavenly rejoicings. The reason, obviously, is that they are self-satisfied and have no right to be, since all have some cause for repentance. Their spiritual inertia and lack of aspiration, even though circumstances have been propitious for their moral development, brands them as personalities of no spiritual vigor, no active faith. But in the turning back of the prodigal son to renew the finer moral life of the home from which he had fled something different is manifest. Here, in spite of the unpropitious circumstances, there is spiritual activity, aspiration, faith. And though it be small and struggling in unfavorable circumstances, the angels rejoice over it.

These sayings of Jesus reveal the thought that it is spiritual inertia, the lack of attention to moral values, that is sin. Active attention to moral values generates a sublime discontent with the level of virtue that is easy to maintain, and an aspiration toward higher ideals. Life is necessarily active, and the moral life is no exception. Unless it is active in pursuit of the good, ever seeking new goals, it becomes dormant and dies. Self-satisfaction is the great enemy of moral progress, for it breeds stagnation. Even the humble cry of the soul that feels itself lost is better than that. It is at least a contribution to some further growth of spiritual life. And where there is life there is hope. Indeed, Jesus goes farther and declares that such spiritual activity " justifies " the individual before God. It is all that God expects of him. Circumstances may have made life too difficult for the achievement of greater perfections of character, but in the aspiration and moral effort that struggle against these disadvantages there is the essential spiritual fact that links his life to the divine. Such attention to moral values and pursuit of them is the essential fact of faith, and he who is thus attentive is " justified by faith apart from the works of the law." Paul, here, was holding true to an insight derived from his master.

But that insight, in the mind of the greater teacher, shows no signs of legalism or of the overemphasis on mere religious belief.

In the light of our best modern knowledge of human motivation we must make the same moral judgment as Jesus attributes to God and the angels. We may praise overt acts to give social encouragement in the performance of them, but the judgment of the moral worth of a personality must be based on the inner attention to values and the response to them. It must recognize that these exist genuinely in unexpected places, even in the feeble aspirations and sometimes futile repentances of the moral outcast. And we must recognize that there is no moral worth in the smug self-satisfaction of self-centered people, however impeccable may be their habits. In brief, true moral worth is summed up in the inner attitude of *faith,* a life of the spirit oriented to what it finds of finest value, a life that may live in honest doubt as well as in unwavering belief. If we may use the terms of the theologians, it is this that is " saving faith "; and the " communion of the faithful " is not a bond of common belief, but a bond of common orientation toward the finest ideal each can see. In so far as that communion is Christian it is because it finds in Christ the concrete exemplification of that ideal.

FAITH AND THE HOPE OF IMMORTALITY

If, with this understanding of the concept of faith in mind, we return to what has been said concerning the conditions of immortality, a still deeper significance is revealed, which is still in harmony with the fundamental Christian insight. In chapter 8 the conclusion was drawn that the possibility of the survival of a personality depends upon its development of an active life reaching out toward values other than those with which the ego is concerned — all of which latter are rooted in tendencies seeking the welfare of the mortal organism. If it be granted, as was urged in that and the two subsequent chapters, that will is rooted, not in the physical organism but in the larger spiritual order of the universe, then it may be reasonably assumed that an organization of will, developed within that larger spiritual order and directed toward goals not dependent on the existence of the physical organism, would go on in pursuit of those goals after the dissolution of the body. Such goals would be the cultivation of truth and beauty through such impacts on the world as remained possible without the body, and assistance in the development of other personalities through such communication as could be obtained. The extent of such possibilities of action we do not know, but it is obvious that they must be much greater than our present knowledge reveals, for our present knowledge falls far short of explaining such control of the mental over the physical as is manifested in everyday purposive behavior.

Thus the extent to which an existing personality is " saved " or preserved for a further life beyond this would seem to depend upon the extent to which it had developed an active system of volitional tendencies concerned with objectives that might still be realized in that further life. Pre-eminent among those objectives would be the good (the further personal development) of other persons; and that further personal development would consist in their active impact upon their world in the creation of forms of beauty, the grasp of truth, and the social co-operation found to be good. But an active system of volitional tendencies of this character is precisely that which manifests the attitude we, in harmony with the most profound element of the Christian tradition, have called " faith." Thus we see the truth in the Christian declaration which, out of a deep insight into its own religious experience, declared that it is faith that saves — faith, not works, and not mere belief. That this insight should ever have been misinterpreted as salvation obtained by believing a creed is a tragedy due to an overemphasis upon the otherwise desirable goal of obtaining and maintaining correctness of theological opinion.

PHILOSOPHICAL SIGNIFICANCE OF THEOLOGICAL DOCTRINE

What, it may be asked, is the advantage gained by showing that conclusions arrived at by objective analysis of religious experience are thus in harmony with the essential insights of the founders of Christianity? One practical advantage may be pointed to: this recognition may make it easier for people of different religious opinions to work and worship together. But there is also a consideration of theoretical importance. Religious convictions that have proved their value in the cultivation of a high and vigorous spiritual life have thereby obtained a certain pragmatic justification of considerable importance. And there is no doubt that, in spite of some concomitant bad effects, this can be claimed for the doctrine of justification by faith. It has liberated and invigorated the souls of millions of men and women, including such vital personalities as Paul and Luther. Its value must surely be due to its being, in some very significant way, a correct diagnosis of the religious life, its disvalue to elements of error in it. What we have done is to show that the disvalues attached to the traditional doctrine are due to its overemphasis upon the importance of mere matters of belief, while its real value lies in the soundness of that essential insight into moral and religious values whereby it is seen that faith is more than mere belief and of greater moral worth than its outcome in good works.

But on this same ground we may be met with a further objection. We have as yet taken no account of the further Christian conviction that the faith whereby a man is saved is not merely the product of his own effort but has been created in him by the hearing of the gospel and the work of Christ. A similar pragmatic justification, with similar qualifications, might be claimed for this part of the doctrine also. So it, too, calls for examination. In this connection it should first be noted that, while Christian experience may be pointed to as positive evidence of the saving power of the gospel of Christ, it constitutes no negative evidence to the effect that such spiritual effects can be wrought in no other way. In spite of a dramatic assertion attributed to Peter, that there is " none other name . . . whereby we must be saved," [11] it would seem that the church of the days when the New Testament was being compiled did not always make this claim. Thus the writer of Hebrews refers to the many heroes of the past whose spiritual achievements are attributed to their faith, and looks forward to their resurrection.[12] The apostle Paul states that Abraham's faith was " imputed to him for righteousness." [13] As he also states that the Gentiles are judged of God according as they observe the law " written in their hearts," [14] it would seem to be his view that a similar faith would be efficacious for them. Among the theories of the atonement later developed by the church, it is true, the greater number attributed to the death of Christ a mystical efficacy such that human salvation would appear to have been altogether impossible without it. But this is not the case with all those theories. In particular, the " moral interpretation," first propounded by Abélard and today widely accepted among Protestants, is purely rational. It teaches that the efficacy of Christ's life and death in the salvation of man lies entirely in the power of his example. This type of theory becomes objectionable if it is suggested that Jesus deliberately chose to suffer in order to set a powerful and moving example. But if we examine the circumstances of the world into which

[11] Acts 4:12.
[12] Heb. 11, especially v. 35.
[13] Rom. 4:20–22.
[14] Rom. 2:14–16.

Jesus was born and the problem with which he was faced, all arbitrariness disappears from the situation; the sheer moral necessity of his personal sacrifice becomes clear and its place in Christian religious experience is established.

Jesus took up the mission begun by John the Baptist as preacher of righteousness. He added to it a still loftier ethic of his own, preserved for us chiefly in the collection of sayings known as the Sermon on the Mount. It was a righteousness that must exceed the righteousness of the scribes and Pharisees, a righteousness intolerant of all forms of exploitation, of the hardness of religious formalism, of racial exclusiveness, of inequity between the sexes, of national bitterness, but tender toward the moral outcast and full of compassion for the afflicted. It challenged the attitudes of the social and religious leaders at many points. It aroused opposition which soon presented the threat of death. Thus, after a brief ministry which had won the devoted attachment of a small band of disciples and a vast popular enthusiasm which everywhere challenged established evils and drew attention to his principles, Jesus found himself faced with two alternatives. One was to retire into relative obscurity, leaving behind him a deep sense of the hopelessness and failure of such ideals as he had preached — a state of affairs worse than he had found. The other was to go steadily forward with his mission until it should lead him to the cross that always, in those days, awaited those who openly challenged constituted authority, whether by force and guile or by truth and love. He chose the latter way because it was the only path that one in his position could consider right. It led him to Calvary.

But after his disciples had recovered from the first stunning effects of the blow they saw in that choice the consummation of his career. And indeed it was that. Without it, his ethics would have stood as the noblest expression of the moral ideal known to man. He had taught that there are no limits whatever to the love, or good will, that human beings should show in their relations with each other — neither race, nor creed, nor caste, nor sex, nor national or personal enmity — and that to this ideal one should be true to the death. But it is one thing to teach ideals and another to *live* them. Had he never himself been put to the supreme test they might have remained as shining ideals without much power, considered too lofty for practical men. But he preached them in conditions in which he was bound to be tested. And when the test came he did not shrink. Thus his personality became the concrete embodiment of his ideals, the exemplification before the world of all that he had taught.

But the significance of this fact escapes us if we think merely of its force as a positive ideal calling for imitation. Its real dynamic in the spiritual life of the world comes from its power to *convict the world of sin*. Here again the insight of the traditional theology is thoroughly sound in fundamentals, even though somewhat distorted in certain aspects. Enough has already been said in criticism of the exaggerations of this doctrine. What is important now is to be clear about its essential truth. For an understanding of that we must go back to what has already been said about faith and the nature of sin.

In our discussion of faith we have seen that it can reach its lowest ebb in the self-righteousness of respectable people as well as in the hardened evil habits of the moral outcast. Society is apt to settle down to the toleration of certain abuses within it which do not affect the great majority, so that the social conscience is not aroused by these things. Then the individual is apt to tolerate in himself what society tolerates in him. If he should reflect deeply enough, the disinterested will to the good would be stirred within him to prick his conscience. But he does not reflect. So the higher growth of personality stagnates at the level already attained. In such conditions of stagnation the ego is apt to expand its demands until the whole of life, including every natural element of altruism, is subordinated to it. This is spiritual death. An active spiritual life requires that there be an acute awareness of the preventable evil in the social order, and a keen consciousness of the obligation to avoid participation in it and actively to oppose it. There must be a similar attitude toward whatever is evil in one's personal past. If the individual fails to take home to himself these obligations there can be no active spiritual life. Something must awaken him to his personal spiritual deficiency, his spiritual inertia, which is sin.

It is here that the power of the life story of Jesus makes itself felt. We have but to reflect upon it and it breaks in upon our self-righteousness to force home to our own consciousness the facts of social evil and personal deficiency. It is its power to stir the human conscience out of smug moral self-satisfaction, and to pierce the protective armor of excuses whereby we defend ourselves, that makes the story of Christ a dynamic for the spiritual regeneration of mankind. In the light of his ideals and his example of supreme devotion, even the finest of human characters must recognize his own personal deficiency. If we frankly face the challenge of Christ it is impossible, at any level of moral development, to slip into the inertia of moral self-satisfaction. The most saintly souls, practicing the contemplation of his example, have found themselves kept morally sensitive, spiritually alive. At the lower levels of personal development, upon which most of us live, a similar meditation can work with equal power.

It was this stimulus to the awakening of an active faith and life of high devotion that the early Christians found in their knowledge of Jesus. Through coming to know him they found such new life in their souls that they said they were born again. They literally lived anew, through the power of the faith that was begotten in the knowledge of Christ. It is no matter for surprise that they called him Savior, for such he was and is.

CONCLUSION

In conclusion we may try briefly to gather up the threads of this study. We began our effort to understand religion by seeking its distinctive characteristics as manifested in its initial phases in the individual consciousness. Here we found that the distinguishing feature is the dawning consciousness of the individual that he is but one of a number of experient agents, and that there is something within him that urges him to be concerned with the good of some at least of these other selves. This factor, in the light of further investigation, we called the disinterested or altruistic will. We found that disharmony with it is the most fundamental cause of the sense of sin, while harmony with it tends to create the sense of assurance. We found that in the natural and inevitable conflicts between the disinterested will and the ego we could see the explanation of all the typical phases of religious experience, including that of the primitive, out of which grew the belief in a spiritual order wider and greater than human society. Thus we saw that this it is that man has called God and interpreted in so many and various ways. This then clarified for us the nature of the religious ideal. We saw that it gave us grounds for a new faith in man to know what it really is that he has called God, and that God, in this sense, is really operative in all; and we saw the value and the need of a great religious society to cultivate and implement this devotion to God.

Next we turned to the question of the philosophical significance of this discovery of the disinterested will, to seek an answer to what Kant called the third of the great questions of philosophy, " What may we hope? " We saw reason to believe that that disinterested will is the factor upon which, as root and foundation, has grown the structure we call personality, and that that structure, being a system of processes responsive to value, could not be conceived as a product or part of an order of physical processes (such as that described by physics and chemistry) in which values play no part. Thus the disinterested will of the individual was found to appear as a factor organic, not merely to the individual organism, but to the wider order of the world. In other words, God was found to transcend the limits of our personalities and to be the creative agency from which our lives arise and in harmony with which they find their good. No reason was found to assert God's immediate control over all the forces of nature, but sufficient reason to believe that nature is not so foreign to him that any tendency within it could continuously counteract his creative will — a will that we know as good because it seeks in and through each of us the good of all.

Finally we found, in this last chapter, that the deepest insights of Christianity have formulated their concepts of the power of God, as it has been felt to be at work in the human soul, in essentially these same terms. Christians have seen unfolding in history a self-revelation of the nature of God, of peculiar force and clarity, in the life and teaching of a succession of religious leaders who gradually developed more and more fully the ideal of a universal good. This revelation — occurring in and to the consciousness of individuals through their participation in a society already permeated by it — they have seen to culminate in the person of Jesus Christ, who thus becomes the central figure of that society. They have found that in and through the knowledge of him individuals are stirred to a new consciousness of the presence of God within them and a lively devotion to the ideal toward which that presence directs them. This attitude they have called faith, and they have found that it releases the spirit from the sense of sin, gives to life an assurance that it is ultimately worth while, and invigorates the spirit in every good work. In that faith they found the salvation of their souls, assuredly for time and, as they hope, for eternity.

Amidst much misconception and misinterpretation we find that our whole analysis of religion endorses these central concepts and attitudes of Christianity as intellectually and morally sound, and finds in them the secret of its power. And, our analysis having been directed purely to the discovery of the facts of the religious consciousness, this endorsement stands, so long as the analysis is sound, whatever may be said of our further theoretical interpretation. Even if that is denied, the religious ideal, the goodness of the divine as found within, the historic leadership of Jesus, and the cultivation and implementation of the ideal in and through the society formed around him — all these remain. Men still will find the salvation of their souls, in all that that can mean for this world, through faith in these things. But if also we can believe, as I have sought to show we can, that these facts point to the reality of a divine life far transcending our own, then faith takes on a richer significance, a brighter hope to lighten the dark places of life, and a deeper note of authority in the call of an ideal that is our own — and yet so much more than merely ours.

Bibliography

The following bibliography is divided into two parts. Part I is a
selected list of references suitable to the interests and needs of the
student who is not specializing in either philosophy or religion.
Part II is a short list of philosophical works bearing upon the
problems of religion, selected as representative of different schools
of thought, but for the most part suitable only for the student with
some training in philosophy. To facilitate reference to varying
points of view both lists are classified according to the position
taken by the writer.

PART I

GENERAL REFERENCE WORKS

WRIGHT, W. K. *A Student's Philosophy of Religion.* New York:
The Macmillan Co., 1935.

BURTT, E. A. *Types of Religious Philosophy.* New York: Harper
& Brothers, 1939.

BRIGHTMAN, E. S. *A Philosophy of Religion.* New York: Prentice-
Hall, Inc., 1940.

BERTOCCI, P. A. *The Empirical Argument for God in Late British
Thought.* Cambridge, Mass.: Harvard University Press, 1938.

WIEMAN, H. N., and MELAND, B. E. *American Philosophies of
Religion.* Chicago: Willett, Clark & Co., 1936.

CONGER, G. P. *The Ideologies of Religion.* New York: Round
Table Press, 1940.

AUBREY, E. E. *Present Theological Tendencies.* New York:
Harper & Brothers, 1936.

UREN, A. R. *Recent Religious Psychology.* London: T. & T.
Clark, 1928.

KERSHNER, F. D. *Pioneers of Christian Thought.* Indianapolis: Bobbs-Merrill Co., 1930.

ARCHER, J. C. *Faiths Men Live By.* New York: Thomas Nelson & Sons, 1934.

LOWIE, R. H. *Primitive Religion.* New York: Boni & Liveright, 1924.

BALLOU, R. O., ed. *The Bible of the World.* New York: Viking Press, 1939.

NONTHEISTIC NATURALISM

SELLARS, R. W. *Religion Coming of Age.* New York: The Macmillan Co., 1928.

LIPPMANN, W. *A Preface to Morals.* New York: The Macmillan Co., 1929.

AMES, E. S. *Religion.* New York: Henry Holt & Co., 1929.

SANTAYANA, G. *Reason in Religion.* New York: Charles Scribner's Sons, 1930.

DEWEY, JOHN. *A Common Faith.* New Haven, Conn.: Yale University Press, 1934.

OTTO, M. C. *The Human Enterprise.* New York: F. S. Crofts & Co., 1940.

LIBERAL THEISM

WHITEHEAD, A. N. *Religion in the Making.* New York: The Macmillan Co., 1926.

STREETER, B. H. *Reality.* New York: The Macmillan Co., 1926.

MONTAGUE, W. P. *Belief Unbound.* New Haven, Conn.: Yale University Press, 1930.

BRIGHTMAN, E. S. *The Problem of God.* New York: Abingdon Press, 1930.

HARTSHORNE, C. *Beyond Humanism.* Chicago: Willett, Clark & Co., 1937.

HICKS, G. D. *The Philosophical Bases of Theism.* New York: The Macmillan Co., 1937.

REID, L. A. *A Preface to Faith.* London: Allen & Unwin, 1939.

PRATT, J. B. *Naturalism.* New Haven, Conn.: Yale University Press, 1939.

BAILLIE, J. *Our Knowledge of God.* New York: Charles Scribner's Sons, 1939.

BIXLER, J. S. *Religion for Free Minds.* New York: Harper & Brothers, 1939.

TRADITIONAL THEISM

MACHEN, J. G. *Christianity and Liberalism.* New York: The Macmillan Co., 1930.

HEADLAM, A. C. *Christian Theology.* New York: Oxford University Press, 1934.

MARITAIN, J. *True Humanism.* London: Geoffrey Bles, Ltd., 1938.

BARTH, KARL. *The Knowledge of God and the Service of God.* New York: Charles Scribner's Sons, 1939.

GILSON, E. *God and Philosophy.* New Haven, Conn.: Yale University Press, 1941.

PART II

NONTHEISTIC NATURALISM

ALEXANDER, S. *Space, Time and Deity.* 2 vols. New York: The Macmillan Co., 1920.

SANTAYANA, G. *Scepticism and Animal Faith.* New York: Charles Scribner's Sons, 1923.

DEWEY, JOHN. *Experience and Nature.* Chicago: Open Court Publishing Co., 1925.

RUSSELL, B. *Philosophy.* New York: W. W. Norton Co., 1927.

COHEN, MORRIS. *Reason and Nature.* New York: Harcourt, Brace & Co., 1931.

REALISTIC THEISM

WHITEHEAD, A. N. *Process and Reality.* New York: The Macmillan Co., 1929.

TENNANT, F. R. *Philosophical Theology.* 2 vols. London: Cambridge University Press, 1928, 1930.

BOODIN, J. E. *God.* New York: The Macmillan Co., 1934.

PRATT, J. B. *Personal Realism*. New York: The Macmillan Co., 1937.

GARNETT, A. C. *Reality and Value*. New Haven, Conn.: Yale University Press, 1937.

MACINTOSH, D. C. *The Problem of Religious Knowledge*. New York: Harper & Brothers, 1940.

HARTSHORNE, C. *Man's Vision of God and the Logic of Theism*. Chicago: Willett, Clark & Co., 1941.

IDEALISTIC THEISM

HOCKING, W. E. *The Meaning of God in Human Experience*. New Haven, Conn.: Yale University Press, 1912.

PRINGLE-PATTISON, A. S. *The Idea of God in Modern Philosophy*. New York: Oxford University Press, 1917.

SORLEY, W. R. *Moral Values and the Idea of God*. London: Cambridge University Press, 1918.

BAILLIE, J. *The Interpretation of Religion*. New York: Charles Scribner's Sons, 1928.

TAYLOR, A. E. *The Faith of a Moralist*. New York: The Macmillan Co., 1930.

DE BURGH, W. G. *Towards a Religious Philosophy*. London: McDonald & Evans, 1937.

Index

Abélard, 315
Activism, 220, 225 ff., 235 ff.
Acts of the Apostles, 37 n., 117, 191 n., 192, 315 n.
Aesthetic experience, 197 ff.
Alexander, S., 227
Al-Ghazali, 37, 41
Altruism: definition of, 53; growth of, 128
American Indians, 70
Ames, E. S., 20, 27, 30
Amos, 114
Andaman Islanders, 60 n., 67
Angus, S., 213 n.
Animatism, 85
Animism, 62 ff.
Appasamy, A. J., 39 n.
A priori, the religious, 48 n.
Aquinas, Thomas, 215, 307
Archer, J. C., 114 n.
Aristotle, 145, 198, 217, 265
Arnold, Matthew, 49, 64
Atonement, 97, 102 ff., 315
Augustine, St., 38, 41, 174, 175
Australian aboriginals, 10, 65, 71, 72, 78

Ba'alim, 86
Baillie, John, 8 n., 26 ff., 49 n., 242 n.
Baptism, 191 n., 192
Barnes, J. S., 165
Barth, Karl, 140 n., 176, 184
Begbie, H., 38, 47
Belief, 8 ff., 29, 45, 64, 69, 80, 178 ff., 248 ff., 301 ff.
Bentham, Jeremy, 252
Bergson, H., 255 n.
Berkeley, 216
Bhakti, 301, 308
Body and mind, 216 ff.

Bosanquet, B., 216, 241 n.
Bradley, F. H., 216
Brahmanism, 93, 104
Breasted, J. H., 93, 129 n.
Brentano, Franz, 220 n., 227
Brightman, E. S., 108, 296–97
Broad, C. D., 227
Brown, W. A., 137 n.
Büchner, Louis, 216 n.
Buddha: *See* Gautama
Bunyan, 38, 41, 43

Calvinism, 14
Caste system, 113
Cecil, Lord Hugh, 168
Ceremonial, origin of religious ideas in, 78 ff.
Character, the, 202–6
Church, the, 65, 147 ff., 182–83, 187, 321; unity of, 179, 187 ff.; vitality of, 192 ff.
Classical literature, 128, 129 n.
Clement of Alexandria, 175
Cohen, M., 220–22
Collective responsibility, 109, 211
Collectivist theory of religion, 65 ff.
Collingwood, R. G., 199–201
Communion, idea of, 96 ff.
Communism, 171–72, 192
Comte, Auguste, 10, 64
Conflict: argument from, 254 ff.; mental and moral, 39 ff., 56, 83, 95, 249
Confucius, 128, 195 n.
Congo pygmies, 67
Conscience, 166, 283–85
Conservatism, 167 ff.
Conservative tendency of religion, 153 ff.
Conversion, 35 ff.
Cooley, C. H., 256

Creativity, principle of, 267
Creeds, 181, 191
Critical philosophy, 1 ff., 3 n.
Croce, B., 199

Democracy, 170, 172, 173
Democritus, 212–13
Deontologists, 274 n., 277 n.
Depravity of man, doctrine of, 175
Descartes, 215, 216
Design, argument from, 107
Determinism, 145–46
Dewey, John, 19, 20, 137, 139 ff., 154,
    177, 185, 196, 223 ff., 237, 256 ff., 265,
    276 ff.
Diffusion of culture, 60, 67
Doubt, 303 ff.
Dreams, spirit theory of, 62 ff.
Durkheim, E., 62, 63, 64, 65 ff., 74
Dynamic tendency of religion, 156 ff.

Ego, the original, 54 ff., 98, 100, 112,
    238, 250
Egoism, 127 ff., 270–75
Egoistic tendencies, 54, 83, 89, 124–25
Egyptians, 66, 85, 93, 129
Elkin, A. P., 67 n., 73 n.
Emergence, 220, 222 ff.
Empiricism, 14 ff., 21 n., 182, 275–76
Epicurus, 129, 213, 253 n.
Epiphenomenalism, 216
Evil, problem of, 107 ff.
Ezekiel, 110

Faith: communication of, 179, 188,
    190 ff.; justification by, 307 ff.; na-
    ture of, 140, 142, 181, 183, 301 ff.,
    317–21
Fascism, 165 ff.
Fertility ritual, 114
Fetish, 64
Fosdick, H. E., 99
Freedom, 147 ff., 181 ff., 188, 194, 297
Freud, S., 80, 289
Functionalism, 233 n.

Galatians, Epistle to the, 118 n.
Gandhi, 189
Gautama (Buddha), 10, 38, 41, 72,
    92, 93, 104, 112, 113, 128, 195 n.
Gentiles, admission of, 117–18
God: goodness of, 107–8, 111, 146, 291,
    297–98, 320; our knowledge of, 51,
    57, 287 ff., 303–4; personality of, 25,
    244 ff., 288; power of, 107–8, 146,
    291 ff., 295 ff., 320; transcendence
    and immanence of, 15, 57, 139 ff.,
    175, 240, 242, 244 ff., 290, 320
Goldenweiser, A. A., 67
Good, moral and natural or situa-
    tional, 131–32, 138
Greek theology, 175
Group, psychology of, 178, 187–88

Habit, 125–26, 202, 257
Haeckel, E. H., 216 n.
Haldane, J. S., 222 n.
Hale, E. E., 43
Hartmann, N., 29, 131–32, 144 ff.,
    264 n.
Hatred, 203
Healthy-minded, 43
Hebrew religion, 94, 104, 109, 114–
    15, 128, 156, 189, 209 ff.
Hebrews, Epistle to the, 183, 307, 315
Hedonism, 131–32
Hindus, 86, 113, 128
Hobhouse, L. T., 164
Hocking, W. E., 165
Hogbin, H. I., 70 n.
Holiness movement, 50
Holt, E. B., 177 n.
Hopkins, E. W., 64 n.
Horton, W. M., 21, 181 n.
Humanism, 10, 48, 72
Hume, David, 107, 216, 228
Husserl, E., 227
Huxley, Thomas, 28, 216 n.

Imagination, 198–202, 205–6
Immortality: Greek theory of, 212 ff.;

grounds of faith in, 239 ff.; Hebrew belief in, 209 ff.; possible condition of, 238, 244, 312 ff.; scientific possibility of, 218–38; value of belief in, 136 ff.
Individual, religion and the, 68, 151–53, 158
Instrumentalism, 19, 21 n.
Integration of personality, 283–86
Intelligence and selfishness, 83, 89, 259
Intentional act, 227
Interaction of mental and physical, 234
International morality, 279–80
Introspection, 228–29
Isaiah, Book of, 210

Jainism, 10 n.
James, St., 183, 307
James, William, 16 ff., 27, 31, 38, 43, 46, 52, 103, 143, 203, 228, 296
Jesus, 97, 105, 106, 111, 116, 124, 136, 156, 157, 159, 175, 183, 189, 192, 212, 295, 309–12, 316–18, 321
Jews, in relation to Christianity, 195
Job, 110, 111, 210 n., 211
John, Gospel of, 58 n., 111 n., 175 n.
Jung, C. G., 40

Kali, 38
Kalou, 70
Kant, Immanuel, 27, 198, 199, 277, 282, 319
Keller, A., 184 n.
Kershner, F. D., 176 n.
Kingdom of God, 116, 117, 159
Koran, 92
Krishna, 86
Kropotkin, P. A., 254–55
Krutch, J. W., 177 n.

Laird, John, 227
Lang, Andrew, 64
Latin theology, 175

Leadership, 180, 187 ff., 192, 321
Legalism, 105–6
Leuba, J. H., 5
Liberalism, 162 ff., 170 ff.
Lipps, Theodore, 199
Logical analysis, 1, 3 n.
Logical positivism, 20
Logos, the, 175, 295
Love, 143–44, 203, 205
Lovejoy, A. O., 227
Lowie, R. H., 67 n.
Loyalty, 143–44, 181, 192, 205
Luke, Gospel of, 118 n., 310 n.
Luther, Martin, 314

McDougall, W., 190 n., 254–55
McGiffert, A. C., 181 n., 192 ff.
Macintosh, D. C., 27 n.
McIver, R. M., 188 n.
Magic, 68, 71, 76, 80
Mahavira, 10
Malinowski, B., 61, 74, 86
Mana, 70, 72, 77 ff., 84
Manitou, 70
Marcion, 181, 189
Marett, R. R., 64, 77 ff., 86, 190
Mark, Gospel of, 212 n.
Marx, Karl, 137, 139, 154, 172
Materialism, 218 ff.
Matthew, Gospel of, 116 n., 118 n., 136 n., 310 n.
Mechanism, 219 ff.
Meditation, 97, 100
Meinong, A., 227
Meno, 3
Mental acts, 227–38
Metaphysics, 12, 107, 182, 294 ff.
Method, philosophical, 1 ff., 3 n., 5 ff.
Micah, 104, 105
Mill, J. S., 132
Mind, theories of, 216 ff.
Minds, our knowledge of other, 264
Mohammed, 92, 112, 156, 195 n.
Montefiore, C. G., 195 n.
Moore, G. E., 227, 252

Moore, G. F., 8 n., 38 n.
Moral awakening, 43 ff.
Moral basis of religion, 19, 23, 26 ff., 39 ff., 47 ff., 66, 72, 74, 76, 81, 87 ff., 94, 112
Moral good and natural good, 131 ff.
Moralistic empiricism, 26 ff.
Morris, C. W., 217, 227, 228 n.
Murphy, A. E., 283
Mussolini, B., 165
Mystery religions, 213
Mysticism, 16 ff., 76, 98 ff.

Naturalistic theory of religion, 69 ff.
Nazi philosophy, 166 n.
Negrito, 60 n.
Niebuhr, Reinhold, 140 n.
Numinous, the, 48 n., 75 ff.

Obligation, sense of, 28, 129, 251–53, 269 ff.
Odyssey, 212
Oman, John, 15 n., 27 n.
Organism, structure of, 230 ff.
Organismic philosophy, 235 ff., 246–47, 262, 295 ff.
Orthodoxy, 180, 183, 184 ff.
Otto, M. C., 137 n., 252
Otto, R., 19, 48 n., 75 ff.

Palmieri, M., 166 n.
Parker, D. H., 284
Paul, St., 37, 39, 50, 103, 106, 174, 247, 251, 307, 309–15
Perry, R. B., 18 n., 220 n., 228 n., 265
Personal development, 127, 130, 133 ff., 137, 237–40, 268, 317–18
Peter, St., 117–18, 315
Phaedo, 214
Phenomenological analysis, 3 n., 6
Philippians, Epistle to the, 58 n.
Physicalism, 220, 222 ff.
Plato, 15, 198, 213, 215
Polytheism, development of, 85–86
Prall, D. W., 199–201

Pratt, J. B., 38 n., 47, 227
Prayer, 98 ff., 293
Primitive religion: moral element in, 66, 72, 74, 76, 86; significance of, 7, 60, 76
Pringle-Pattison, A. S., 27 n., 137 n., 216
Process, mind as, 217
Prophet and priest, 91, 104
Psalms, 211 n., 308
Pythagoras, 93, 213

Qualities, theory of, 224–26, 230 ff., 235, 237 n., 262–63

Radin, P., 61 n.
Ramakrishna, 38, 41
Rashdall, H., 108 n., 131 n.
Rationalism, 8 ff.
Rauschenbusch, W., 160
Religious experience, definition of, 6
Respect, 203
Revelation, 90 ff., 293–94, 320
Revelation, Book of, 118
Rivers, W. H. R., 64
Rohde, E., 213
Romans, Epistle to the, 106 n., 111 n., 307 n., 309 n., 315 n.
Romanticism, 14
Ross, W. D., 251, 274 n.
Royce, J., 216
Ruskin, John, 199
Russell, B., 28, 219

Sacrifice, 96 ff., 104
Sadhu Sundar Singh, 38, 251
Salvation, 114, 116, 136 ff., 313–18, 320, 321
Schleiermacher, F., 14 ff., 19, 27, 30, 48
Schlick, M., 276, 278–80
Scholasticism, 15, 215
Self: conflict within, 39 ff., 46, 51 ff., 102 ff.; growth of, 46, 54, 203; the higher, 17, 38, 46, 54

Self-interest, 126, 270 ff.

Self-sacrifice, 53, 82, 134 ff., 141, 259, 273

Self-surrender, 47, 52, 98, 250

Sellars, R. W., 242 n.

Sentiments, 203

Shand, A. F., 203

Sharp, F. C., 270–71

Simpson, J. Y., 137 n.

Sin: Jesus' interpretation of, 105; sense of, 22, 103, 176, 317–18

Sleep, 234

Smith, T. V., 283–84

Social gospel, 160

Social nature of religion, 20, 23, 30, 51, 54, 65 ff., 82, 83, 112 ff., 151 ff.

Social pressure, 147, 275 ff.

Social, two senses of the term, 257–58

Socrates, 3, 3 n., 4, 93, 213, 214

Sorley, W. R., 27 n.

Soul, theories of immaterial, 210 ff.

South African Bushmen, 67

Space, 232

Spencer, H., 216 n.

Spinoza, 15, 72, 265

Spirit: origin of belief in, 62 ff.; primitive conception of, 62

Stace, W. T., 270 ff.

Stalin, 172

Starbuck, E. D., 42 ff., 52

Stout, G. F., 227

Streeter, B. H., 39 n.

Subconscious, the, 17–18, 234, 246

Substance, theory of, 215–17, 235, 287

Suggestion, 204

Symbolistic empiricism, 19 ff.

Synoptic philosophy, 1, 3 n., 8 ff., 294

Syrians, 86

Taylor, A. E., 27 n.

Teleology, 29, 145–46, 292

Tender-minded, 12

Tennant, F. R., 27 n.

Tennyson, Alfred, 305–6

Theodore of Mopsuestia, 175

Theology, philosophical significance of, 314 ff.

Thomas à Kempis, 99

Time, 232

Todas, 64

Toleration, 181–87

Tolstoi, L., 38, 41, 43, 251, 266

Totemism, 66

Tough-minded, 12

Transmigration of souls, 92

Tribalism in religion, 112 ff.

Trinity, doctrine of the, 295

Troeltsch, E., 18, 48 n.

Tylor, E. B., 62 ff., 74

Universalism in religion and ethics, 112 ff.

Upanishads, 93

Values: argument from, 261; objectivity of, 231, 264 ff., 285, 292

Vedic poems, 64

Ward, James, 16, 217

Webb, C. C. J., 69 n.

Westermarck, E., 62, 69 ff., 77, 256, 276, 281–82

Whitehead, A. N., 27 n., 68, 230 n., 296–97

Wieman, H. N., 19 ff., 27, 30

Will, altruistic and disinterested, 30, 52 ff., 87, 95, 98, 100, 101, 108, 119, 123 ff., 128 ff., 173, 249 ff., 261, 268, 286–87, 319

Will to believe, 11, 222

Wishful thinking, 103, 112, 306

Yahweh, 114, 115

Zoroastrianism, 128